# BEER SCHOOL

## BOTTLING SUCCESS AT THE BROOKLYN BREWERY

Steve Hindy and Tom Potter

**WILEY**

John Wiley & Sons, Inc.

Published by John Wiley & Sons, Inc., Hoboken, New Jersey
Published simultaneously in Canada

For general information on our other products and services or for technical support, please
contact our Customer Care Department within the United States at (800) 762-2974, outside
the United States at (317) 572-3993 or fax (317) 572-4002.

Wiley also publishes its books in a variety of electronic formats. Some content that appears in
print may not be available in electronic books. For more information about Wiley products,
visit our web site at www.wiley.com.

Library of Congress Cataloging-in-Publication Data

Hindy, Steve, 1949-
    Beer school : bottling success at the Brooklyn Brewery / by Steve Hindy and Tom Potter.
        p. cm.
    ISBN-13: 978-0-471-73512-0 (cloth)
    ISBN-10: 0-471-73512-4 (cloth)
    1. Brooklyn Brewery—History.  2. Brewing industry—New York (State)—New York—
History.  3. Beer industry—New York (State)—New York—History.  4. Brooklyn (New
York, N.Y.)—History.  I. Potter, Tom, 1955–  II. Title.
    HD9397.U54B744   2005
    338.7'66342'0974723—dc22
                                                                          2005012268

Printed in the United States of America

10  9  8  7  6  5  4  3  2  1

*This book is dedicated to our wives, Gail and Ellen,
and to our children, Bill, Sam, and Lily.
Without your love and support there would have
been no book to write and no business to write about.*

# Contents

# Foreword

A warning: Three things are bound to happen as you read this book. First, periodically, you will become thirsty. Prepare your refrigerator. Second, you will want to visit the Brooklyn Brewery for a tour. Prepare your itinerary. And finally, if you have ever considered starting your own business, you will be inspired—and scared. Prepare yourself.

As someone who began a start-up company in 1981 with three men and a coffeepot, Steve Hindy's and Tom Potter's story rings true as an honest accounting of the sheer determination—and good luck—required to nurture a business from conception to maturity—and the inevitable mistakes that are made along the way. But their success story is about more than the birth of a brewery; it's about the rebirth of a borough. In so many ways, the Brooklyn Brewery symbolizes—and helped to create—the renaissance that has taken hold in Brooklyn.

When Steve and Tom leased an old ironworks building in Williamsburg in 1994, the once thriving industrial district had long lost its vitality. For decades, manufacturing jobs had been moving out of Williamsburg and overseas, leaving behind abandoned warehouses and crumbling buildings. To many, Brooklyn seemed to be dying. But Tom and Steve believed in Brooklyn's history—its rich tradition of brewing and its wealth of cultural icons and institutions: Walt Whitman, Jackie Robinson, and all the Dodger greats, Coney Island and the Cyclone, the Brooklyn Bridge—to name a few. They understood that Brooklyn is more than an address; it's a spirit, an attitude, an identity. And they bet—correctly—that hometown pride would lead New Yorkers to embrace Brooklyn beer as their own.

In the more than 10 years since the brewery opened, Brooklyn beer has become a popular and successful brand, and Williamsburg has grown into one of New York City's hottest residential neighborhoods. Steve and Tom helped make Williamsburg hip—sponsoring block parties and music festivals and opening the brewery to tours and Friday night happy hours. But as the area changed from a decaying industrial center to a vibrant residential neighborhood, its antiquated zoning regulations prevented the development of new housing and sealed off the waterfront from residents.

As the city began the process of rezoning the area, community input was solicited. Steve and Tom helped residents participate in the discussion by hosting a public meeting at the brewery attended by city officials. In May 2005, with strong support from the community, the city completed the largest waterfront rezoning in its history, which will result in new housing along a waterfront esplanade. In addition, the plan creates a special industrial park to ensure that manufacturing companies—like the Brooklyn Brewery—can continue to succeed and grow in the area.

More than opening their doors to community events, Steve and Tom have taken an active role in Brooklyn's civic life, sponsoring fund-raisers for Prospect Park and exhibits at the Brooklyn Historical Society. New Yorkers, especially myself, are particularly grateful for their support of the Jackie Robinson and Pee Wee Reese monument commissioned for KeySpan Park, home of the Brooklyn Cyclones. Steve and Tom are helping to bring the monument to life by generously donating $1 from every case and $5 from every keg that they sell of Brooklyn Pennant Ale '55.

*Beer School* is the story of the incredible challenges—most of them unanticipated—that entrepreneurs experience and the hard road that is traveled from planning to profit. But Steve and Tom have done more than build a profitable business; they have played an integral part in revitalizing Williamsburg and fostering Brooklyn's renaissance. In doing so, their public-spirited brewery has become part of Brooklyn's identity. I tip my hat, and lift my glass, to them both.

Michael R. Bloomberg
New York City
June 2005

# Preface

## STEVE AND TOM INTRODUCE THE BROOKLYN BREWERY

The Brooklyn Brewery is among the top 40 breweries in the United States, selling nearly 45,000 barrels of beer in 2004. With 17 years in business, the company has risen above many multinational giants to become the number six draft beer in New York City and a virtual institution in Brooklyn, a borough of more than 2 million inhabitants. How did we, Steve Hindy (a journalist) and Tom Potter (a banker), with no experience in the beer business, turn a hobby into a multi-million-dollar business and develop both a beer brand and a distribution company in the most competitive beer market in the United States?

It wasn't easy. We started, textbook style, with a well-researched business plan and $500,000 raised from family, friends, and an ever widening network of people who invested in the Brooklyn Brewery. We soon learned that starting a business was an all-consuming enterprise that tested us, our relationship as partners, and our relationships with our families and our community. As partners, we were essentially married. Our only child was the Brooklyn Brewery, and we faced many challenges in raising that child, the same way parents wrangle over how to raise their offspring. More often than not, we agreed on how to proceed, and we were thankful for such a strong partnership that could withstand the burdens and anxieties of building a company. When we didn't agree, the very foundation of the company was threatened. Employees took sides. It got nasty.

We learned that when we could not find a conventional way to get something done, we had to make our own way of doing things. Sometimes we succeeded, and sometimes we failed miserably. We learned the value of maintaining a focus on the main purpose of the company.

We learned that we were attempting to become part of an industry that was dominated by large multinational corporations with tremendous resources at their disposal—companies that greatly value a presence in New York City because it is the center of the world's financial institutions.

We learned that start-up companies have some important advantages over large companies. The media and many other businesses are always rooting for David over Goliath. Exploiting these advantages is essential to success.

We learned that our investors' initial concerns about the Mafia in New York were not unwarranted, and that no company is too small to find itself a target of such threats. We learned that protecting your business and its employees sometimes means that you might have to look down the barrel of a gun. It is your business, and there is no one else to turn to.

We learned that entrepreneurs have to articulate a dream, inspire their followers to believe in that dream, and work tirelessly for its realization. But we also learned that entrepreneurs have to let go of control of the dream and allow their followers to take ownership.

We learned that the conventional wisdom of "getting in on the ground floor" of a successful business does not always mean that you are going to enjoy the fruits of that business. We learned that banks and venture capitalists are not always the preferred way for an entrepreneur to finance an enterprise.

We learned that selling a successful business is a perilous undertaking, even when there are competing buyers.

Along the way, we have had others turn to us for guidance, and we've been regularly questioned about how we built our business. As our seventeen year partnership comes to a successful end, we thought it was time to write a book and share the lessons we learned with others who dream of starting a business. We also graded our performance in key areas of our business. Our cumulative average was a B. That's not bad when you consider that 80 percent of new business ventures get an F.

We hope you will find our story helpful as you set about bottling your own success.

Steve Hindy and Tom Potter
Brooklyn, New York
July 2005

# Acknowledgments

It's fun to write a first-person account about the founding of a successful business. "If you want a flattering history, you've got to write it yourself" is our motto. But we've tried to be honest about our failures as well as our successes, and share both the lows and the highs in our relationship as partners.

We also hope that we've adequately shared the credit for the Brooklyn Brewery's success. It was never just the Tom and Steve show. The early support of dozens of visionary investors got us off the ground. Mentoring from Milton Glaser, Charlie Hamm, and Bernard Fultz helped keep us on track. Early support from family, friends, and colleagues and substantial, and timely, financial support from Jay Hall and David Ottaway allowed us to pursue our ambitions. And perhaps most important, the business has thrived on the imagination, hard work, and dedication of its employees and managers since 1987.

We're fortunate to have had a chance to work with you all, and we'll always be grateful for your amazing contributions.

# CHAPTER 1
# Steve Tells How Choosing a Partner Is Like a Second Marriage

My head was thumping and I was drenched in sweat when I was jolted awake on a fresh sunny morning in May 1984 by the blasts of two mortar shells in the parking lot outside my second-floor room at the Alexander Hotel in East Beirut. Lebanese hotel workers were inspecting the damage to the cars in the lot—shattered windows and punctured tires. None had caught fire. No one was hurt. The mortar shells were a Beirut wake-up call from the Palestinians and Lebanese leftists on the other side of the nearby Green Line that divided the city. Nothing like a mortar blast to make you forget you have a hangover. *Mawfi mushkila*— no problem—the uniformed deskman would tell me when I trudged downstairs for breakfast with David Ottaway of the *Washington Post* (who would later play a major role in the Brooklyn Brewery). Well, no problem, unless your car was hit. I walked outside and picked up a piece of shrapnel from the parking lot—a fitting souvenir of my five-year assignment in the Middle East for the Associated Press.

I keep that shrapnel fragment in my office at the Brooklyn Brewery as a reminder of my last day in Beirut.

## THE LIFE OF A FOREIGN CORRESPONDENT

My wife, Ellen Foote, had declared a month earlier that she had had enough of being the wife of a foreign correspondent in the Middle East. She had spent two years with me in Beirut, giving birth to our son, Sam, in May of 1980, and three years in Cairo, where she delivered our daughter, Lily. Ellen had endured many dangers in Lebanon. There had been machine gun fire through the thick wooden door of our 140-year-old home in Beirut. Rockets had landed right beside the house, and often flew over the house and into the sea. Once, when I was away covering the Iranian revolution, guerrillas fired rocket-propelled grenades at the American embassy, just across the street from us. A month before the birth of Sam, I was abducted while traveling with a United Nations patrol in south Lebanon. Two Irish U.N. peacekeepers with me were tortured and killed in what turned out to be a vendetta. A third was tortured and released, and I carried him to safety. In my five years, I also covered the hostage crisis in Iran, the Iran-Iraq War, the Israeli invasion of Lebanon, and the massacres in the Beirut refugee camps. Ottaway and I were sitting in the grandstand behind Egyptian president Anwar Sadat when he was assassinated at a military parade in 1981. It was not a career for the faint of heart, and Ellen endured this life like a real trouper. But she firmly declared "no" when AP offered me my next posting in Manila, Philippines, where President Ferdinand Marcos was facing growing popular opposition.

So ended my career as a foreign correspondent. After nearly six years, I decided that my family and their safety meant more to me than my career as a journalist. Besides, there were not many foreign correspondents I admired or wanted to emulate. The best of them, like Ottaway, Tom Friedman of the *New York Times,* and Robert Fisk, then of the London *Times,* combined some sort of scholarship with the grind of daily journalism. They had studied the Middle East and their work reflected the historical context of the events unfolding before our eyes in the 1980s. They wrote books. Most correspondents, including me, were rogues and adventurers addicted to the Big Story. Most were divorced, getting divorced, or getting remarried. Most drank too much, or took drugs, or stopped drinking and became real psychos. We all started out thinking we knew who the good guys were and believing we were on their side. My personal goal, never stated in the presence of my colleagues, was to foster understanding and make the world a better place. But the more wars I covered and the more I learned of the roots of conflict, the less sure I became of who the good guys were—and the less sure I was of the nobility of my role. Journalists, particularly war correspondents, are in a grueling competition to see who can tell the best story, and sometimes that is incompatible with doing good. Except in rare cases, as they get older, war correspondents become insufferable, cynical windbags.

## MY LIFE AS AN ENTREPRENEUR

My career as a war correspondent, however, did much to prepare me for my next career—as cofounder of the Brooklyn Brewery. The determination, focus, and endurance required to get a story is similar to the single-minded determination required to start a business. The necessity of responding quickly to unexpected events is similar to the flexibility the entrepreneur needs to respond to problems—and solving problems is the entrepreneur's trade. The distance journalists need to establish from the stories they are covering is similar to the distance entrepreneurs need to maintain between themselves and the pressures they are under. Journalists need to maintain a kind of buoyancy in the same way entrepreneurs need to maintain a sense of optimism about their venture. The overarching goal in business—to make money for yourself and your investors—certainly is not as noble as the journalist's goal of making the world a better place, but it is more attainable and, with a special effort, it can bring some good to the world.

## THE ART OF HOMEBREW

In Cairo, I became friends with Jim Hastings, the inspector general of the Cairo Office of the Agency for International Development, which was responsible for spending $2.3 billion in aid to Egypt annually under the terms of the Camp David Peace Accords between Egypt and Israel. Before Egypt, Jim had been in Saudi Arabia and had acquired a fascinating hobby; homebrewing. Jim made beer at home. In Saudi Arabia, alcoholic beverages are forbidden in a strict interpretation of the Muslim holy book, the Koran. King Saud banned alcoholic beverages in 1954 when Americans flooded into Saudi Arabia to develop the oil fields. At the same time, Aramco—the Arab-American Oil Company—issued a pamphlet to its employees explaining to them how to make their own beer, wine, and liquor at home. I since obtained a copy of this crudely mimeographed guide to homebrewing from a former Bechtel Construction Company executive who was one of the ringleaders of this bootleg operation and, years later, invested in a start-up microbrewery in California.

The tortuous title of this recipe book is:

PERFECTED TECHNIQUES
ON THE EBULLITION
OF
SUGAR, WATER & SUITABLE CATALYST
TO FORM
AN ACCEPTABLE ARAMCO
ASSIMILATIVE IMBIBABLE
POTION
APPROPRIATE FOR CONSUMPTION

I can only guess it was thus named to dampen any suspicion about its contents, perhaps as an inside joke about the flowery, convoluted indirection often employed by Arabic speakers. Whatever the background, Hastings and his friends made very good beer. It was dark and rich and hoppy, and had much more in common with the great beers of Europe than the fizzy mass-market beers of America.

Thus I developed an enthusiasm for homebrewing, or at least for drinking homebrewed beer. I could not yet make my own beer because I had no source for ingredients. Jim and other American diplomats got their malt extract, hops, and yeast through the diplomatic mail. My hobby had to wait until I returned to America.

## RETURNING HOME

In 1984, Ellen, Sam, Lily, and I settled into a two-bedroom apartment in the Park Slope neighborhood of Brooklyn. With two children, Ellen and I could no longer afford our old Manhattan neighborhood on the Upper West Side. I took a job as assistant foreign editor at *Newsday*. My colleagues at AP bought me a homebrewing kit as a going-away present, and I began making my own beer at home.

My first batch was a disaster. The tool for capping the bottles was a crude metal gadget called a "hammer capper." The hammer capper fit over the uncrimped bottle cap. The brewer then hammered the capper, crimping the cap onto the bottle. I broke 30 of 48 bottles in my first batch. At one point in the frustrating process, I became enraged and began striking the capper with far too much force. The kitchen floor was covered with shards of glass. I was cut and bleeding and tired and angry. Ellen took the children to the back of the apartment while I swept up the mess. The beer that resulted had an unpleasant malt character, as if someone had slipped a few drops of cod-liver oil into the batch. But I stuck with my new hobby, comforted by the mantra of homebrewing guru Charlie Papazian, author of *The Complete Joy of Homebrewing* (Harper Resource, 2003): "Relax, don't worry, have a homebrew."

Homebrewing enabled me to approximate the world of great beer I had experienced as I traveled through Europe—the malty ales of England, where the beer was served at cellar temperature; the wholesome, almost food-like lagers of Bavaria, which seemed perfectly appropriate at noon. In my college days, I was puzzled by the bad taste of American beer when I reached the bottom of the bottle or can. Why should the last ounce taste different than the first? English ales and German lagers tasted great to the last sip. Could it be that American beers only tasted good when they were cold? In 1984, Beck's was my favorite commercially available beer, but even it seemed metallic compared to my homebrewed concoctions. I became an adequate homebrewer, learning to brew with raw ingredients, malted barley, and flower hops, as well as malt extract and pelletized hops. Apart from a few accidents—such as a five-gallon carboy exploding on top of our refrigerator, spewing sticky unfermented wort onto the ceiling and sending it cascading down the sides of the fridge—I learned to make good beer. Like all homebrewers, I craved approval. Beer must be shared. I served my beer to my friends and neighbors and, on Saturdays when the top editors were not in the office, to my colleagues at *Newsday*. On weekends, my kids helped me sterilize the bottles. The pleasures of homebrewing are a lot like those of cooking, but the product is even more uplifting than food.

I subscribed to the homebrewing magazine *Zymurgy* and began to read about the small breweries on the West Coast that were producing, on a small, or *micro*, scale, all-malt beers like those I was making at home. I read about Jack McAuliffe and New Albion, the first of the microbreweries. I read about Fritz Maytag, scion of the washing machine family, who had revived the Anchor Brewing Company in San Francisco, and Ken Grossman, a former bicycle repair shop owner who had built a brewery in his garage to make Sierra Nevada Pale Ale. I met Bill Newman, a former state budget office employee who started Newman's Albany Amber in an English-style brewery in Albany, New York. In 1982, in New York City, Matthew Reich, a former banker, had started New Amsterdam, a rich malty lager beer that he brewed under contract at a regional brewery in Utica, New York.

I was happy in my job at *Newsday* while growing more successful at my hobby of beer making. Being an assistant foreign editor seemed like a dream job—I could work with *Newsday*'s nine foreign correspondents and travel a couple of times a year on special assignment. But it lacked the adventure of my years abroad. I was restless. I also envied those guys starting breweries. Starting a brewery . . . what an incredible enterprise. Why couldn't I do that?

As a young man in southeastern Ohio, I had run a very large newspaper delivery route. I had won a statewide newspaper and magazine sales contest, becoming "Most Popular Newsboy in Ohio" and winning a two-week trip to Brazil. I won every candy and greeting card contest my church and the Boy Scouts held. I won my high school golf championship in upstate New York. My dad had worked for big companies all his life and ended up bitter about being replaced by "college boys" and put out to pasture before he was ready to retire. My two grandfathers both ran businesses—a supermarket and a cinema—and I was always envious of their confidence in themselves. I hadn't been to Harvard Business School, but I always harbored a conceit that I could succeed in business if I put my mind to it.

But, really, what did a journalist know about starting a business—let alone a brewery—in the most competitive beer market in the country, if not the world? Clearly, I needed help. And help came from a serendipitous source: my downstairs neighbor in Brooklyn, the best customer for my homebrew, banker Tom Potter. As I look back on the evolution of the Brooklyn Brewery, I am struck by the role serendipity—or as some would say, dumb luck—played in the development of the company. David Ottaway would eventually become our biggest investor, and his two sons would join the company and eventually become my partners. The chemistry that developed between Tom and me was a critical piece of luck. Our relationship was vital to the sound development of our company. My enterprise, drive, and activism always were balanced and tempered by Tom's patient, calculating, and analytical mind. All of our best decisions were the result of a dialogue between our very different ways of approaching problems.

In retrospect, the ideas Tom and I developed in the early days of the company were crucial to our success. Our relationship began as a friendship. My wife, Ellen, an editor, and Tom's wife, Gail Flanery, an artist, had become friends through their involvement in the local public schools attended by our children. In 1985, Tom and Gail purchased the two-bedroom apartment below ours in a cooperative apartment building on Eighth Street, on the block bounding Brooklyn's wonderful Prospect Park. The Park Slope neighborhood of Brooklyn was being revitalized by a flood of young couples like us, many with young children, who had been priced out of neighborhoods in Manhattan. Eighth Street was on the far edge of that revitalization. Today, it is in the heart of a prosperous neighborhood. Property values have increased five times since we bought our apartments.

## FRIENDS BEFORE PARTNERS

Tom and I quickly became close friends. Tom was 29 years old and I was 36. We shared a passion for reading. He had majored in English at Yale, and I at Cornell. He was very articulate and thoughtful. We ran together in the park. We played tennis and golf together, and we raised our kids together. On summer weekends, it seemed Tom and I always shared child care duties. Tom was not a beer enthusiast, but he liked my homebrew. Neither of us was making much money, and homebrew was cheap. In the summer of 1986, I was brewing beer about once every two weeks. We would sit in Tom's backyard drinking homebrew and watching the Mets on a beat-up black-and-white television set. Unlike many summers, that was a fun summer to watch the Mets, because they were on their way to a World Series championship. My children, Sam and Lily, and Tom's son, Billy, played in a sandbox.

In 1986, I was following the progress of New Amsterdam Brewing Company, one of the first start-ups in the East. Founder Matthew Reich had gotten lots of publicity for his venture. His New Amsterdam Amber Beer was delicious. Reich had started out in 1982 brewing beer at the F.X. Matt Brewing Company in Utica, New York, a 100-year-old regional brewery with a lot of excess capacity. His elegant black-and-gold label depicting New York's original name and proud heritage as a seaport was showing up in supermarkets and restaurants. Reich was raising money to build a brewery in Manhattan. His confident, smiling face appeared in articles in the *New York Times* and *New York* magazine. About the same time, the Manhattan Brewery, a brewery restaurant, successfully started up in Soho. In Albany, Bill Newman's four-year-old Newman Brewing Company was thriving. All these ventures seemed to be successful. They were developing a new market for domestic beer brewed to the standards of imported beer—100 percent malted barley, no corn or rice, lots of rich and flavorful hops, resulting in richer-colored and -flavored beers.

It seemed to me that Brooklyn, with 2.5 million inhabitants and a proud, storied history, would also support a brewery. Tom was skeptical. He had recently completed a master's degree in business administration at Columbia University. Among other things, I think they taught him that you should never start a business based on your upstairs neighbor's hobby.

One rainy day, daydreaming as I ran on the road that wound through Prospect Park, I passed a runner wearing a sweaty old T-shirt that said "Breweries of Brooklyn" in classic Victorian font. I lacked the presence of mind to stop at that moment, but I ran into the same guy on the other side of the park. I stopped him and asked about his shirt.

"Oh this," he said, panting. "It's a book I wrote. It's been out of print for 10 years."

"I'd like to talk to you," I said. "I'm starting a brewery in Brooklyn."

"Yeah," he said skeptically. "You and everybody else."

His name was Will Anderson, and he was a crotchety sort of guy, a collector of breweriana and, fortuitously, author of a lovingly written book about Brooklyn's brewing history. His cramped Brooklyn apartment was a jumble of old beer posters, signs, and beery bric-a-brac. He said he was moving to Maine soon, but not soon enough. Brooklyn, he very wrongly declared, was going to hell. He had only one copy of *Breweries of Brooklyn* left, and he agreed to let me photocopy it.

## FINDING THE HISTORY

The book made me an instant expert on the history of brewing in Brooklyn. Will had painstakingly documented the history of 28 of Brooklyn's breweries. He had visited and photographed many of the old brewery buildings. The former Federal Brewing Company on Third Avenue was being renovated as apartments; the Fallert Brewery housed Roman Furniture; the old Schaefer Brewery housed a lumberyard, a kosher winery, and a yeshiva. The 28-acre Rheingold Brewery plot was mostly bulldozed. Other former brewery buildings housed small manufacturing businesses. Brooklyn had been known as "the borough of churches," but it might have been called the borough of breweries. In 1898, when Brooklyn became part of New York City, there were 48 working breweries within its borders. As late as 1962, Brooklyn brewed 10 percent of the beer consumed in America. Schaefer and Rheingold had closed their doors in 1976, ending the wonderful history of brewing that began in New Amsterdam in 1613, with a Dutch brewery on the southern tip of Manhattan.

On weekends, Tom and I drank homebrew, and I began to dream out loud about starting a brewery in Brooklyn. I argued that Brooklyn occupied a special place in the history of American brewing. Brooklyn also was a special place in America and the world; it deserved to have a beer named after it. I pointed to the success of Reich, a former banker, and Newman, a former state bureaucrat. If they could do it, why not us? Tom was intrigued by my research, but not convinced. He grudgingly admitted that there was a brewing tradition in Brooklyn. He even learned that his father-in-law had been a security guard at the old Schaefer brewery. But that did not mean we should start a business. Look at the brewing industry, he said: The big breweries and distributors are getting bigger, and the small are getting swallowed up. How could we compete in that environment?

More and more articles about microbreweries were appearing in the press. William Least Heat Moon wrote a rhapsodically romantic article, called "A Glass of Handmade," about the trend in *Atlantic Monthly*. Wasn't that proof enough?

Not for Tom. Sitting at my desk at *Newsday* one quiet Saturday in the summer of 1986, I did an electronic library search of the word *microbrewery*. The result was a half-inch-thick stack of articles about the growth of this new industry. Reading glowing news articles about Anchor and Sierra Nevada, about Hart Brewing in Seattle and Newman and New Amsterdam, it was clear that something new was happening in the beer business. These articles—and his growing taste for my homebrew—caught Tom's imagination. I was subscribing to *Zymurgy*, published by the American Homebrewers Association, in which I learned of a conference of small brewers to be held in Portland, Oregon. Tom decided to attend the microbrewers conference in Portland. At that time, there were only 33 microbreweries in the United States. All were represented at the conference, most by their founders. And all were eager to talk to the quiet banker from New York wearing a Brooks Brothers suit. Little did they know that he longed to chuck his suits and join the beer revolution.

## AN IDEA BECOMES A REALITY

Tom returned from Portland believing that we could start a business. He said he had been impressed by many of the entrepreneurs he had met in Portland. It was not just a bunch of wild-eyed homebrewers. These people were serious about making money, he said. I was thrilled. Tom represented many talents I thought I did not have. Like me, he had majored in English in college, but he had been to business school and had some firm ideas about how a company should be structured. A member of a championship high school debating team, he was very persuasive when he applied his mind to an idea. He also had a very earnest and intelligent manner—you would not hesitate to buy a used car from Tom. When we began doing the research for the business plan, he avidly tackled the numbers—projections of case and keg sales, estimates of sales in Brooklyn and beyond. I worked on the sales and marketing strategy, basically answering the question "Why build a brewery in Brooklyn?"

I had no idea how to go about raising money. Tom's dad, David Potter, had been vice president for research and development at General Motors in the company's heyday. Prior to that, he had been undersecretary of the Navy in the Ford and Nixon administrations. For me, this answered an important question: How were we going to raise money? It seemed to me that Tom's dad and his cronies would be the best initial target for us.

First, we had to figure out what kind of presence each of us wanted to have in terms of general roles in our business. Because of our respective past careers, we agreed on some broad roles: I was to be Mr. Outside—the salesman, the marketer, the public relations man; Tom was to be Mr. Inside—the numbers guy, the strategic thinker, the brains of the outfit. These roles worked very well for us for many years, but not forever. As the company grew over the years, the lines between these roles became blurred.

We shook hands on this arrangement, but thanks to Tom, we did something more, which every entrepreneur who has a partner should do: We enshrined our relationship in a partnership agreement that clearly outlined our fifty-fifty shares in the general partner position in the Brooklyn Brewery Limited Partnership. In a limited partnership, the general partner has all the voting shares; the limited partners invest money but have no management role. The partnership agreement outlined buyout procedures should either of us want to terminate our agreement and leave the company. The agreement also provided for life insurance policies on each of us that would buy out our wives for $500,000 should either of us die. It was a sound beginning.

The agreement was sort of like a prenuptial agreement. It is an appropriate analogy. A partnership is very much like a marriage. In a partnership, you pledge to work with another person through success and failure, until you decide to part ways. The partnership agreement outlines a method for parting ways without destroying the company. It is an essential part of any partnership that hopes to maintain a balance of trust and harmony as the business prospers.

## LESSON ONE
## EVEN A DOG CAN SHAKE HANDS

In the movies, business relationships often are consummated by two eager, honest, hardworking guys shaking hands on a fifty-fifty deal. I suppose partnerships like this can work, but in my experience, they are very dangerous to both parties. Over the years, we watched many partnerships fail in the beer industry, and elsewhere.

One such case involved a prominent microbrewery in the East. The founder had developed a brand and was brewing beer. But he had fallen behind many other start-ups. He lacked marketing and sales know-how. So he partnered with someone who had marketing and sales experience. Together, they developed a second brand, a lighter beer that they theorized was more accessible to the average beer drinker. The idea seemed reasonable enough. The microbrewing segment had mostly ignored this style in favor of darker, heavier ales and lagers. The new product was 100 percent malted barley—like other microbrewed beers—and would compete directly with imports like Beck's and Heineken, not with Budweiser and Coors. The brand had a good name and a snappy label. Brooklyn Brewery distributed the brand, so we had a ringside seat for this project. The partners contracted with a brewery in the Northeast to produce their brand, and we received a few hundred cases in our warehouse in Brooklyn. But no sooner had we started selling than the partners ran into problems with their contract brewer. I believe the problems predated the new brand introduction. They found a new producer in the Northeast. The partners ran low on money, and the brewer refused to produce more beer. The partners had a falling-out, but both started calling us for orders. The founder forbade us to buy beer from anyone but himself. We had no idea who was controlling the brand. When I told the founder I had been dealing with his former partner on a regular basis, he insisted this must stop, and he threatened to sue. In the meantime, the brand was floundering. No one was selling the beer. It was an ugly mess.

## Get It on Paper

Two men who had eagerly embraced each other less than a year before were now refusing to speak to each other and telling two different stories about their deal. The handshake that had sealed their partnership was forgotten. Their only recourse was the courts, but they would be spending lots of money on legal fees to decide the ownership of a brand that was stillborn. They had no sales. They also had no partnership agreement and therefore no basis for resolving their dispute. A partnership agreement might not have been the answer to all their problems, but it would have forced them to define their relationship at the outset and given them a set of parameters to work within when trouble did arise. This process might have resulted in a sound foundation for their company, or it might have forced a realization that they should not be in business together at all. I have no idea who was right and who was wrong, but at least, with a partnership agreement, if the relationship dissolves, there's a mechanism in place to make it amicable and fair.

This is not an uncommon situation. Any issue or dispute that comes between partners is bad news for their business. Employees choose sides and exploit the differences the way children play parents off each other. Valuable time is wasted. I have watched several undocumented partnerships fall into ruinous disputes. For instance, a very talented chef friend of mine partnered with an older man who owned many buildings in Brooklyn in the 1980s. The older man had always dreamed of having his own restaurant. When the restaurant was up and running, the chef ran the show and his partner was happy to greet customers every night and roam around the restaurant talking with customers through the evening. On the face of it, it was a brilliant partnership. But then one day, the older man's daughters became interested in the restaurant. Eventually, differences developed between the older man and his daughters on the one side and the chef on the other. They parted ways and fell into a terrible legal battle.

"The lesson I learned is that in the absence of any partnership agreement, the guy with money, the guy with his name on the deed, wins," said the chef later. ★

## TOM WEIGHS IN

When Steve brought me his idea to start a brewery in Brooklyn, I was skeptical both about the idea and about him as a partner. Even as I warmed to the idea, I still had doubts about Steve.

I talked to my dad about the situation because he had a lifetime of experience in business management. I weighed his opinion carefully. Listening to me describe the idea and my potential partner, he sounded the alarm. This was going to be a very tough business to succeed in, he said, and in my partner I was potentially saddling myself with someone whose only contribution was the original idea. I might have to pull the brunt of the managerial load myself, and for a long time. Was I ready for that?

Steve didn't look like the ideal partner in 1986. For one thing, he was my upstairs neighbor and a friend. I was skeptical about turning a friendship into a partnership. More likely, I thought, the process would turn our friendship into a messy brawl. I could imagine us as a *Honeymooners* episode: Ralph and Norton start a brewery! He also didn't have much business experience. He was a journalist, and journalism was a romantic field but one not known for business discipline.

My dad's skepticism was well grounded, but dads aren't always right. And in measuring Steve, I thought I saw some latent skills. For one thing, he had managed an editorial staff of 25 while a foreign correspondent in the Middle East. Experience in managing people, even if not in a bottom-line-driven environment, was good. And something seemingly minor, which my dad dismissed as irrelevant, intrigued me. In his youth, Steve had been voted "outstanding newsboy" in Ohio. Steve was convinced he could be the salesperson and manager we would need. Though he had no professional sales experience, I was inclined to think he did have the aptitude. Moreover, I knew that I did not. In the end, Steve sold me on his salesmanship.

Most important, before either of us actually committed to the business, we began to work together, thinking through the idea privately and talking to others about it. During this preliminary feeling-out period I noticed that we thought a lot alike. We were on the same wavelength. We had similar judgments about people, priorities, and how to shape the business. It also became clear that we worked well together. In meetings, we fell naturally into complementary roles. I could sense when to shut up and let Steve carry the ball, and when I was on a roll, he gave me room. I had always respected Steve and definitely began to feel that I could trust him in business, at least to work hard and pull his weight.

My insistence on a written partnership agreement came mostly from my previous experience as a banker. I viewed it as standard operating procedure. But given my initial private doubts about Steve, I also saw it as important protection for us both if things blew up.

I'd have to say my early expectations for Steve were pretty modest. Luckily for me and for the business, I had underestimated him by a wide margin.

**Our Grade:**   A. Yes, some of it was luck, some of it was instinct, but in retrospect we did well in choosing each other as partners. Choosing the best partner is key to making a new business venture succeed.

# CHAPTER 2

# Steve Discusses the Importance of Building a Solid Team

## THE ENTREPRENEUR'S LOT

Starting a business is an exhilarating, heady experience. It is the dream of many Americans, young and old. It is an integral part of the whole idea of being an American. Freedom, enterprise, hard work, believing in an idea—these are bedrock American values. But relatively few Americans ever start their own businesses. Why? Because it is a very scary proposition and it is very difficult to succeed. By some estimates, 8 of 10 businesses fail in the first year. When we started the Brooklyn Brewery, both Tom and I read *Inc.* magazine religiously. *Inc.* is one of those publications that really glamorizes entrepreneurship. A particularly strong editorial that captured our imaginations was entitled "Entrepreneurial Terror." The author, Wilson Harrell, was publisher of *Inc.* at the time. He recounted his World War II experience as a combat fighter pilot shot down behind enemy lines in France. He was rescued by members of the French Resistance, who gave him refuge on a family farm. Periodically, the Germans would search the farm, looking for resistance fighters. Discovery of any role in the Resistance meant certain death. When his French hosts got word that the Germans were coming, they buried him on his back in a shallow grave in a field on their farm. A piece of straw sticking up through the earth was his only source of air to breath. He lay quietly underground while jackbooted German soldiers tromped around the fields, thrusting their bayonets into the ground to detect any buried partisans. Harrell said this experience was very similar to the life-and-death thrill of starting your own business.

Harrell wrote in a later column that entrepreneurial terror was not a once-in-a-lifetime experience, but rather the perpetual lot of the entrepreneur. Harrell told of his first business representing Kraft Foods in selling their products to military bases in Europe and the Middle East. One day, the president of Kraft told Harrell that the company was thinking of taking over the sales operation in Germany with its own people. Harrell boldly replied that if he was losing Germany, he would give up the rest of his brokerage business.

He said it took Kraft a month to make up its mind. "During every moment of those 30 days and 30 nights, I lived with a terror as vivid and as horrifying as anything I had experienced in combat," wrote Harrell. Finally, Kraft backed down and awarded him a new contract.

"That experience anointed me 'Entrepreneur' and inducted me into 'The Club of Terror,' " he wrote. "The experience taught me another entrepreneurial secret: The elation you feel after a terrorizing episode is payment in full for the suffering. That 'high' is an emotion especially reserved for those of us who start companies. It is food for our spirit—the sustenance that keeps us going from one encounter to the next."

Harrell's column was an inspiration for Tom and me. We faced many scary moments over the years, both spiritual—staring at the brink of bankruptcy—and physical—staring down the barrel of a 9mm pistol. When you start a business, it is not only your money and your investors' money that is on the line, it is your dream, your idea. Failure is terrifying, but it can result not only from your own shortcomings but from forces outside your control. Fear of failure is a powerful motivator and, depending on the circumstances, can either hold you back or push you forward.

## IN THE BEGINNING, EVERYONE PITCHES IN

When you are starting a business, you stand a little taller than you ever have. Instead of being an assistant foreign editor at *Newsday,* like me, or an assistant vice president at Chemical Bank, like Tom, you are a founder of a company. You become the president or the CEO of the Brooklyn Brewery Limited Partnership. Even though this entity has no employees, no plan, no money, you still gain respect from your peers. Even in the earliest stages of planning, you feel the prestige and power of being your own boss. Your colleagues begin to look at you in a different way.

Starting a business is a creative process that is fed by everyone around you. Everyone has advice for the entrepreneur. Everyone close to the entrepreneur feels they have played some role in the making of a business. The process of building a company becomes your life, sweeping up the ideas of everyone you know, particularly your loved ones and friends. If you are not careful in the way you manage this process, you may lose them all. Many marriages and friendships fall victim to the passion of the entrepreneur.

I was constantly discussing the business with my wife, Ellen, and she helped me develop some of my best ideas. Even my children felt a connection to the business. In the late 1980s, Sam and Lily used to help me package my homebrew at our apartment in Brooklyn. We had a little assembly line at the kitchen counter. First they passed me a bottle to sterilize, then to fill with a siphon, and finally to cap. The bottles were then packed into a case to ferment and condition.

When Tom and I made our first test brew at the F.X. Matt Brewing Company in upstate New York, the brewery sold us 1,000 cases of beer bearing an old F.X. Matt holiday beer label. We did not yet have government approval for our own label. We stored the beer in a warehouse in an old brewery building about five miles from our homes in Brooklyn. We used to drive from the warehouse to our home with 22 cases of beer packed into the trunk of my Chevy Citation. We would put the bottles in a plastic kid's swimming pool in the basement of our building, fill it with water, and soak the labels overnight. Then Tom, his son, Billy, Lily, Sam, and I would sit on concrete blocks in the basement, scraping the holiday beer labels off the bottles with our fingernails and applying black-and-white versions of our label on the bottles. We used these bottles to try out our beer on prospective consumers and bar and restaurant customers. That was the extent of our market analysis back then. Many people kept those black-and-white labeled bottles. Recently, one sold at a charity auction for more than $100!

All in all, Tom had learned a good deal about market analysis at Columbia. He knew that starting a business would cost much more than our personal time and the $500,000 in start-up funds we were trying to raise in the beginning. As time went by, I took to telling questioners that ours was a "product-driven" company, that we eschewed traditional market analysis. Part of this new method would be depicting our brand to best reflect our product.

## Branding Our Identity

One of the first tasks we faced was to develop a logo for the company and a label for the brand. Anyone who lives in New

York knows artists and designers, so there was no shortage of people wanting to design our label, and Tom and I were very good at getting people wound up about our idea. Our original sales pitch was a combination of Brooklyn nationalism—which appealed to the many people like us who were flocking to Brooklyn at the time—and hard-nosed numbers about the beer market in Brooklyn. The first name we envisioned for the product was Brooklyn Eagle Lager. This was based on the *Brooklyn Eagle* newspaper, the legendary daily once edited by Walt Whitman. At parties in our Park Slope neighborhood, we talked up our idea and the wonderful history of brewing in Brooklyn. We said we wanted a dynamic, emblematic label, the sort of image that every Brooklyn guy would want tattooed on his arm someday. Several of our friends developed elaborate presentations of labels and logos for us to review, based on our ideas. They became passionate advocates of our ideas as they listened to our plans. They were deeply disappointed when we rejected their proposals in order to find just the right logo. Some are still sore to this day.

I was uncomfortable with my friends' designs. I didn't know what I wanted, but I knew I had not seen it yet. The more I thought about the logo/label, the more I realized that this was the most important decision we faced at this early stage of the business. We were busy working on a good business plan, but we also needed a quality symbol of our enterprise to put before potential investors. We needed an image that would inspire confidence and desire in investors.

I called Maureen Healy, the wife of a friend of mine and a graphic designer. She expressed great interest in our project and said she would like to work on it. But cautious of hurting more friends, I asked her to hold off. What I really needed was the names of some design firms, so Maureen introduced me to some other designers. One evening, I hosted a couple of young designers at our apartment. I interviewed them for about an hour. When they left, Ellen said to me, "Do you realize that those guys could hardly get a word in edgewise for all your gushing about the business? Why are you selling *them*? They should be selling *you*."

This was a revelation, and it explained some of the discomfort I had been feeling about this process. Thus far, every designer I had met loved our idea, told me I was brilliant, and said they wanted to design our logo. But no one had really told me anything about what a label should be. After all, what did I know about designing a logo? I began to develop a sense of the enormity and complexity of the problem I faced. At the time, I was working the 10 A.M. to 7 P.M. shift at *Newsday*. So I began to use my mornings to visit design firms in New York City. All in all, I interviewed more than 25 firms. I met many talented designers at their Manhattan studios, but no one was giving me anything to think about. Furthermore, they were expensive. In 1987, the lowest price I could get for developing what I came to know as a "corporate identity" was $40,000. Most were higher. Tom and I were hoping to raise $500,000, and we had budgeted $20,000 for the design fees. Was I going to break the budget on my first effort? One evening, I was stewing about this when my wife Ellen said, "Why don't you try and see the very best designers in the city? I'll bet the best in the world are here. You are a reporter. You don't mind calling anyone, anytime. Find out from Maureen who the best are, and call them."

Maureen gave me the names of a half a dozen major firms. Ellen was right. The best firms in the world are in New York City, and most wanted to talk to us. In the summer of 1987, Tom and I were entertained at lunch by a partner and his staff at Pentagram, a brilliant English firm with a large office in New York. Over a catered meal of fettucine Alfredo, we looked at projections of Pentagram's work. In particular, they showed us the Watney's Red Barrel brand they had developed for a venerable English brewery. At Chermayeff and Guismar, an associate showed us the work of Ivan Chermayeff and Tom Guismar, who had developed the Mobil Oil logo many years before and had also created logos for an impressive list of Fortune 500 companies since. Even though we said our budget was $20,000, we got the red-carpet treatment from these and other firms. The only exception was Milton Glaser, Inc., the legendary designer of the "I Love NY" logo, *New York* magazine, and a volume of other commercial art that had put its mark on our generation.

"Do you know who Milton *is*?" said a snobby, highly protective receptionist when I called and quickly explained why I wanted to talk to him. I told her I had heard that he was pretty good and that, I said, was why I wanted to talk to him.

"Absolutely not," she replied. "He doesn't talk to anyone who just walks in the door."

This rejection brought out the reporter in me. I became determined to meet Milton Glaser, partly because I knew his work and partly because I was determined to get the one that thought he was "too good for me." I began calling daily and I got on a first-name basis with the receptionist. She seemed to be charmed by my persistence, in spite of herself. Eventually, she sent me a press kit about Milton. The sheer bulk of his PR seemed designed to scare me away. There were profiles in *Time* magazine and the *New York Times,* as well as listings of his historic work. But this only spurred me on. I continued to call the receptionist daily, talking about the weather, the news, anything to develop a relationship with her. Eventually, I wore her down.

"You aren't going to give up, are you?" she said one day. "Okay. Here he is."

She put Milton on the line, and I blurted out our plan for Brooklyn Eagle Beer. "That sounds like fun," said Milton. "Come in and see me."

There is no way that Tom and I could have afforded the normal fees of any of these firms. But to our surprise, Milton and the other big-time firms agreed to work for a small stake in our company and fees that essentially covered their costs. I since have learned that big firms rely on major corporate accounts for their bread and butter, but they sometimes take on interesting projects because they are fun for the creative people in the firm. Milton Glaser was a different type of special case. After a career of successes, he was only working on projects that gave him satisfaction, and I was happy that Brooklyn Brewery was one of them.

The difference between Milton and the other firms was that Milton said he would be working on the project personally. He would be our daily contact, not some unknown associate. We happily retained Milton as our designer.

In our first design meeting, I was determined not to be intimidated by Milton and instead to get all my ideas on the table. I talked about my desire for an "emblematic" label, a label that would become a symbol of a "new" Brooklyn. I talked about the Brooklyn Bridge, about the Brooklyn Dodgers, about Brooklyn as a fountainhead of people and ideas for America. Milton listened patiently, then exhaled and replied, "Save something for me to do."

Milton put his stamp on our project in that first meeting. He convinced us that we did not need an eagle in our name, noting that a successful St. Louis brewer already used that classic American symbol. "You have name enough in Brooklyn," he said. "Brooklyn is recognizable the world over, and somehow it fits with beer. Lay claim to Brooklyn."

Two weeks after the initial design meeting, Milton unveiled the logo that we use to this day. I must say, Tom and I were underwhelmed. The greatly anticipated logo was a shock. There was no Brooklyn Bridge. There was no soaring eagle. Instead, he gave us an elegant "B" that almost seemed to float like a full, white sail against an infield of green surrounded by a white ring and the words "Brooklyn Lager."

Sensing that we were stunned, Milton said, "Don't say a word. Take this home and show it to your wives. Put it on the counter in your kitchen and live with it for a while."

After a couple of weeks, the brilliance of the design definitely began to sink in. The "B" at once evoked the nostalgia of the Brooklyn Dodgers while being a fresh symbol of Brooklyn, a burgeoning center of art and culture in New York City. The copperplate font of the words "Brooklyn Lager" and the two gold dots that somehow nailed down the emblem gave the label a sort of classic, urban feel. It looked like the logo of a company that had been in business for decades and in fact has made many people believe that our company is actually an old Brooklyn institution.

In addition, Milton's name immediately added prestige to our young business. When we put the Milton Glaser–designed Brooklyn logo on our business plan and Milton in our list of key collaborators, potential investors were instantly impressed.

### Finding a Brewmaster

The consulting brewmaster we hired also became an important member of our team—both for his brewing expertise and for the credentials he brought to our initial business plan. Stealing an idea from our rival, New Amsterdam, we decided to begin by brewing our beer at an existing brewery in Utica, New York. Brewing 16,000 gallons of beer in a commercial brewery is considerably different from brewing 5 gallons of beer on your kitchen stove. I had some ideas about the beer we should brew, but I was not about to brew 7,000 cases of beer without the assistance of a professional.

When Tom attended the small brewer's conference in Portland, Oregon, he met a brewery engineer named John Bergmann, who had worked for New Amsterdam and several other beer start-ups. John eventually introduced us to William M. Moeller, a fourth-generation German-American brewer whose grandfather had brewed beer in Brooklyn at the turn of the last century.

Bill Moeller was senior brewmaster at C. Schmidt and Sons Brewery in Philadelphia. He had taken early retirement but was eager to be part of a new venture like ours. "For 35 years, I have listened to brewery owners tell me to make a beer cheaper and faster," said Bill. "This is the first time in my career that an owner has ever told me to make the best damn beer I can make." Like Milton, Bill agreed to take a share of the business as his primary compensation. We also agreed to pay him a daily rate for his work, plus any expenses.

Bill, Tom, and I developed the recipe for Brooklyn Lager, our first product, from the notebooks of Bill's grandfather. Over a two-month period, the three of us tasted many homebrewed variations of Brooklyn Lager in the basement of Bill's home in Boyertown, Pennsylvania, before settling on a recipe for the beer.

Our Brooklyn Lager was 100 percent malted barley. It used much more hops than mainstream beers, and it was dry-hopped, meaning hops were added during the aging process to give our beer a fragrant aroma. We also naturally carbonated the beer by adding unfermented beer to the tanks during aging. It was an impressive formula, and it clearly was an alternative to the mass-produced beers that dominated the American market. Our beer was built with the intent of competing with the imports—and it commanded an import price.

Bill was our first brewmaster, but it was clear he would not be the man who pulled on his boots and worked day-in, day-out in the brewery that we someday hoped to build in Brooklyn. That position would eventually go to a brewer a few years later who would one day be known as one of the great brewmasters and authorities on beer in the country: Garrett Oliver.

I first saw Garrett in 1987 at a December meeting of the New York City Homebrewers Guild at the beer bar Brewsky's on Manhattan's Lower East Side. It was a cold winter evening. I had been invited to speak to the homebrewers about plans for the Brooklyn Brewery. I arrived early for the 8 P.M. meeting, but Brewsky's was already filled with avid homebrewers. There seemed to be many professional people among them—lawyers, engineers, college professors, and the like. They all were passionate about homebrewing. Most had samples of their beers with them and were only too eager to share them. Just about everyone I met asked if I had been introduced to Garrett yet. Garrett had the reputation of being among the best of the homebrewers. He had been one of the founders of the New York City Homebrewers Guild in 1986, and he had designed the intricate crest of the organization. Indeed I had not met Garrett yet, but my anticipation grew as 8 P.M. came and went.

Garrett made his entrance at about 8:20 P.M. There was a stir at the door as he was greeted by the other members. I was ushered to the door to meet him. I was surprised to see a tall, handsome African-American man wearing a cape and knee-high, buckled, black boots. (Garrett since has corrected me: It was not a cape. It was a nineteenth-century French lieutenant's greatcoat which he had draped over his shoulders.) I was very impressed by his singular style. Among all these brewers, Garrett clearly stood out, and he was very comfortable with that. I was introduced to Garrett, and I gave him some of the background about the Brooklyn Brewery. He introduced me to the crowd. Standing on a chair, I told them about our plans. There were many questions about the profile of our first beer, about my background, and about the history of brewing in Brooklyn. People were disappointed that we were not planning to build a brewery in Brooklyn immediately. I explained that we had determined it was more important to focus on getting our beer distributed before investing in a plant in the city. After many tastes of homebrew, I was preparing to leave, when Garrett approached and thanked me for coming. He presented me with a bottle of his Christmas homebrew. As I recall, it was a raspberry stout. And it was a most impressive package. It was a 12-ounce bottle with a parchment label depicting the baroque New York City Homebrewers Guild logo. Across the cap was a scarlet ribbon affixed to the bottle by a wax seal. I had never seen a more elegant bottle of beer.

At the time, Garrett ran the back-office operations of one of New York's most prestigious law firms, Rogers & Wells. (Among the partners in Rogers & Wells was former secretary of state William Rogers and former secretary of state Cyrus Vance.) We launched Brooklyn Lager in the spring of 1988, and after that, one of my college friends, who was a partner at Rogers & Wells, invited me to do a beer tasting for the firm. At the tasting, many of the partners suggested I officially meet Garrett Oliver, their resident brewer. Garrett complimented me on my presentation, and on the Brooklyn Lager that I served. Afterward, I began to run into Garrett at more and more homebrewing events I attended. We soon became friends—and drinking buddies.

As we were entering our second year of business in 1990, Garrett quit his job at Rogers & Wells to start work with the Manhattan Brewing Company, a brewery restaurant in Soho that was one of the first such establishments on the East Coast. I am sure he took a whopping salary cut to become the assistant brewer there. He was apprenticed to Mark Witty, an Englishman who had been a brewer at Samuel Smith's in Yorkshire, one of the companies that we were distributing in New York City by 1991. Mark and Garrett made fantastic beers at Manhattan Brewing Company, but the company struggled under several owners who seemed unable to balance the necessity of making great beer with running a great restaurant at the same time.

Over the next few years, Garrett and I had many conversations at homebrewer meetings and at American Institute of Wine and Food beer events. We always invited Garrett to participate in our beer tastings. He told me of his conversion to better beer during an extended stay in Great Britain. Garrett said he could not come home to mass-produced American beer after developing a taste for English bitter. We had passionate discussions about beer and brewing. In the early morning hours of a homebrewing meeting at a bar on the Upper West Side, I recall us shouting at each other during a discussion of whether the big national breweries should be part of an association of small breweries. I honestly forget which position I was advocating, but I do remember that Garrett had very strong opinions about beer and brewing, and so did I. His homebrews were fantastic. To this day even, he opens some of his presentations by referencing the mystical properties of yeast and saying, "I am on a mission from God."

It was clear to me during our many intense conversations that Garrett should one day be our brewmaster. In the early 1990s, as we began planning to finally build our brewery in Brooklyn, I began to talk to Garrett about coming to work for us.

### Hiring Legal Counsel

Another key member of our team turned out to be our lawyer, our general counsel. When we first began telling people we were starting a brewery in Brooklyn, the most common reaction was: Are you kidding? What about the mob? Organized crime is a very real force in New York City, and in Brooklyn in particular. It is much weaker today than it was 15 years ago, thanks to the work of Rudy Giuliani and other prosecutors, but it still is a force, and if you fall into its clutches, you have some very difficult choices to make. It was clear we needed an answer to investors' questions about the mob. They wanted to know what we would do if the mob tried to tap into our business. No one really knew anything about how this might happen, but they wanted us to assure them we could handle this rough-and-tumble aspect of Brooklyn. My experience as a war correspondent in the Middle East went some way toward assuring people of our ability to handle difficult situations, but they wanted more local knowledge.

Eventually one of my colleagues at *Newsday,* Josh Friedman, introduced us to Nick Scoppetta, a former deputy mayor for law enforcement under Mayor John Lindsay. (Nick later served in Giuliani's administration and as Mayor Michael Bloomberg's fire commissioner.) Scoppetta had earned fame as the prosecutor in the celebrated police corruption case upon which the movie *Serpico,* starring Al Pacino, was based. Nick's law partner, Eric Seiff, had been chair of the New York State Commission of Investigation. Together, they hired a very capable financial firm to help Tom and me shape our limited partnership offering. Vickie Schoenfield, the partner at the financial firm who would work with us on our offering documents, had expedited countless limited partnership offerings, mostly in the real estate field. She was very, very impressive.

Nick said he did know a good deal about the structure of organized crime in New York, but he stressed that he did not know exactly what he would recommend if we were approached by the mob. It didn't matter. We at least had an answer to the question: What about the mob? The answer was that Nick Scoppetta was our general counsel and he would be advising us on such problems, should they arise. Many investors were satisfied. They were impressed that we had an answer to that question.

Scoppetta answered our investors' question about the mob, but we discovered we needed more specialized legal expertise when it came to dealing with the New York State Liquor Authority and the federal Bureau of Alcohol, Tobacco and Firearms (now known as the Tax and Trade Bureau). Beer and other alcoholic beverages are regulated heavily by the federal, state, and sometimes local governments. Knowledge of rules and bureaucrats is essential.

When our application for a brewer's license began languishing in the offices of the State Liquor Authority at 250 Broadway, I made a personal visit to the offices to investigate. I found our 18-inch-thick application sitting on the desk of a woman whose office was filled with similar piles of paper. There were piles of paper on every flat surface in the room. Some sheets had fallen on the floor. It looked like a scene from Charles Dickens's novel *Bleak House,* which illustrates a legal case that swallows up all the client's money before it is resolved. I shuddered to think of the time I had spent resending materials to the authority. I wondered how many of those "lost" documents were on the floor.

I befriended the woman who occupied this office and offered to help her process our application. She was a very nice person, and she and the other ladies at the authority appreciated the doughnuts I brought them that morning. I went to the office every day for a couple of weeks and worked to make sure our files were in order. They gave me a desk, which they called "Mr. Hindy's desk." In time, we completed our application, and a higher-up at the agency recommended a law firm that specialized in the beer industry. Scoppetta eventually went back into the government. Today, we have an excellent general counsel, Steven Gersh, who handles most of our corporate work, another firm that handles most of our New York and federal licensing, and yet another firm that handles most of our out-of-state licensing and relations with distributors.

Interestingly, the nice woman I met at the authority eventually retired and went to work as a consultant for one of our law firms. Having the right legal team is very, very important.

## Contract Brewing

Another key member of our team was the brewery in upstate New York where we were going to brew our beer, the F.X. Matt Brewing Company. Matt's is a proud, family-owned brewery that started in business 100 years before us, in 1888, but had recently fallen on hard times trying to compete with the national breweries. It was led by F.X. Matt II, an intelligent, proud, irascible man. When I first called him in 1987 to ask about contract brewing, F.X. angrily rejected my proposal, basically saying,

"What makes you think you can sell beer just because you make five gallons on your kitchen stove? My family has been doing this for 100 years and we are having a very hard time." Thinking perhaps I had a chemistry problem with F.X., I asked Tom to call him as well, but he got even less time on the phone than I did.

That year, we had gotten much better receptions from C. Schmidt and Sons in Philadelphia, probably because Bill Moeller had formerly supervised the brewing team there. We also talked to the Pittsburgh Brewing Company, and Bill made inquiries for us at several other breweries in Pennsylvania. We visited many of these facilities and were about to sign a deal with Schmidt, though in my heart I felt that Matt's made better beer and was better able to employ the kind of processes we envisioned for our recipe. Bill Moeller also agreed. Stewing over this one night, Ellen suggested I call F.X. one more time.

I screwed up my courage and made a second call. F.X. launched into a diatribe about people like me trying to get into a very complicated and difficult business. He sang the praises of Matthew Reich, the founder of New Amsterdam, and then as an afterthought asked me what I did for a living. I told him about my background as a foreign correspondent.

After a pause, he said, "Really? I always wanted to be a journalist." It turned out that F.X. had majored in English at Princeton and wrote poetry as a hobby. We talked about journalism and literature for the next 15 minutes, and he invited Tom and me to come to Utica. Finally, I felt that I had found the magic password—my background as a journalist—the "open sesame" to 100 years of brewing experience and wisdom.

### Creating a Sales Team

From the start of the company, I was performing the marketing and publicity tasks while Tom was securing funds, but we still needed a salesperson. Our first salesperson came from the staff

I worked with on the foreign desk at *Newsday*. His name was Mike Vitale, and he was a part-time clerk on the desk. At 21, he monitored the wire services and did chores for the editors on the desk. His full-time job was running the accounts receivable department, collecting money, for a Long Island electronics firm. Mike was a witty, fast-talking young man, a born salesperson. Day by day, Mike followed the progress of the Brooklyn Brewery. Eventually, his father invested in the company, and Mike left the electronics firm to became our first employee.

With the hiring of our first salesperson, our team was complete. It was impressive, and it gave me greater confidence in my abilities and my instincts.

## LESSON TWO
## IS IT A BUSINESS OR A *FAMILY* BUSINESS?

The seeds of the first crisis of the partnership between Tom and me were sown on the night we decided to start the company. In 1987, Tom and his wife, Gail, and Ellen and I met in Tom's living room to discuss the venture. Tom explained that starting a business would be a perilous undertaking, particularly because we both had families to support. We would be working long hours for little pay, probably less than we were making at our present jobs, and there was no guarantee of success. On the contrary, most such ventures failed, but we still had some good ideas and believed we had a good *chance* to succeed.

Tom said he had always wanted to start his own business, and this was the idea he was looking for. I said I was restless in my job at *Newsday*. The two-hour daily commute to my office on Long Island was deadly. I needed excitement, and what could be more exciting than starting a brewery in New York City? I said I was certain a brewery could take hold in Brooklyn—New York's largest and most storied borough—with more than two million people. Unnecessarily, I launched into my selling mode. Brooklyn was an undervalued place. Its main institutions were the Brooklyn Museum, the Brooklyn Academy of Music, and the Brooklyn Botanic Garden. The Dodgers were gone, and there were few symbols for Brooklynites to identify with. If we developed the business the right way, we could become another great Brooklyn institution. "Brooklyn is a proud place," I said. "People in Brooklyn are proud of their town. When asked where they live, they say 'Brooklyn,' not 'New York City.' If we can establish our beer as a symbol of that pride, we can succeed."

Tom and I waited for a reaction. Gail said she had faith in the two of us and favored the plan, and Ellen said she was confident we could succeed. So we decided to start the Brooklyn Brewery, but within minutes I said something that jarred Tom: "Well, I'm very happy about this. I think the only way I will ever get to be president of anything is to start it myself."

"Who said you were going to be president?" Tom asked.

This was our first small power struggle. After considerable discussion about each position and its merits, we agreed that Tom would be chief executive officer and I would be president. When we became a corporation, Tom would also be chairman of the board. Of course, the titles seemed virtually meaningless at that point to us. Our fifty-fifty relationship was more clearly defined by the partnership agreement and by our handshake agreement that I was Mr. Outside and Tom was Mr. Inside. But titles are never really meaningless—and anyone who says he doesn't care about them is kidding himself. Proudly, though, our original structure has stood the test of time. For the next 16 years, I would be president and Tom would be CEO.

Then came the words that still haunt me to this day. Tom said to Gail and Ellen, "Do either of you want to be involved in the business?" I was startled. Tom and I had not discussed the possibility of our wives, or other family members, working in the business.

Gail immediately said she did not want to be involved. "No way," she said, shaking her head vigorously. "I don't want to work with you guys. I see enough of you as it is."

Ellen, however, said she might want to work for the company. I was shocked. We had never discussed the possibility of her working in the business. At the time, she was doing freelance book editing at home so she could be with Sam and our infant daughter, Lily. Ellen had worked in publishing during her years in New York, Beirut, and Cairo, but she was not sure that it was her life's work. She had viewed our return to New York from the Middle East as a chance for her to play the careerist role in the family—and here I was starting a brewery. She had been intimately involved in the idea development of the business, and she saw this as a possible job opportunity for her.

I instantly convinced myself, and resolved to convince Ellen, that we should work together in the Brooklyn Brewery. I then developed plans for Ellen to be office manager of the company, making $24,000 a year. At home, I worked to sell this idea to Ellen and also tried to sell it to Tom. Ellen accepted the idea with some hesitation, but Tom balked. He said we could not afford, and did not need, an office manager at this time. Tom and I planned to pay ourselves $48,000 each in the first year. (In reality, it would be much less.) At the time, we hoped to be able to hire our first salesperson in the early part of 1988. Tom was right, but he also was reneging on his offer of a role for Ellen in the company. After much angry argument between Tom and me, Ellen did not come to work for the company. It took many years for the bitterness of this episode to dissipate among all of us. I could hardly blame her for not joining us. Tom should never have offered our wives jobs before discussing it with me, and I should have rejected the idea before it was even said aloud in front of them.

Barely two years later, in 1989, both Ellen and Gail would come to our aid when the company had trouble making payroll. Ellen helped in the office, and Gail helped us sell Brooklyn

Lager in the trendy Soho neighborhood of Manhattan, where she had many old artist friends.

## Who Will Be Involved?

When you start a business, you should decide up front if it is going to be a family business or a merit-based business. In other words, are family members going to have the edge in seeking jobs in the company, or are jobs going to be rewarded to the best possible candidates? Thinking back, the question of family involvement should have been discussed at the time we signed the partnership agreement.

In the beer industry, some of the most successful companies are run by family dynasties. The president of Anheuser-Busch is August Busch IV. The company has been run by a Busch since 1876, but the Busch family has not had controlling interest in the company since it went public. Coors is controlled and run by the Coors family. Miller is a merit-based company now owned by South African Breweries. (There is a famous story about Jack McDonough, the president of Anheuser-Busch, leaving the company to join Miller. When August Busch III asked him if there was anything he could do to keep McDonough, the executive replied, "Yes. Adopt me.")

Eventually, Tom and I agreed that the Brooklyn Brewery was a merit-based company, not a family business. Anyone joining the Brooklyn Brewery knows he or she has a chance to be president or CEO someday, no matter that their names are not Hindy or Potter. Two painful experiences taught me the importance of this principle: first, the harrowing experience with my wife (who is now principal of a highly-respected middle school in New York City), and second, with our talented brewmaster, Garrett Oliver. A few years ago, I made the mistake of asking Garrett to hire my son to work in the brewhouse. Sam was an 18-year-old taking a year off from school before starting college. He was working in the warehouse and driving trucks for us. It is very arduous work, particularly in the winter. Sam had expressed no particular interest in brewing, but I wanted him to learn the basics anyway. I compounded my mistake by pointing out to Garrett that many of the most successful companies were family run. Garrett was clearly threatened by my words and was very angry. Over lunch he said he was absolutely opposed to hiring someone just because he was related to me. He said that he was proud of the reputation of the Brooklyn Brewery and his role with the company, but that he had a thick file of resumes from experienced brewers who wanted to work for the Brooklyn Brewery. Many had offered to work for next to nothing to get experience with Brooklyn. His team worked hard, and they were proud of their beers and their company.

"What sort of message would this send to the guys working in the brewhouse now?" he asked.

This was a bitter pill for me to swallow, but Garrett was right.

Once again, I could have averted a lot of aggravation and heartache if Tom and I had stipulated up front that the Brooklyn Brewery was not going to be a family business. We eventually decided that if a family member wanted a part or a position in the business, they would be subjected to the same processes as outside applicants and be hired only on the basis of their merits. To date, none of our children have expressed their own interest in working at the brewery. ★

## TOM WEIGHS IN

The most common form of organization in the world is the family business, and it has been forever, for obvious and primal reasons. Certainly a family business works well when a company is small (and sometimes even for larger businesses), but it's not what I wanted for the Brooklyn Brewery.

First, I had a partner. Two families are one too many for a family business. Second, we were going to have outside investors. That meant we would have to put their interests first, not ours. I didn't want any confusion about that. And third, I didn't like the idea of putting such specific expectations on our kids. The world is a huge and wonderful place: Why push your child into the one thing you happened to do? I once served on a Venture Bowl panel with Moira Forbes, one of the younger generation of the famous magazine family. She cheerfully acknowledged that she owed her job at the magazine strictly to enlightened nepotism—though in her case, she also happened to be an exceptionally able young woman. The magazine was lucky to have her. Nepotism works well in some families and for some businesses, but it was not what I wanted for mine.

I don't think Steve and I ever saw completely eye to eye on this. When I asked at our first sit-down if our wives wanted to be involved, I thought I was asking if they wanted to help out temporarily. I didn't realize my open-ended question would open a larger can of worms between Steve and me. Later, our wives did in fact work for the company. My wife, Gail, worked (for Steve, which I thought lessened the nepotism issue) in 1988 as our first Manhattan salesperson. She got our first bar and restaurant customers in Manhattan (and some of them are still customers), but she hated it and begged off after a few months. Ellen, Steve's wife, worked for me in our office, as Steve explained earlier. I don't know if she also hated it, but she stuck it out and helped us considerably in 1988 and part of 1989. That is what I initially had in mind, but Steve saw it as having potentially more ramifications than that.

It would come up again 10 years later, in the summer of 1998. On my first day back from a vacation I learned that Steve had hired his son, Sam, to work temporarily in the warehouse as an extra stock picker and driver. My heart sank. Steve had hired him in my absence and without talking to me.

Sam just needed a summer job, Steve explained. What was the harm in that? We had hired the sons of friends before, so why not our own sons? Our company now had over 75 employees, so an extra guy in the warehouse, more or less, didn't have to be a big deal.

But this episode created a rift between Steve and me, and employees who resented working with a son of one of the bosses used the situation to exploit the differences between Steve and me. I tried to let it slide. Only it turned out not to be just for the summer. Sam decided to take the year off before starting college. I was pretty sure this didn't reflect a sudden rush of enthusiasm about working for the Brooklyn Brewery.

Against that background, how could Steve have possibly proposed to Garrett that Sam should work in the brewhouse? The brewhouse was a much smaller, tighter group than the warehouse crew, with little room for slack. And again, probably knowing what I'd think, Steve didn't tell me about his proposal until after the fact.

Working at a menial job was a powerful motivator for Sam. He learned that driving a truck and delivering beer in New York City is no picnic. He went on to college and found things he much preferred to do and that he was good at. For the company, this episode wasn't a big deal—just a footnote that the old-timers remember—but it did confirm all my doubts about nepotism and family businesses. In most cases, searching for the best person for the job should be priority number one.

**Our Grade:**   On clarity about whether or not we were a family business, I give us a D. On putting together a good team in spite of that, Steve and I get a B. Over the years, we attracted some great people despite our sometimes unclear purpose.

# CHAPTER 3

# Tom Talks About Creating the Business Plan: A Money-Raising Tool and More

Weaving throughout Steve's experiences of finding design and brewing experts and thinking about how to best staff our new business were my similar experiences of discovery. We were in this together, always working at something and constantly discussing our ideas and actions, our successes and failures, in shaping our dream of starting the brewery.

As a young English major tucked into an ivy-covered college, I'd dreamed of writing the Great American Novel. Ten years later my target had shifted. In the fall of 1986, while living in Brooklyn, supporting a family, and trying to start a business, I was feverishly motivated in a different direction. I was going to write the Great American Business Plan.

The business plan was where the idea of the Brooklyn Brewery began its transformation into the business of the Brooklyn Brewery. The plan was the bridge from Crazy

Idea to Commitment to Crazy Idea. It was what allowed Steve and me to quit our jobs and turn our backs on our previous careers.

## WHAT KIND OF BUSINESS IS THIS PLAN FOR?

Business plans serve different purposes at each stage of a company's development. For a brand-new start-up like the Brooklyn Brewery, though, the first business plan is not just a document. What might appear to be a mundane 40-page report is really the dramatic result of months of imagining the world anew. It's the founders' distilled brainstorm of strategy, structure, management, and motivation. For Steve and me, the business plan represented green fields and blue sky. It contained dozens of crucial elements brought together in balance, and hundreds of other elements considered but necessarily rejected.

Brewpub or brewery? Production in-house or contracted out? Distribution in-house or contracted out? On our initial management team did we need an experienced professional brewer? Bookkeeper? Sales manager? Were our ambitions local, regional, or national? Would our beers be available only on draft? Only in bottles? Or both? Would our first beer be an ale or a lager? In a historic style or a created one?

About the only way to think clearly about so many complicated and interrelated ideas is to produce a written business plan. Where more than one founder is involved, like Steve and me, this is where we would find out whether we were thinking along the same lines. A cluster of amorphous possibilities are whittled down into a single plan of attack. General ideas are made specific. In it are the mission of the company; the proposed structure of the company, including ownership, management roles, and raising capital; and the operating structure and financial assumptions. It asks the question: Are we all on the same page?

This stage involved enormous creativity and analytical ability. Each question had multiple possible answers, and most of them were not clearly right or wrong. Any decision in one area influenced decisions in others. An approach on, say, the financial side (how much money will we try to raise?) would have implications on the operations side (how can we physically get the beer to market?). The process put together complementary answers that did the best job possible of making use of our assembled skills and resources. For every good idea there might be 10 possible business plans, but Steve and I were trying to create the strongest, most integrated plan for us. We needed a plan that best addressed our specific regional competition and our own personal strengths and weaknesses.

A real business plan allows ideas to move to the next stage: personal commitment. The founders look at each other and agree to hold hands and jump. Jumping might be quitting your job, or it might be raising money and taking on a role of financial responsibility for other people's money. The business plan is more than a planning document. It becomes your legal and moral contract when incorporated into an offering document. In it you explain exactly how you will spend money that has been committed to you. The commitment you are honoring might also be one of time. When you hire your first employees, they will want to know what they are signing on for, and the business plan maps that out.

But before you write the plan, you need to do your research.

## PROWLING THE CONFERENCE

I was standing in a hotel ballroom in Portland, Oregon, in 1986, wearing my Brooks Brothers pinstripe suit and carrying cards identifying me as an assistant vice president of Chemical Bank. Surrounding me, in just 5,000 square feet of carpeted meeting space, was the entire U.S. small brewing industry. It was the second annual small brewers conference, sponsored by the fledgling *New Brewer* magazine, and in attendance were either the owner or the brewmaster (often one and the same) of each of the 33 small breweries that had sprung up across the country within the last few years.

Most of these people were from the West Coast. Beginning with the New Albion and Anchor Steam breweries in northern California, each start-up had seemed to spur another. From the Bay Area, through Oregon, and up to Seattle, the movement had spread. It was still such a fledgling industry that it seemed every owner knew every other owner. The beer market was so vast (and their own presence so small) that there was not yet much worry about competition from each other. Each little brewery was a tiny boat on a huge heaving sea, and the conference gave them an opportunity to form groups and exchange survival tips. As a measure of the category's newness and a harbinger of impending growth, wannabe brewers outnumbered actual brewers by a wide margin.

Apart from consultants and equipment suppliers, there were no industry veterans. The founders were a motley crew: former teachers, social workers, and unemployed homebrewers were all newly minted commercial brewers. The dress code, to my banker's eye, looked something south of casual. Everyone was talking to each other with great animation about mysterious subjects such as the specific gravity of best bitters and new methods of spent grain removal. I thought: What am I doing here?

Initially I just kept my mouth shut to hide my ignorance. I went from booth to booth, learning what I could and giving out my banker business cards. People who took my cards asked what I was doing there, and I'd just say, "Research." Most assumed I was there as a professional, perhaps looking to finance these new start-ups. Within a few hours I realized that I was the only banker at the conference, at least the only one giving out cards, and I was becoming increasingly popular. The brewers and consultants were eager to answer my questions.

At night I fell in with a group touring the handful of exciting new Portland breweries. With the conference in town, Widmer, BridgePort Brewing, and Portland Brewing were each serving their beers and proudly pointing out equipment innovations. Experimentation and adapting old equipment to new purposes to save money were the order of the day. One of my new friends there was an industry consultant named John Bergmann. He gave me a private running commentary on the pros and cons of each of the brewery designs.

I learned that John was one of the few real pros at the conference. He had graduated 30 years earlier from M.I.T. and the United States Brewers Academy, and had worked in the industry since. He was now a consultant to breweries large and small, old and new. His clients included New Amsterdam, which was at that time the largest and most successful start-up brewery on the East Coast. He told me a little about his work for them, and I was impressed.

I confided in John that a partner and I were thinking of starting our own brewery in New York. He was enthusiastic, in the fashion that consultants are always enthusiastic about the possibility of a new client, and we agreed to stay in touch. His own field was in brewery design and construction, but if we were looking for someone to consult on recipes, he had some trusted colleagues. Later, through John, we would be introduced to our first brewer, Bill Moeller, who had been a classmate of John's at brewing school.

I had come to the conference with many questions. I had been serious enough about possibly starting a brewery to pay my own way across country, but I'm by nature pretty cautious. By the time I left, though, I had a lot of promising contacts and a few important answers. The most important answer was: Yes, we can do this. My growing confidence and excitement were based on an insight that was not original and that later proved to be only partly correct. I concluded that the primary appeal of the small brewers was that of geography. Their competitive advantage only began with the quality of their beer. It was crucial to go to the next step and develop local roots, to inspire affection and loyalty from their hometown. If that was true, then the best place to start a brewery was where you found the best potential local base. Where would a lot of people root for the home team?

In 1986, small breweries were beginning to open up like crazy. It seemed every big city and most medium-sized cities could probably support a local brewery. Portland and Seattle were each already supporting a handful. The movement was much newer and smaller back East, though New York already had two start-ups, and we might become the third. But I thought we had an important potential advantage over our existing and potential regional competition. Our advantage, I reasoned, could be Brooklyn.

It seemed to me that Brooklyn was both big enough and small enough to support us. Big enough: Though only one of five boroughs that make up the city of New York, it had the largest population. In fact, if it were a stand-alone city, it would at that time have ranked, with over two million residents, as the fourth-largest city in the United States. But it was also small enough to notice us, *and* it took great pride in its unique history. It had endured some tough economic times in the 1960s and 1970s, but by the 1980s it was just beginning to show signs of revival. Perhaps it would be hungry for a new local success story. The two other New York City breweries were in Manhattan; we would be the first in Brooklyn and, if we were good enough, perhaps the last.

Brooklyn also had a wonderful brewing history. I didn't know much about promotion—that was Steve's end of things—but I knew we would have a lot to work with. A rich history would give us angles to promote. We wouldn't be just a start-up, we would be carrying on an important tradition.

When I came back to New York from Portland, I was bubbling with enthusiasm. Steve had already been convinced that we should start our own brewery. Now I was convinced, too. I told my wife, Gail, that I really thought this could work. Steve and I talked for hours about our next steps.

Up until this point, I had been ambivalent about the business potential. I wasn't sure if this was just another good idea, or the one to jump on and convert into a business. Now I was on fire. I had to organize my thoughts in writing. The serious research began.

## VISITING THE COMPETITION

There were fewer than a dozen new breweries on the East Coast in 1987, but each was operating with a different philosophy and business model. We were determined to visit as many of them as we could. Most were quite friendly, as fit the community-of-brewers vibe of the time. Others were somewhat less so.

The very first microbrewery in the East was founded in 1981 by Bill Newman and his wife, Marie, in Albany, New York. When we called to ask for a visit, they were gracious. Bill spoke with a missionary zeal about his love for English beer and showed us his English-style brewhouse. Bill learned to make good and very traditional beer under the tutelage of the British consultant Alan Pugsley, and he refused to compromise with anything modern. Bill made beer totally by hand and expected one to drink it at "cellar" temperature, as was traditional—and which, for an American, meant "warm." Consequently, Bill struggled to sell beer.

Though largely forgotten now, Newman's example was hugely influential in the East Coast microbrewery scene. Consultant Pugsley became the Johnny Appleseed of British brewing systems, eventually installing over 40 breweries and brewpubs. By 1987 his breweries already included Geary's and Shipyard in Maine, among others. Consequently, many of these breweries started out brewing pretty similar beers. It seemed each of them had a flagship pale ale, supplemented with a porter and a stout.

And most of them used Pugsley's favorite Ringwood yeast, making them taste even more similar. It didn't matter for local fans of each brewery. They were getting very good beer. Only if you traveled and tried each of them did you realize that they were all good, and all strangely similar.

We also went to Philadelphia to talk with Jeff Ware, the founder of Dock Street Brewing Company. It was a brand-new start-up, and it seemed very promising. In addition to brewing beer under contract, Dock Street was to become a brewpub, a restaurant serving its own beer. Jeff had been a restaurant manager, so he actually knew something about what he was setting out to do. That put him in rarefied company in the early days. We thanked him for giving us advice, and he smiled and admitted he wasn't sure if it was a good idea to talk to potential competitors or not. But, he said, he had been in our position, asking many of the same questions a year earlier. He noted that most of the brewers he had talked to had been friendly. Matthew Reich from the New Amsterdam brewery was the main exception. Matthew had insisted on charging Jeff by the hour for advice. Jeff had paid but resented it, and after thinking about his resentment decided he'd be more generous when others, like Steve and me, might come to him.

In the car on the way home, Steve and I chewed over Jeff's experience with Matthew Reich. The founder of New Amsterdam seemed to have a pretty formidable personality: How would he view us? On the one hand, we were trying to start a brewery in New York, his hometown. And we were trying to steal as many of his good ideas as possible. On the other hand, we reasoned, he was already big, and we would be little. He was in Manhattan, and we would be in Brooklyn. There was nothing for him to be concerned about.

I don't know if Jeff was right or wrong about the wisdom of being generous with advice, but I know I appreciated it. For many years after, Steve and I tried to reciprocate with others who came to us. I liked our small industry's feeling of community. Though, I must admit, there came a time in the mid-1990s when it seemed like everyone was getting into the business and asking for help. The occasional request became a torrent of phone calls and written requests, and we started saying no. It was a sign of changing times, of an intimate niche industry growing larger, more competitive, and more demanding.

## Historical Breweries Tour

In addition to visiting the new microbreweries, we wanted to visit the older regional breweries. There were still about a dozen of them fighting to survive in the East. For most it was a losing battle, but a few, like Yuengling, F.X. Matt Brewing, and the Lion Brewery, would find a way. Access to these breweries proved a little trickier. They did not share the communal friendliness of the new microbrewers. They were skeptical, competition-hardened veterans who didn't think much of people like Steve and me. They all knew each other, but didn't much care to know us.

When we hired Bill Moeller in early 1987 as our professional brewer, it opened up additional brewery gates for us to visit. Bill was a veteran and respected brewer from a family of brewers. He had been going to brewmaster conferences for practically his whole life. He had seen the East Coast brewing industry shrink from hundreds, in his youth, down to dozens at the time of his early retirement from the Schmidt brewery. With the brewery pool contracted, all the remaining brewmasters at the traditional breweries knew each other well. Bill had contacts everywhere. We were delighted to take advantage of them. For his part, he was delighted to be working on a project for a really premium beer. When we told him that all we cared about was quality, his eyes lit up. For years brewery owners had told him to make their beer cheaper. We were telling him that we wanted a better beer, no matter how much it cost.

When we visited the older regional breweries it was with two thoughts in mind. First, to learn as much as we could about the industry in general. And second, to find a specific brewery that we could use to produce our beer under contract. We targeted those within one day's drive of New York City that were flexible enough to make good beer.

One of the breweries Steve and I wanted to visit was Yuengling. The oldest brewery in America, it had been brewing beer in Pottsville, Pennsylvania, since 1829. Since Bill Moeller lived in Pennsylvania, he set up the appointment and agreed to meet us there. Steve and I piled into in the car in Brooklyn and talked nonstop for four hours, barely looking at the map to check progress. When we arrived in town, none of Bill's directions seemed to make sense. We eventually stopped and asked a town policeman, who looked amused.

"The Yuengling brewery, in Pottsville?" he said. "Well, now, take a left here, and then drive north about 60 miles. You're in Pottstown. Pottsville's up that way." Sheepishly, we turned around and arrived at the brewery considerably later than scheduled. But Bill had waited for us, and he introduced us to Yuengling's brewmaster, Ray Norbert. Ray gave us a detailed tour of the old brewery and its famous cave cellars. We were entranced. Brewing history came alive as we walked through the brewery. Bill was asking Ray technical questions, some of which I could only partly understand, but I absorbed as much as possible. We met Dick Yuengling briefly. He was wearing blue jeans and a polo shirt and working in the bottling room. He didn't have too much time for visitors. He had bought the brewery from his father two years earlier and was driven to keep it alive. This did not seem like a sure thing in early 1987. His family brewery had been in decline for many years, and the odds of turning around the fortunes of an older brewery were long indeed.

After our Yuengling tour, the three of us ate lunch, and Bill told us that he admired the Yuengling brewery, but he didn't think they would be receptive to brewing beer under contract for us. Despite the fact that they needed additional volume, Ray had told him privately that they were determined to brew only their own beer and add to their volume only by increasing house-brand sales. It seemed a stubborn position to take, not only disappointing from our point of view but a mistake from theirs. History proved them right, however. Their stubbornness was rewarded with exponential growth over the next two decades, the only older brewery to enjoy such growth.

Bill joined us as we visited other breweries, as well. He patiently explained brewing techniques and the intricacies of production facilities. His presence not only got us into breweries, but helped us decipher them.

When we narrowed down our choices of contract brewing facilities, the Matt brewery became our favorite. You'll remember Steve's mention in Chapter 2 of the monumental struggle to find an in with F.X. Matt II. The location, reputation for quality control, and flexible production capabilities of the Matt Brewery were decisive. When we told the Matt Brewery that Bill would be our brewmaster and would represent us during the brewing of our beer, they had mixed feelings. They didn't like the idea of a contract brewer (one that, like us, would be making our beer in their brewery) looking too closely over their shoulder. It was a proud and private operation. But if we had to saddle them with someone, they seemed glad that Bill was our guy. From their point of view, Bill was a fellow professional who knew commercial operations on a true commercial scale. He wasn't just another damned homebrewer with big dreams.

Working on a shoestring, we tried to save as much money as we could when visiting breweries. That included crashing on floors with friends instead of paying for hotels, when possible. I had a friend who had recently moved to the country just outside Utica, New York, so when we met Bill to visit the Matt Brewery I arranged for us to borrow some floor space. Bill was older than my father, but he didn't complain about the rough accommodations. The next morning I found him awake bright and early, freshly shaved and smiling, and talking politics over a cup of coffee with my friend.

## THE GREAT AMERICAN BUSINESS PLAN (CIRCA 1987)

In 1987, even more than now, background industry research still meant libraries. The Internet was not available, and Google did not exist. Steve had been able to generate a valuable compendium of newspaper stories from *Newsday*'s Nexus database, but we needed more. To put news stories into an industry perspective, and to create a business context, we needed basic research. Five years out of Columbia Business School I still had my student ID, though, of course, it had expired. Fortunately no one looked too hard at it as I bustled in and out of the business school library there. I also began haunting the Brooklyn Business Library, a unique branch of the Brooklyn Public Library located on Cadman Plaza near Brooklyn Borough Hall. It had a surprisingly strong collection of journals and periodicals, including ones from the brewing industry.

The writing of business plans, like the rest of the business world, was being transformed by the growing availability of personal computers in the 1980s. When I first joined Chemical Bank in 1983, computers were mostly confined to information technology departments in large corporations. I knew of personal computers—Apple was well established, and IBM had just introduced its seminal PC—but I didn't own one, and I didn't know anyone who did.

At the bank, we began to have access to word processing, but we still wrote memos on Selectric typewriters. We fixed our mistakes with clumsy correction tape and rejoiced when Wite-Out became available. A small secretarial pool was meant to serve junior officers, but knowing how to touch-type gave some of us the great luxury of independence and the ability to work brutally ambitious hours. Financial statements were prepared using adding machines or calculators, with each line entered longhand. "Spreading" financial statements was to us an accounting term, which meant standardizing several years' worth of individual statements and comparing them closely, line by line, to detect and highlight trends. Early computerized spreadsheets like VisiCalc and Lotus were out there, but hot-shot junior officers were just beginning to get access to them.

Business tools taken for granted now were just on the horizon then. Transmitting information from office to office meant sending paper documents by the post office, interbank courier, or messenger service. Forget about e-mail—unless you were a physics professor or a general, you probably hadn't heard of it. Fax machines were beginning to be introduced, but hardly anyone had one yet. Our bank office was proud to have one (painfully slow, with curling thermal paper), but none of our customers did, so it was useless in communicating with them. We used it mostly with other bank departments. Federal Express was a wild success with its new overnight delivery service, but it was so expensive (and there were so few other options) that it quickly became a budget-buster, requiring senior approval, as vice presidents grappled to contain costs.

By 1987, I had taught myself the basics of WordPerfect and Lotus and knew that they would make a huge difference in writing a business plan. The only problem was that they required a computer. I couldn't use the bank's computers, didn't have my own computer, and didn't know anyone in New York who would lend me one. I did have a friend, however—Steve Edelson—who had recently graduated from Stanford Business School and, on hearing of my plans, offered to let me borrow his nearly new Apple II. It's hard to overstate how generous an offer that was. I could hardly believe when it arrived from California. It was like a gift from heaven, and I got busy.

## Getting the Market's Passing Grade

Writing a business plan feels a bit like writing a college term paper. At 40 or 50 pages including exhibits, it might be about the same length; a considerable amount of research is involved; and you might take the equivalent of a semester to finish. Of course, the grading system is different. Instead of subjective comments and a letter grade from the professor, your final business plan feedback will be coldly objective. Did the plan allow you to raise the money you need? Did it lead to a viable business? And there is no grading curve. Welcome to the harsh world of business pass-fail, where, unfortunately, the majority of business plans simply fail. So—how to get the market's passing grade?

Actually putting your thoughts on paper is a powerful process. On our return from the Portland, Oregon, convention, I knew it was time to get organized and get writing. We still had lots of research to do, but the process of writing actually helped organize the research. Seeing what we had, on paper, made clearer what we still needed to do.

I had some advantages when I began to write. The first came out of business school. I attended Columbia at a time when entrepreneurial studies were an insignificant afterthought. Nearly all of my friends and classmates were eagerly heading off to successful careers working for major corporations in finance and marketing. Those of us who dreamed of starting our own businesses were in a crackpot minority.

Out of the hundreds of classes Columbia Business School offered at that time, there was only one true class for us—just one that specifically addressed how to start a business. Taught by the now legendary professor Ian C. MacMillan, it was extremely practical. The class formed into groups; each group chose an idea for a new business, got the idea approved by Professor MacMillan for practicality, and then set out to write a business plan. As the semester proceeded, we learned what each section of a standard business plan looked like and how the sections worked together. There were no tests and no papers, apart from the actual plan.

The entire grade was based on two things: the final plan and our presentation. For the presentation, Professor MacMillan would recruit professionals in our specific industry to sit in as surrogate venture capitalists. They would hear the initial presentation and then take an hour to ask questions and probe for weaknesses. For students, this was an intimidating session, to say the least. All the time we were writing our plans we knew that real professionals—successful managers in the field we proposed to enter—would ultimately be grilling us. It no longer felt like an academic exercise. Pros who knew far more about our industry than we did would be rendering an unsentimental verdict. This was outstanding training. It closely mirrored the real world, giving us invaluable practice and practical experience. Professor MacMillan's approach was innovative at the time, though it seemed to me to get little respect from the rest of the more academically inclined school. Of course, more than 20 years later, business schools have embraced this exact concept. Business plan competitions have sprouted up at schools across the country, and entrepreneurial studies have rightfully moved into the mainstream. Columbia now boasts that entrepreneurial studies are a core element of its MBA program, and the former academic director of its Lang Center for Entrepreneurship is now dean of the business school. It's a sign of real change.

Past experience gave me another advantage as I set about writing our Brooklyn Brewery plan. My years as a credit trainee, analyst, and young banker turned out to be great training. Part of that training was writing hundreds of memos analyzing various businesses. I was an English major in college and may have thought I knew how to write, but as a banker I labored to learn a very different style. I discovered that business writing is most persuasive when it is least flamboyant.

I learned that an even surface tone beats enthusiasm every time. As a lending officer, I wanted to do deals, I wanted my boss to read my credit memo and sign off on the proposed loan. But the bank taught me that my boss's trust—the reader's trust—was established with patience and thoroughness instead of rah-rah boosterism. Each memo included sections on the proposed credit's weaknesses, as well as its strengths. I knew I wanted to achieve the same thing with our Brooklyn Brewery business plan: Establish trust first; sell second.

Sometimes Steve and I disagreed over how to say things. Usually he'd accuse me of being too cautious, and I'd accuse him of overselling. In the end, of course, every business needs both caution and enthusiasm, as does every business plan. The challenge is to find the right balance, which Steve and I achieved through lots of communication and trust.

## PRIMER FOR PLAN WRITERS

The typical business plan for a start-up will be made up of about a half dozen separate sections. An executive summary will take one or two pages. Then might come one or two pages describing "sources and uses" of financing, which specify exactly how much money is sought and what it will be spent on. Next will be a description of the market and a definition of the opportunity at hand, a frank look at competitors, a description of how the company will operate and what its advantages and disadvantages will be, a section on key managers and advisors, and financial projections.

Over the last 30 years or so, this format has become fairly standardized. Despite what some books may tell you, there is no exact right or wrong structure. Still, trying to get too creative with the format is probably a mistake. People who read lots of business plans, just like people who read lots of resumes, aren't looking for a creative format. They want something familiar and comprehensible. As the writer, you will want to cover all of the obvious bases but also leave the reader intrigued and interested in learning more. The purpose of a business plan, as with a resume, is not to answer all possible questions. It is simply to get the interview.

Here are some specific tips that can help a writer shape a strong business plan. Tip number one: Trust the reader. Your job is to present the facts, pro and con, and trust the reader to get as excited as you are. In your mind, do the positives of your plan far outweigh the negatives? The reader wants to be reassured that you are being as fair, as thorough, in presenting the negatives as you are the positives. If all a reader sees is blue sky, it will feel wrong; there is no such thing as a can't-miss, perfect idea. Of course, you, as the writer, have the huge advantage of always being able to get the last word in. After you've presented a negative, you always can present ways to address the concerns, lessen possible impacts, and explore flexible alternatives that may be available.

Did the Brooklyn Brewery business plan instruct the reader? Of course. But I was also looking for a guided discovery process. I assumed that readers would not be persuaded by dictate but by reason, thoroughness, and a sense that the plan presented enough information for them to draw their own conclusions—conclusions that would be more strongly held than any I could have drawn for them. "Guide but trust" was my motto.

Tip number two: To the extent possible, avoid the word *conservative*. When a business plan says that it "conservatively" estimates this or sales will "conservatively" reach that, most readers get a suspicious twitch. When using the word *conservative*, you're trying to feed the reader a conclusion and shortcut the private analysis. It doesn't work. Readers will come to their own conclusions, wherever you try to lead them. The reader is thinking: Don't tell me that's a "conservative" estimate; just give me the facts, and I'll tell *you*. So present your best estimates and label them as such. Then point out why they might be too high or, better yet, too low. (Did we use the "c" word in our plan? Well, yes, maybe once or twice. But we did keep it to a minimum.)

Tip number three: You won't convince everyone, so don't try. In fact, it's highly unlikely that you will convince even one person in four that your plan is good enough to deserve their money or their time. If everyone around you tells you they think you've really got a winner, congratulations—you're surrounded by people who love you. That's a good thing, but just don't start believing them.

The hard truth is that every new idea initially looks like a long shot. You can't convince everyone, but you can convince enough people to raise enough money to get started. Perhaps you need 25 investors. Maybe you need two venture funds. Maybe you just need one father-in-law. Most people will say no, but that's okay—there are a lot of people out there. (Well, maybe not a lot of such fathers-in-law.)

You are searching for what you will come to identify as the intelligent reader. An intelligent reader will get it and understand that there are risks in investing in a start-up. They don't want or need you to pound them over the head with your conclusions. For example, your plan may suggest that you will bring together blue from here and yellow from there and the result will be a useful green. You don't have to use boldface headings that say **green** or heavily drawn arrows pointing to **green**. You don't need to say **green green green**. Allow the reader the thrill of discovery; it is the most powerful and subtle form of selling. *Green,* the intelligent reader will think, *how exciting! How do I invest?*

## IS IT TIME TO QUIT YOUR DAY JOB?

In February of 1987 our business plan was done and our lawyers were busy converting it into an offering document. Lawyers should enter the picture only near the end of the business plan process. I hope that you don't need a lawyer to tell you how to meet the business opportunity. For instance, Steve mentioned our law firm, Scoppetta and Seiff, in Chapter 2. Scoppetta and Seiff was attractive to us not for their corporate work or for working with start-ups, but rather for their knowledge of how to deal with the mob. They actually contracted out most of the securities work, which was fine with me because the woman doing the work was good, and I didn't think we actually needed much corporate advice yet. But as the lawyers were preparing the offering, I struggled with a serious choice. When the offering was ready, should I quit my job to try to raise money full-time? Or should I stay at the bank and hedge my bets?

I'm normally a cautious guy, but I couldn't see trying to do both things at once. For one thing, I wasn't sure it was ethical to be working at the bank while I was soliciting my fellow workers for investments and while my attention was clearly elsewhere. Maybe more important, I was as keyed up as a racehorse at the starting gate. I could no longer pay attention to my bank business. It didn't seem important anymore. I could hardly bear to think of going to work.

The economic environment that winter seemed to make the choice a little easier. After a tremendous boom in the early 1980s, values in New York real estate were headed for a fall in 1987. Congress had passed a massive tax law overhaul in 1986, which took away some of the tax advantages of commercial real estate, and it was hard to justify the high-flying purchase prices that buyers wanted to finance. I had declined to do certain deals because the valuations seemed wrong, but other banks would do the deals, which initially left me scratching my head. Later on, it left those other banks with some pretty bad loans.

There wasn't much to do at my job, I reasoned, and there was lots to do if we were to get the Brooklyn Brewery up and running. I talked it over with my wife and with Steve, and made the decision to leave the bank. I wasn't sure if it was the right thing to do or not, but it seemed the only real choice. The business plan I had written was now beginning to direct my life.

My wife was tremendously supportive. Gail had one basic question: "If it doesn't work, can we lose the house?"

"No," I said confidently. "If it doesn't work, I can always get another job."

That was it in a nutshell. I was 32 years old in 1987. The bank had given me great training and experience. It had promoted me at each step as quickly as bank policy allowed. My annual bonuses, while puny by investment bank standards, were high for a young commercial banker. My performance ratings had always been tops. I was among the first of my peers to be anointed an assistant vice president, and I was pretty confident that I'd become a full vice president within another couple of years if I stayed. But I didn't want to stay a banker. I wanted to own my own business. And if it didn't work out, I knew I could always find another job.

In a perfect world, I would have been better prepared. I could have waited a bit longer and put some savings away. Or perhaps I could have taken a leave of absence instead of simply quitting. But at that time, I wanted to gamble and commit myself fully. I wanted the feeling of being totally dedicated emotionally to getting the Brooklyn Brewery up and running.

I walked into my boss's office and gave four weeks' notice. She wasn't entirely surprised at my leaving, only at what I was leaving to do. Not too many bankers were quitting to start breweries. I came out of her office, breathed a huge sigh of relief, and began to tell my colleagues in adjoining cubicles what I had planned. Surprisingly, not one of them told me I was crazy. Most were nearly as excited for me as I was for myself, and the idea of starting not just my own business, but my own brewery, enchanted them. I took it as a good omen that beer was different. Beer was going to be special.

## MONEY: WHERE, HOW, AND HOW MUCH

One main goal of the business plan was to raise money. But what would our target be? Where would we raise the money? How would we solicit the investment? And how much money would we need to get the business off the ground?

Since I was a banker, many friends assumed Steve and I would look for bank financing. Even as I was writing our plan, though, I knew the Brooklyn Brewery would not want money from a bank. We were envisioning a high-risk venture. We expected to lose money the first year and, at best, break even the second. We would plow all eventual profits back into the business to fund the most rapid growth possible. It just wasn't a strategy a bank would be comfortable with, and I didn't want a bank looking over our shoulders. Banks care only about risk and downside, since they don't share in the upside.

Instead of using my banker's background to raise money from a bank or using contacts, I hoped to use what I had learned at the bank to put together a sound plan and to be convincing when selling it to individual investors. The financial structure of the plan, and our business, assumed that all of our investment would come from moderately wealthy individuals, or angel investors. I had rejected out of hand the idea of trying to raise venture capital. For one thing, venture money in those days was a tiny fraction of what it is now—there were far fewer sources of it, and most weren't interested in modest ideas like a microbrewery. By its very nature, a microbrewery is not a "big" idea. We conceived of success as eventually becoming perhaps a $7 to $10 million mature business. Venture funds like ideas that can scale up and get huge.

I also was leery of the control I knew we'd have to surrender to win venture money. It seemed to me that venture funds were the ultimate professional investor and would doubtless negotiate hard terms while demanding some measure of control to protect their money. I preferred structuring an offering targeted to individual investors as a take-it-or-leave-it deal. I felt we could find enough amateur investors to raise the capital that we needed by offering a fair deal but maintaining control.

I considered all the standard business forms, such as corporations and general partnerships, but the one that intrigued me was the more exotic limited partnership. In this format a single general partner runs the business and accepts total risk, while limited partners are removed both from management decisions and from liability beyond their original investment. As a banker, I had financed many real estate limited partnerships and I had seen dozens of limited partnership offering documents. I knew I could adapt this format to our business goals.

Early draft plans envisioned raising $875,000. On the one hand, it didn't seem like a lot of money to me. At the bank I had personal signing authority for up to $1 million. On the other hand, I knew it would be a lot harder asking for money than giving it out. And it was hard to figure where exactly we were going to raise it. Neither Steve nor I came from particularly wealthy families and we hadn't identified any big spenders as likely benefactors. Trying to add up potential investment amounts in my head, I kept petering out after a couple of hundred thousand. Reluctantly, we lowered the target amount to be raised to $500,000. It was still more ambitious than most of the other breweries starting up, but it meant that even if we raised the full amount we couldn't do everything we would have liked right away.

### Asking for Money, Hat (and Plan) in Hand

We had about 125 offering books printed up. Each book started with stern warnings and disclosures. In essence, it said that the founders had no experience in this business and there was a strong chance we would fail completely. No one who couldn't afford to lose all of their money should invest. Then came the good part. The business plan described how we thought we could build a great company and get rich. Finally, it ended with more dire warnings and disclosures. It was easy to tell which parts we had written and which parts our lawyers had written.

After much agonizing, we ultimately decided to try to raise a minimum of $300,000 and a maximum of $500,000 in $20,000 units. We agreed to sell partial units if necessary. We gave ourselves eight months to raise $300,000, the minimum amount we felt we could begin our business with. Before we reached the minimum, all investment proceeds would be held in escrow by our lawyer. If we didn't raise $300,000 by the end of 1987, we would give all the money back untouched—but I didn't think that would happen. At least, I hoped not.

I numbered each of the books and accompanying subscription documents, which were what someone who invested had to fill in and give back, along with the all-important check. Steve and I gave out books to our friends, relatives, and colleagues. Then we arranged to meet with them and would proceed to describe the unique investment opportunity they were being offered. Sometimes Steve or I would meet alone with a potential investor, but usually we double-teamed them.

We developed our own version of the good cop/bad cop routine. Steve would be full of open optimism and boundless enthusiasm. I would present the risks and acknowledge legitimate concerns in cautious, banker's fashion. Of course, I was burning with excitement inside, but investors seemed reassured by the conservative exterior. The complementary nature of our public personas made for an effective presentation for Steve and me. It was a good balance.

Each time someone agreed to invest, it was a huge victory. As confident as we tried to appear, the truth was, we were still secretly amazed that anyone would actually give us money. When we'd get a subscription package with a check, it was validation for our plan, our idea, our dream. I'd look at the check in private wonderment, then I'd give it to the lawyer to deposit into the escrow account.

The first two months of raising money were exciting. Beginning in April, and throughout May, a number of people enthusiastically signed up. We reached $100,000 in commitments, then $150,000. Halfway to escrow! It seemed that we were building momentum. Unfortunately, what we were really doing was picking the low-hanging fruit. Many people we had specifically targeted as potential investors did, in fact, invest. Some did not. But the remaining pool of potential investors seemed to be shrinking, and we still had a long way to go.

Investment slowed to a trickle throughout the summer. I was making telephone calls, following up with friends of friends and acquaintances of acquaintances. Steve and I each went through our Rolodexes twice. I cashed out my meager savings and burned through it by the end of June. From then on, I was living off my credit cards and feeling increasingly tense.

By the beginning of October we had crept up to just over $260,000 in escrowed funds. We were so close to our goal that I couldn't imagine giving up, but I was also nearly out of personal financial running room. My mother, who had limited resources, had already agreed to make a modest investment. Now I reluctantly asked her if I could borrow some money to live on for another couple of months. She sent me a check for $5,000. I also began to make discreet inquiries with friends about job possibilities at different banks, just in case.

Then came the call that put us over the hump. Charlie Hamm, president and CEO of Independence Community Bank, said that his bank would put in $40,000. I was dumbfounded. We had met with Charlie a month earlier and been enormously impressed. His bank was the largest based in Brooklyn and he seemed to know everyone of influence in the borough. But I had to tell Charlie that we weren't looking for loans, we were looking for equity investors. He had waved off my objection and just kept asking questions.

When he called, I had to ask, "You mean $40,000 in equity, right?" He said that was correct. He explained that his bank would set up a special-purpose subsidiary to make this one investment, which would come out of his marketing budget. Then he would immediately write off the entire investment as a marketing expense, so he wouldn't have to bother to justify it to bank regulators. I had never heard of a bank doing that before or since. Charlie Hamm proved to be a unique banker, and his confidence in us was both thrilling and humbling.

His investment offer came in the nick of time. We didn't know it yet, but the stock market was about to plummet and drag all investor confidence down with it. Culminating a long bull run, the market had peaked in late August of 1987, with the Dow Jones reaching 2,722. It had fallen a bit over the next six weeks to just over 2,600. The Monday after Charlie Hamm's call, October 19, the stock market crashed. It lost over 500 points, or almost 20 percent of its value, in one day. It was an even steeper one-day decline than during the crash of 1929.

Over the next few days, the Dow Jones dropped below 1,800 and the market decline had reached 30 percent. Worried investors were seriously speculating about not just a financial recession but an actual depression. Certainly no one was in the mood to consider a risky investment in a new brewery. With the commitment from Independence Bank coming in just under the wire, we broke escrow, but barely. We were in business. Without it and being so close to the market crash, we would have been finished. It would have signaled the end of the Brooklyn Brewery before it had even started.

## LESSON THREE
## THE BUSINESS PLAN WON'T BE GRADED ON A CURVE

The business plan is a matter of life and death to the business—and, by extension, to the dreams of the founders. To a new business, money is like oxygen. Will the plan allow the business to raise enough money and give it enough breathing room to get started? And does the plan set out an initial structure and strategy that will let the business take initial forward steps and survive the first year? Or does it instead include some crippling birth defect that will hobble the business from the start?

Results are brutally objective. You will raise enough money, or you won't. The business will survive, or it won't. Survival may not describe your lofty dreams, but unless the business survives the first year, it can't adjust, grow, or search out alternatives. Dreams can be achieved, if time allows. If your plan gives you the means to survive the first 12 months, good work. There are no bonus points for style, elegance, hard work, or good intentions. Raise the money you need and survive; then, and only then, will your business plan earn a passing grade. And that's the only thing that matters.

Even though I took the reins on building the business plan and initiating a lot of the capital-raising activities, Steve was instrumental in bringing in a substantial amount of our first-year investments as well. We both discovered quickly that there was more money out there to secure, but we'd eventually have to forage widely to find it. ★

## STEVE WEIGHS IN

There is money out there, but it's not in banks. The process of raising money provided Tom and me with some of the biggest surprises—and thrills—of our entrepreneurial experience. Until we started the Brooklyn Brewery, my particular experience in raising money had been limited to begging for money from my parents. And I did not have a great record at that. Thankfully, Tom had had some experience with large sums of money, signing off on loans and deals at Chemical Bank. This gave us a jump on trying to get our heads around finding capital for our own business purposes.

When Ellen and I returned from the Middle East, we had $40,000 in savings. It doesn't seem like much when you're trying to raise more than

$300,000 to start a new business, but it was still a blessing. We had been able to save this amount not because AP paid so well but because we paid no income taxes to the United States or to Lebanon and Egypt during our years abroad. When we started looking for a place to live in New York City, we quickly realized we could no longer afford Manhattan. So we began looking in the up-and-coming Brooklyn neighborhood of Park Slope. Eventually, we found a two-bedroom cooperative apartment for $89,000. For about $20,000 more, we could have gotten a similar-sized apartment on a much nicer block. Ellen and I each approached our parents, who had hinted they would be willing to help us out, but after much aggravation, we realized they were not so willing to help. One minute they had to balance any help they gave us with help they might give our siblings. Then they wondered why we didn't buy something we could afford, and then they wanted to come and see the apartments. We gave up.

Ironically, two years later, in 1987, when I was raising money for the brewery, my father and mother were the first to invest, with $20,000.

"Finally, you're going to make some money with that Cornell education," said my dad, optimistically. He had never been a fan of my journalism career. I can still remember my humiliation when I proudly told him of my first job with a daily newspaper, the Geneva *Times* (New York): "Six years at Cornell and you are making $100 bucks a week . . ."

Tom and I set out to raise money in the spring of 1987 by showing our offering documents to anyone who would look at them—chiefly colleagues from work. In the end, I garnered 10 investors from *Newsday*, bringing in a total of $95,000, and another $105,000 from family and friends. Tom raised $105,000 from his professional and personal friends and family. Once we tapped out people we knew, we began to pitch referrals. That is where the rest of the money came from. We presented our plan to potential investors in bars and diners around New York. We visited some people in their homes on weekday nights. We did a beer tasting and pitch to a group of potential investors at the Montauk Club, one of Brooklyn's last private clubs, an ornate masterpiece of architecture modeled on the Ca' D'Oro in Venice. We began calling our presentation "The Tom and Steve Show." I told the story of my interest in beer, and Tom impressively laid out the business plan. I was as flabbergasted as Tom when these prudent amateur investors wrote out checks to us. I had the feeling they were investing more in us—and in our partners Milton Glaser and Bill Moeller—than in the actual plan, but they all said they understood the perils of investing in a start-up, and some really did.

One of the initial investors, an electrician from Long Island, told us of investing in a dental clinic, which folded when the entrepreneur-dentist fled to the Caribbean.

"How do I know you guys aren't going to disappear?" he asked. That is a difficult question to answer. All we could do is ask for a character reference from the *Newsday* employee who had recommended us. The electrician invested.

One of our key early investors, who would later become the biggest investor, was David Ottaway, the *Washington Post* correspondent in Cairo, who had been a close professional and personal friend of mine during my years in the Middle East. I did not think to ask David to invest until I was spurned by another *Washington Post* reporter, John Randal. Randal had invited me to a Boxing Day party at his mother's impressive Fifth Avenue apartment in Manhattan. I took my offering documents along and offered them to John as I was leaving the party. He took a quick look at the plan and said, "I don't have the kind of money it takes to do this. But why don't you talk to your friend David Ottaway?" I did, and David, to my surprise, invested $10,000.

The investment of Charlie Hamm of the Independence Community Bank (which Tom explained earlier) was a huge, maybe decisive, boost. Charlie, a handsome, enthusiastic man bubbling with ideas, embraced our business plan. He said he believed Brooklyn was poised for great growth and he felt that our business could be part of that future. Charlie offhandedly coined our first slogan, "We Serve Brooklyn," by picking the words out of my mouth during my presentation.

"If you guys work very hard, and stick with this idea, then in 10 years, you will be an overnight success," said Charlie. He was right.

I quit my job at *Newsday* in September 1987, after returning from a month-long assignment in the Persian Gulf. By early October, we had raised $300,000, the minimum amount needed to begin putting our plan into effect. Then, on October 19, 1987, the stock market plummeted. Investors lost up to 50 percent of the value of their portfolios. Up to that moment, the dips and rises of the U.S. economy did not seem to have any appreciable effect on our venture. The U.S. economy was international; we were local. But after Black Monday, even small investors were obsessively calculating their drastic, if mostly paper, losses. No one was investing in anything at the end of 1987, and especially not a start-up by two inexperienced, unproven entrepreneurs. We were dead in the water . . . for the time being.

In September 1987, we had rented offices at 230 Fourth Avenue in

Brooklyn, a storefront on a ragtag commercial strip of automotive parts stores, car washes, oil-change businesses, plumbing supply stores, and fast-food outlets. We had to have an office address to apply for our brewer's licenses. Tom and I set up our desks at the new office, erected a Brooklyn Brewery sign over the door, and began work on the copious applications for brewer's licenses from the U.S. Bureau of Alcohol, Tobacco and Firearms and the New York State Liquor Authority. It was a cold Thanksgiving and Christmas that year. The licensing process was arduous. We learned that we had to get detailed financial disclosure statements from all our investors. They also had to get fingerprinted. The process was designed to ensure that no illegally gotten funds would be invested in a brewing enterprise. As far as we knew, none of our investors had any shady connections, but they were not happy about disclosing their personal finances to the U.S. BATF and the New York State Liquor Authority. Our phones were not ringing. It seemed to be raining a lot.

On one such dreary cold day in January 1988, I got a call from Bernard Fultz of Middleport, Ohio, my hometown. Middleport is the middle port on the Ohio River between Pittsburgh and Cincinnati. That was probably important about 100 years ago, but history had long since passed Middleport by. When I left Middleport at age 16, it had a population of 3,300. In 1988, the population was slightly less than that. Bernard had been our family lawyer. He was a close friend of my father, who had helped him get elected Meigs County district attorney many years before. At my dad's suggestion, I had sent Bernard a prospectus several weeks before.

"How are things out there in New York?" asked Bernard in an upbeat tone. I brought Bernard up to date on my life and then presented the state of the company in as positive a way as I could. He said that he thought we had an interesting plan, and he wanted to invest. I said great, and began to explain how to fill out the offering documents. He politely interrupted me by saying he had a client who also was interested in investing. He asked if I had ever heard of Jay Hall. He said Hall was a man who had done quite well in the coal mining business, beginning as a truck driver delivering coal to the power plants on the Ohio River, buying his truck, and then gaining ownership of all the trucks, buying a mine, and then buying lots of mines. Hall liked our idea and was interested in investing, he said.

I said, "Great," and began to explain how to fill out the offering documents, again. Bernard said Hall's resources were much larger than his own. Hall wanted to invest $50,000. I blurted out, "$50,000?" and Tom came running to my desk, asking who I was talking to. Bernard asked me to send him another set of offering documents so he and Hall could send us checks.

In business, Hall is called an angel investor. An angel investor is someone who likes an idea for reasons known only to him- or herself and is not afraid to take a chance. Without Hall, the Brooklyn Brewery might never have succeeded. At key points over the next six years, he invested a total of $2 million, becoming our biggest investor and saving us from ruin several times.

On one occasion, when Jay invested $1.2 million, we met him and Bernard in a hotel in Columbus, Ohio. Jay is a man of few words. He has had great success as an entrepreneur and an investor. He is an admirer of Warren Buffett and, like Buffett, has a penchant for enigmatic comments. (At the height of the Internet boom, Buffett told an interviewer, "The Dilly Bar is more certain in 10 years than any software." The Dilly Bar is a product of the Dairy Queen company.) Jay allows his attorney to do most of the talking. At this meeting, Bernard explained that Jay was impressed that Tom and I had left promising careers to start the Brooklyn Brewery. He was impressed that I had worked a year at the brewery with no pay while working nights at *Newsday*. Bernard said that Jay was encouraged by our enthusiasm for our dream. He noticed that we never looked back at our difficulties, but rather forged ahead with the conviction that the Brooklyn Brewery would succeed.

Hall listened patiently and then with a mischievous grin on his face, said, "Hell, Bernard, the only reason I invested in this thing in the first place is because Steve is from Middleport."

America is an amazing place, where fortunes have been made in the smallest towns as well as the bigger cities. There is a fundamental belief in entrepreneurship, in enterprise, and there are people out there who are willing to back an idea that catches their fancy. You just have to be dedicated enough to your ideas to find the right people. Banks and venture firms will rarely invest in a start-up, and if they do, they typically want to own the lion's share going forward. If you are raising money for a start-up, leave no stone unturned. There may be an angel hovering somewhere in your world.

**Our Grade:** I give us an A+ for the business plan and raising money. "The Tom and Steve Show" became a very polished presentation. Ultimately, raising money became one of our most important skills.

# CHAPTER 4

# Tom Asks, "What's the True Mission of the Business?"

Imagine you're the leader of a wagon train. You've led your brave band through the wilderness for the better part of a year. Now it's a quiet night, and you're sitting at the fire alone, reflecting. And what you're thinking is: *I've really screwed this up.*

Maybe you're not lost, exactly, but the original plan doesn't seem to be working. You are way behind schedule, having encountered some unanticipated detours, and food is running short. You consider your three main choices. One is to continue straight ahead. Bull through. But that thought gives you a queasy feeling and a sick stomach, because you've seen the trail ahead, more clearly than anyone else, and you have a growing, silent, informed feeling that you won't make it. The second choice is to turn around and go back home. You are trying to picture yourself telling everyone, "I'm sorry, I guess it just wasn't meant to happen"; though an almost unbearable thought, it would get everyone back a little bit poorer, but alive. The third choice is to strike out in an entirely different direction. Sure, you might be thinking, the original trail washed out, but there might be an alternate route. With a little luck, a little flexibility, we could still make it. We could change directions. Couldn't we?

Well, pilgrim, this is why you are the stuff of movies. You wanted to be a hero, didn't you? Everyone is counting on you to get this decision right. They trust you (mostly). They want you to be right. They want you to be optimistic, but also realistic. If there are good alternatives, no one wants to give up. But what is a good alternative? What are acceptable risks? They'd like to be consulted, but they don't want to take a vote. They want leadership. They want direction. They want it from you.

What should you do? When the reality of fresh experience stomps on those old business plan assumptions, something has to give. Your sleep, surely, will be the first casualty. This is one of the most crucial, agonizing, confusing decisions you might have to make. For Steve and me, it was.

Sometimes discretion really is the better part of valor. When I read of people who turned back at the right and crucial moment, I'm always impressed at their discipline and professionalism. The mountain climber who has spent a month climbing Denali and gets within 500 feet of the top but then turns around because of impending bad weather. Tremendous! Every now and then a start-up business will fold early and give most of the money back to its investors. Sorry, the founders are saying, our original idea was wrong. Exceptionally brave! Or a money management fund will distribute everything back to investors, saying, "Unfortunately, we don't see anything that we can do with your money better than you can." Fantastic! That's the manager I want directing my investments.

But sometimes a turnaround doesn't have to mean turning

back. Sometimes you can find another way through the wilderness. It probably won't be a shortcut, but there just might be another path.

## FACING A QUIET CRISIS

We faced such a situation in the period between 1990 and 1992. We were up and running, and to the outside world it looked like we'd made a good start. We were selling some beer and getting some good public attention. Under the surface, though, our prospects looked bleaker. We were losing money and we weren't growing much. We had a small foothold in the market but couldn't seem to expand it. Our wholesale distribution was limited and acted as a chronic constraint. We weren't gaining traction and were running out of time. We had to face the question: Could our original business model work?

In our initial offering plan, we didn't have an explicit mission statement. However, in the executive summary that introduced the plan, we did a pretty good job of describing, succinctly, what our company would be. In March of 1987, we had defined ourselves as one would with a mission statement:

> The goal of the Partnership is to start a regionally oriented Brewery in Brooklyn that can gain and defend a 3% market share ($6,000,000) or more of the Brooklyn beer market within 7 years. [We] will pursue a niche on the highest end of the beer market by initially establishing a single premium brand, "Brooklyn Lager." It will be a fresh, copper colored, full-bodied beer which will be brewed according to the Reinheitsgebot, the Bavarian purity law of 1516, using only ultra-high quality malted barley, hops, yeast and water. Unlike America's major breweries, we will use no adjuncts, such as rice or corn grits, and no chemical additives will be used. Production initially will be contracted out to a nearby regional brewery, under the direction of the Partnership's brewmaster and according to the Partnership's strict specifications; [we] later hope to split production between a small

brewery to be established by the partnership in Brooklyn and the contract brewery. The emphasis will always be on craft and quality, and on linking Brooklyn Brewery's image to the resurgence of Brooklyn pride.

In retrospect, we did a pretty good job of articulating our vision at such an early stage. Our original aspirations endured and still ring true, but note one huge hole: We were silent about how, exactly, we were going to get this beer to the market. We didn't bother to directly address distribution, and by 1990 we were struggling with how to deal with it.

To give some perspective, just two years later, and five years after our original offering plan, we were raising money again, for the third time. I began writing yet another business plan, but this time the executive summary would be strikingly different. It would demonstrate just how radically we wanted to redefine ourselves. Here was how we saw ourselves in April of 1992:

The Brooklyn Brewery's goal is to become the dominant supplier of gourmet beer in New York, and to produce internationally recognized beer for sale in upscale markets around the world.

We will build on our present $3.0 million sales pace and 70% annual growth rate to become at least a $6 million company by 1994. We will focus short term efforts on our core New York market.

We will strengthen our current position, as New York's leading distributor of gourmet beer, into dominating the category. Brooklyn Lager will be the single category leader, and we will control two thirds of all beers in this category by 1994.

We will become the first company in the United States to fully integrate brewing, distributing, and retailing beer within a major market. We will build a 5,000 barrel draft brewery, taproom, and a retail outlet in 1992, and add up to 10 more retail outlets by 1997.

This integration will bring with it a high profile and positive identity, gross profit margins nearly double those of other brewers, and unique Federal beer tax savings and State licensing savings.

We will go public, if market conditions permit, in 1995, raising a targeted $5 million. With this additional capital, we will expand both within and outside of New York, from the current eight states and five foreign countries to reach all of the United States and at least 20 foreign countries.

Our goal is $20 million in sales by 1997, with significant additional growth beyond that.

Reading this now, 13 years later, in 2005, I still catch my breath at the ambition of it. In just a couple of years we had gone from puzzling over how to survive to boldly trying to conquer the world. And while we didn't achieve all that we aimed for (we never did open the retail accounts, for instance, or go public), we actually did achieve much of the rest of it. How? By embracing distribution as an opportunity, not as a problem.

## DISTRIBUTION: GREAT DETOUR OR GREAT OPPORTUNITY?

Considering how little, at first, we wanted to hassle with distribution, it's ironic that it became our most important issue. Distribution would become the Brooklyn Brewery's great detour, sort of the way America became the great detour of Christopher Columbus. It wasn't what we were looking for, but it was what we bumped up against. And this terra incognita was much bigger than we initially thought. Responding to the distribution challenge shaped and defined our company, more than any other issue, for our first decade. Some parts of business are sexy. Some, like distribution, are not. It's often the dull parts of business that are the most crucial.

Some of the most profound early advice we received was from Sophia Collier, an entrepreneur who lived on our block in Brooklyn. She had cofounded Soho Natural Soda, the first of what would later be called the "new age" beverages, in her kitchen a decade earlier. Steve and I sometimes saw her walking down our street and I longed to talk to her, but I was a bit in awe of her success and too shy to approach. However, Steve, a reporter used to interviewing big shots and never overly impressed with them, went right up to her and suggested a meeting. To my surprise, she readily agreed and sat down on a Saturday morning in my living room to share her experience with us.

She told us her story—how she had originally tried and failed to introduce her innovative product through health-food distributors. "Take it back," they had told her after a couple of months. "This stuff won't sell." She tried soda distributors and failed; then beer distributors, and failed again. Convinced that her product could sell if given a chance, she bought a van, had her distinctive checkerboard label painted on the side and back panels, and started peddling her sodas herself store by store. Slowly she learned in which stores the soda was most likely to succeed, the important price points she had to hit, and how to merchandise her sodas. With this hard-earned knowledge, she eventually made it work.

"I know you guys don't want to hear this, " she said. "I know you are all excited about creating and marketing your own beer. But the smartest thing you can do is also to distribute it yourself, because no other distributor will pay attention to your product the way you can. No one will tell the story the way you will; no one will capture the imagination of the retailer the way you will. And you learn so much from being in direct contact with your customers—you'll see it all firsthand. When you sell through a distributor, all your information comes through his sales reps. When you do it yourself, you'll get the unvarnished truth."

It was excellent advice that we didn't want to hear. We didn't see ourselves as a beer distributor—we wanted to start a brewery. Sophia had convinced us that it would be smart to do our own distribution when we first started, but not forever.

Beer distribution is a tough and grinding business. Especially in New York City, rolling trucks through the crowded streets and delivering bulky boxes to countless small but picky customers, all for a thin profit margin, didn't seem like our kind of job. Making beer and promoting it sounded like more fun. Delivering it was simply heavy lifting.

## Distributing from Brewers Row

Our first warehouse was located in the former Huber-Hittleman brewery. One of Brooklyn's first breweries, founded in 1842, it originally anchored a once-famous Brewers Row of a half-dozen nineteenth-century breweries along Meserole Street. It was a wonderfully evocative rambling wreck of a building, 150 years old and looking older. Patched together from different buildings on the sloping street, none of the floors exactly matched each other. The ground floor was a maze of concrete ramps between narrow wooden beams. The owner of the building, Henry Von Dam, had agreed to swap a year's rent on second-floor space for a partnership interest in our new company, saving us a cash outlay—but we soon discovered that the savings came at a high cost.

Von Dam only allowed forklifts to load and unload on the street in front of the building. All movement of pallets inside the building had to be done with a hand-jack. Since each pallet weighed about 2,000 pounds and none of the floors were level, we would strain to push the pallets uphill and then strain to control them as they threatened to barrel downhill. The hand-operated freight elevator was not a precision instrument. Getting it to stop within a couple of inches of our second floor was a major accomplishment, and then we would struggle to push our hand-jack and one-ton pallet in or out. On the ground floor, in a room off the main entrance, were stacked dozens of plastic tubs with stenciled skulls and crossbones. When we asked a little nervously what was inside, Von Dam impatiently told us, "Just never you mind about those. Harmless, really. Don't touch them."

Von Dam never bought anything new. Everything was scavenged and repaired. His two forklifts were each Korean War vintage and barely held together with electrician's tape and the considerable patience of Van Dam's handyman, Charlie. It was not unusual for both to break down at the same time, leaving us temporarily unable to load or unload. Once, in desperation, I walked down our industrial street looking for a spare forklift. A jobber business down the block was running a half dozen lifts that morning, with one standing idle. I walked through the garage door and asked to speak to the boss. As he looked up from his paperwork I explained that both our forklifts needed repair and I had a truck waiting to unload. Could I borrow one of his for an hour? He looked at me impassively, then said, "Sure, why not." He went back to his paperwork. I tried to look nonchalant but was slightly amazed. It was the industrial equivalent of borrowing a cup of sugar from your neighbor.

Even before our year wound to an end, we longed for a real warehouse. One the one hand, it was a cost we couldn't really afford, but on the other hand, we didn't have much choice. We couldn't keep operating out of Von Dam's. After hunting around, we found a 4,000-square-foot space near our offices on the fringes of Park Slope. We swallowed hard, then signed a lease on the space and another lease on our own forklift. We warily committed more resources to the distribution side of the business.

## First Blush of Enthusiasm

After we left Von Dam's place in 1989 and took the 2nd Street warehouse, we were incredibly charged up. The warehouse made our life much easier, and our nearby office was a beehive of frantic activity. We felt we were hitting on all cylinders for the first time. We were making the beer, selling the beer, delivering the beer, and trying to get paid for the beer.

Initially we decided to concentrate our sales efforts only on Brooklyn. This fit our idea that Brooklyn would be our home base within New York City, from which we later could grow and expand. I thought of Brooklyn as our high hill, defensible and giving us a view of the surrounding territory.

Although we limited ourselves to Brooklyn, we did try to sell in virtually every neighborhood within Brooklyn—not only the upscale brownstone neighborhoods like Brooklyn Heights and Park Slope, but the gritty neighborhoods of East New York, Bedford-Stuyvesant, and Crown Heights, and the largely blue-collar enclaves of Bay Ridge and Sheepshead Bay. Each of us sold beer—even me (though I was probably the worst beer sales-person ever), delivered it, and collected money. Most of the neighborhoods were slightly discouraging, and some were downright dangerous.

Just at the time we started selling and delivering Brooklyn beer, a series of armed truck robberies had started up. Coke and Pepsi trucks were being held up at gunpoint by tough kids. Sometimes the drivers would be shot. Twice within a year, drivers were shot along De Kalb Avenue, across from the large housing projects. I remember delivering beer there, alone in our van with the Brooklyn Brewery logo painted on the side, and feeling that the logo resembled a big, fat target. We had safes put in our trucks, with prominent signs saying "Driver Has No Access to Cash." The safes and signs were all we could do, and it didn't seem like much. I tried to picture the scene: A crack-addled tough guy shoves a gun up my nose and demands all my money. I point at the sign and the tough guy nods and says, "Okay, catch you later?" I didn't like to picture that scene.

Even our neighborhood around the office was tough, espe-cially at night. The crack epidemic was then raging in Brooklyn, and young hoodlums used to hang out at a deli across the street, using the pay phone to arrange their deals. On the corner next to us was a small tobacco store owned by a gentle man, Ish-war Aggarwal, who had been a scientist in India before emi-grating. He was an earnest entrepreneur who enjoyed exchanging business advice with us. One morning we learned that Ishwar had been shot dead in his store, a hundred feet from our office, the previous evening. There was no point to it: a brief argument; a kid left, came back with a gun, and killed him.

## When Is a Battery Charger Worth More Than Your Life?

When running a small business, phone calls that wake you up are invariably bad. On an early Sunday morning I had a call from our warehouse landlord, Ron Fatato. He had never called me at home before.

"Tom," he said, "are you awake?"

"Sort of."

"I thought you'd want to know this. One of my other tenants up the block just called me to tell me that someone broke into your place. They saw a guy taking stuff out. They didn't know your number so they called me."

Now I was really awake.

"Thanks," I said, jumping up. I pulled on pants and raced out to my car. The warehouse was only a few minutes away. When I arrived, our front pedestrian door was wide open. The truck entrance was still closed. I turned on the lights and saw how they had entered. Someone had broken a skylight and wiggled through security bars, dropping down onto a truck parked below it, then onto the ground. They must have been very skinny to get through the bars.

I ran around to see what was missing. One of our three handtrucks, five cases of beer from off of an otherwise full pallet, nothing from the office—was that all? Then I noticed that the battery charger for our electric forklift was missing. I couldn't believe it. Why steal that? It seemed useless without the forklift. Why wouldn't a thief just take the whole forklift? Yet without the charger, the forklift itself was useless. And replacing the charger would be very expensive at a time when we were barely scraping by. My heart sank.

I ran to my car and quickly drove up and down every street within 10 blocks, looking for someone with either our battery charger or our beer rolling along on our handtruck. I didn't see anyone. I tried to think. I could call the police, but I knew that it could be a long time before they responded to this kind of nonviolent crime. I still thought I had a chance to catch the guy. What would the thief do?

Maybe he'd try to sell the beer. Since it was early on a Sunday morning, there were only a half dozen likely places, mostly small delicatessens. I started going into each one, looking around for anything suspicious, then running out and on to the next one. On the third try I found what I was looking for. A handtruck with our decaled logo, holding five cases of Brooklyn Lager, was back in a corner. No one had unloaded it yet.

"Where did you get that?" I demanded.

The owner shrugged. "Who are you?" he asked.

"I'm the guy that beer was stolen from. You just bought stolen goods. Who'd you buy it from?"

"I don't know what you're talking about."

I walked over to a pay phone on a wall and called the police. I told them, in a loud voice, what happened. They said they'd send a squad car.

The owner and I stood glaring at each other. For a long time no one talked.

"How do you know it's yours?" he said finally.

I pointed to the decal on the hand truck. He didn't say anything. Then I pointed to the batch numbers stamped on the outside of each of the cases.

"See these?" I asked. "These are individual lot numbers. These are the cases that were stolen." Actually, each lot number covered several thousand cases, and there was no way to identify individual boxes, but I figured he wouldn't know that. He frowned and tugged on his beard. I was beginning to make an impression.

"I didn't know they were stolen," he said finally, trying to be reasonable.

"Come on," I said. "Someone walked in here at 7 A.M. on a Sunday morning and asked if you wanted to buy five cases of beer and a handtruck, and you didn't know it was stolen? No way. What did you pay for it, anyway?"

"Forty dollars," he admitted.

"It was worth two hundred and forty dollars, and you know it. That's a felony, by the way. Over one hundred dollars. That means you could lose your liquor license."

I had no idea if it was a felony or not, but I wanted to know who he had bought it from. I wanted my battery charger back. We lapsed back into silence.

When the police finally arrived, a half hour later, they took down my information. No one was killed, no one was hurt—it was just another petty crime. One of the cops took me aside.

"Look, you got your stuff back. This guy doesn't know anything. Are you going to press charges?" he asked skeptically.

I explained about the battery charger. He listened, and then turned to the store owner and spoke with him in rapid-fire Spanish. Finally he turned back to me.

"He says he doesn't know anything about your battery charger. I told him he was a stupid son of a bitch for buying stolen beer, and it could get him in serious trouble." In a private voice, he added, "But really, I doubt it." He gave me his card and some advice before he drove off. "Junkies have been stealing metal stuff to sell to scrapyards. You might check around."

I was alone with the owner again. "Look," I said, "all I want is to get back the other thing this guy stole, my battery charger. I really need it. Maybe you'll see this guy again. You tell him that I'll pay twenty bucks to get it back, no questions asked. He should talk to Tom. That's me. Okay?" I handed him my business card. He nodded.

Two days later a skinny, dirty man with sad eyes came to the warehouse and asked for me. He said that he had an acquain-tance who had just told him about stealing a battery charger. He happened to know where this charger was. He could tell me—and wasn't there a reward involved?

I said I didn't want him to tell me, I wanted him to show me. I'd pay him $10 now to get in the car with me, and $10 when he showed me the place. He directed me to Bond Street, then a grimy, litter-strewn industrial wasteland just off of the Gowanus Canal. From the car he pointed to a gloomy warehouse and scrapyard, but he refused to get out of the car.

I went back to the office to get Steve, and we determined to go back together. It was just getting dark when we walked into the open warehouse together. Three rough-looking guys were moving heavy metal around. As soon as we got inside, we could see the battery charger along a back wall. The guys looked up at us, and we stopped.

"You've got our battery charger," I said.

"I don't know what you're talking about."

"That battery charger," I pointed. "It was stolen from our warehouse a few days ago. We reported it to the police. We want it back."

There was a tense silence. I didn't know what to expect, whether they'd laugh at us, give us a beating, or just throw us out. Two of the guys were looking at the third for direction. All of them looked pretty big.

The boss stared at us, calculating. Finally he shrugged.

"Take it," he said simply.

## DISTRIBUTING FOR OURSELVES

Within a few months, we wanted to start selling outside of the borough of Brooklyn, but at the time we didn't imagine that we could stretch our self-distribution past its borders. Instead, we sought out existing beer distributors that might be interested in our product. In the greater metropolitan New York area there were a couple of dozen choices, though most covered only a certain part of the territory. One might cover only the Bronx and Westchester counties, for example. Another might cover only Queens and Manhattan. The geographic patchwork was confusing, and it was a challenge for any brewery to put together a network of distributors that could cover the entire area.

When we looked at these distributors, it was not a pretty picture. Just as the brewery industry had recently consolidated down to a few large players, so had the beer distribution industry that depended on it. Distributors of the successful breweries, primarily Budweiser, were growing and flush with prosperity. Most of the rest were shrinking and just trying to survive. Some were adding juice lines. Some were adding bottled water. Some were selling out, and some were simply disappearing.

We learned right away about the fragility of beer distributorships from one of the first we ever visited: a small distributor called Pilsner Bottling. It had been a family business passed down from father to daughter. The daughter and her husband ran it in 1986, as Steve and I were first researching our business plan. They had recently moved into a nice, medium-size warehouse, a step up from their previous place. Sales had been growing, driven by Anchor Steam.

Steve and I were impressed with the couple. They were very generous with advice when we met, and they also seemed like genuinely good people. Steve and I played poker with the husband several times, soaking up his industry expertise. Within only a few months of our meeting them, however, they announced they were selling out. They had lost the rights to a key product. They couldn't keep up with rent in their new warehouse and they were giving up and moving to Vermont. It was a mild shock to us, but the passing of small distributors has turned out to be the rule rather than the exception.

Most of these small distributors were family businesses, often dependent on a single person. If something happened to him or her, the business could fold. For instance, a former German race car driver, Dieter Steinman, had started importing German beers in the 1960s. He sold throughout New York but concentrated his efforts on the large German communities, especially in Queens and Nassau counties. At one point, we reached an agreement with him and began selling his products to restaurants in the city. Not long after, I remember getting a call telling me that Dieter had died in a car crash. His creditors were moving quickly to liquidate all of his inventory. A few days later, I went out to his warehouse and examined the product for sale, putting in bids for much of it. I felt like a vulture picking through the bones. There are few things as lonely as an auctioneer in a warehouse, selling off decades of hopes and dreams in one afternoon.

When we first wanted to sell beer on Long Island, we tried to find a good distributor. We tried Alon Distributing, run by Joe Nola. It was a small company that mostly resold other distributors' beers. It was happy enough to take on any new beer that it would have exclusively—even an obscure, expensive beer that no one had ever heard of, like ours. But it had a hard time selling a new beer. It was the kind of very small company that could fill orders, but if there were no orders it wasn't going to generate any. After a few months, we got the idea and moved on.

Next we tried Midway, a much larger distributor that had the exclusive rights to a long list of secondary beers. It was the classic "all-other" house of that time, so called because it didn't have the rights to any of the major products like Budweiser, Miller, or Coors. It tried to survive by bundling as many as possible of the other beers. Most of their beers were vaguely familiar names from the past: Rheingold, Schaefer, Schmidt's, Pabst, Stroh. These were supermarket beers that had once been mighty sales volcanoes but now were growing old and spent, selling for rock-bottom prices to old men who were past caring what it tasted like.

The distributor was run by Billy Flommer, who had a real tough-guy reputation. Our Midway experience was going to prove painfully educational.

We introduced our beer to their sales staff of 40, and began to lose ourselves in what our manager, Mike Vitale, later dubbed "stupid math." *Boy,* we'd think, *if each of those 40 salespeople just sold 10 cases a week that would total 1,600 cases a month!* We'd been doing only a couple hundred a month with Alon. In the first month it seemed we were indeed on a roll. We sold over 1,000 cases. Unfortunately it was not to last; sales declined each month from then on after the pipeline was filled. We learned not to trust stupid math.

Still, we did better than another beer introduced by Midway at the same time as ours, an Israeli beer called Macabee. We were slightly intimidated by Macabee's ad budget of $2 million for the New York television market. How could we compete with that kind of spending? Pretty well, as it turned out. Despite its breathtaking spending, Macabee never sold more than 100 cases a month for Midway. That was another lesson: In New York, ad money can simply disappear, with no trace and no discernible benefit. Even $2 million was essentially a drop in the New York bucket, guaranteeing nothing.

Flommer at Midway also schooled us in the fine art of dragging out payment. Our first check didn't bounce, but was drawn on an obscure Pennsylvania bank that took two weeks to clear it. Then we'd get checks that weren't signed. Instead of simply replacing them, Midway would insist on our returning them to be signed, which would usually eat up another several days. Then they began issuing postdated checks.

Our sales declined. Afraid of Midway owing us so much money, we decided to leave and distribute ourselves temporarily on Long Island until we could figure out something else. We didn't know that "temporarily" would mean the next seven years or so. We were lucky to leave Midway when we did because within three months of our leaving, they ended up going out of business. We thought about what they had owed us not long before, and shivered. It might have sunk our little company.

## DISTRIBUTING FOR OTHERS: STICKING OUR TOE IN THE WATER

We had been distributing beer for ourselves for just a year when we were first asked to distribute other beers, too. The requests came from two companies. The first was Phoenix Imports, a small importer of specialty Belgian beers like Corsendonk and Dentergems. The second was from the relatively new Philadelphia microbrewery, Dock Street. Both companies had already been selling small amounts of beer in the New York market but felt that their distributors weren't doing an adequate job. Jeff Ware of Dock Street explained that he had only about six steady customers in the city, and he'd be happy if we just made sure that those customers got beer when they needed it. If we could find another six customers that would be a bonus.

Since we were selling Brooklyn beers to several hundred customers by then, that didn't sound too hard. We certainly weren't professional distributors yet and our geographic reach was quite limited, but we must have looked better from the outside than we did from within. As the new guys, we tried to overcome our rookie mistakes by giving great customer service and doing it quickly. Since the other distributors did not yet appreciate specialty beer, which was all we cared about, we had a small competitive advantage in this niche.

Why did we agree to distribute other beers? Wouldn't they just compete with our own? They were questions with far-reaching implications, and we kept thinking about them in the years that followed. As we learned more, the pros and cons became ever more complex, but initially the answer was simply that we needed the money. To run trucks and support salespeople cost money. It didn't cost much more to sell and deliver 15 cases of beer than 10 to any one customer. The extra profit margin dropped right down to the bottom line, and the decision to distribute other beers didn't seem like a big deal because it was only a few other added beers . . . at first.

## Embracing the Detour

In early 1991, Steve and I went to Vermont with our two managers, Mike Vitale and Ed Ravn. We needed a retreat to talk strategy. We all knew we were struggling financially. During the drive up and drive back, four days' round-trip, we talked and argued nonstop about how to turn our finances around. Should we quit our distribution experiment and focus only on brewing and marketing our own beer? Should we stay on our current half-in, half-out course? Or embrace distribution fully, expand our territory, and seek additional brands aggressively?

We still didn't really want to be distributors. It was hard, hard work, but we had observed that where we distributed ourselves, we were growing, and we felt confident we could keep it up. But when trying to work through other distributors we were finding nothing but heartache. Not only were they not selling our beer, but we were constantly afraid they would go broke owing us money and forcing us to go broke, too.

Feelings ran high in Vermont, and so did the stakes. At one point, Steve and I offered to essentially give our nascent distribution company to Mike and Ed if they would run it. We'd focus on the brewery; they would focus on the distributor. They declined, wanting to stay part of an integrated company, brewery and distributor. I'm sure they felt the brewery would ultimately be worth more. Ironically, 10 years later the distributor would be twice as big as the brewery in sales, but we had no inkling of that then. So we made our decision: We'd be a brewer and a distributor. We'd take back the distribution from others to do it ourselves, even though it would stretch our geographic reach. We didn't know exactly how we would accomplish the logistics, but we plunged ahead. We were betting the company on a new strategy.

## 1991, THE LONGEST YEAR OF MY LIFE

By the end of 1990, it was clear that the United States would shortly be going to war. Iraq had invaded Kuwait. President George H. W. Bush began to assemble an international coalition. Experienced Middle East foreign correspondents like Steve, especially those who spoke Arabic, were suddenly much in demand.

Meanwhile, the Brooklyn Brewery was slowly growing broke. We had committed to a new strategy and we hoped sales would grow, but we were still a long way from breaking even. We had raised a bit more money in an internal debt offering, and that gave us breathing room, but we urgently needed to cut costs. One way was to give up our small but comfortable offices on Fourth Avenue, moving quarters into the tiny cinder-block room inside our warehouse. It would be uncomfortable but would reduce our rent obligation substantially. The second way to save money was for Steve to go back to work for *Newsday*.

When he told me that *Newsday* had offered him a job, I had profound mixed feelings. On the one hand, we needed to save money. In the past year, Steve and I had each skipped two months of our own salaries so we could make payroll for everyone else. I thought I could run the company on my own, and Steve would still be available on a regular part-time basis to help out. But on the other hand, I felt abandoned. The company was nearly bankrupt, and I privately thought there was perhaps a fifty-fifty chance of survival. If it went down, Steve would have the security of a full-time job while I would be left satisfying creditors—company and personal—as best I could. I had seen some bankrupt companies up close and I was under no illusion about what the endgame looked like. It would be me in an empty office at a phone for months, trying to collect as much of our accounts receivable as possible, in order to pay off debt, as a matter of honor.

Ultimately, I supported his leaving. It was the right thing to do because we needed to save money. Steve worked hard to keep contributing to the brewery, coming in to help almost every day before or after his *Newsday* work, but during all of 1991 I had to work like a maniac. With the help of Mike Vitale, Ed Ravn, Jim Munson, and Rich Nowak, we kept the doors open. They did most of the selling and delivering, and were my heroes. Their dedication was unbelievable. I did most of everything else they didn't do. I loaded trucks in the morning, organized the warehouse, answered the phones, and did all of our accounting. Halfway through the year we hired an office assistant to help out. When Steve was able to come back to the brewery full-time in 1992, I was grateful.

Conditions while he was gone were difficult. After we'd given up our office on Fourth Avenue, we were reduced to working out of a 10-foot by 15-foot cinder-block office carved into one side of the warehouse, with no outside windows and no heat. It was always dark inside and in the winter it was cruelly cold. Portable electric heaters were nearly useless. I bought a kerosene heater—of the type used on construction sites—and would blast it on for 2 minutes right outside the office door. Then we'd slam the door shut, endure the fumes, and be warm for only about 15 minutes. We wore fingerless gloves so our hands could still feel enough to write.

Gail was worried about me, but I told her I was fine. And in fact, I believed I was. Of course, my hair was turning gray; I contracted stress-induced shingles, and I was generally wound tighter than a drum. Once I fainted on the bathroom floor—the only time in my life—but I decided that it was just the flu and a coincidence, even though I was constantly fending off creditors, soliciting new suppliers, and sweating out Friday payrolls. But sales began to grow again, led by our distribution arm more than our own brewery, and we began to make real financial gains. I could begin to see the logic of how we might ultimately succeed. The vertical integration of brewing and distributing looked increasingly powerful to me with each passing day. Our new strategy was working. Hope is a powerful tonic.

With conditions being difficult, we needed a chance to blow off steam. An opportunity came with our inaugural Brown Out, celebrating the second arrival of our seasonal beer, Brooklyn Brown Ale, in 1990. We decided to have a warehouse party for fun and promotion. It was strictly illegal—we were licensed as a brewer and wholesaler, not a bar, but we figured we were so small no one would notice. Steve arranged for the event to be a fund-raiser for Brooklyn's Prospect Park, putting a sheen of respectability on an otherwise dubious shindig. The park's director, Tupper Thomas, came and had a great time, along with a couple hundred of our other best friends. We danced all night to our favorite band, the Blue Chieftains, drank too much beer, and forgot about our struggles for an evening.

Word got out that the Brown Out had been the coolest party in Brooklyn, so we did it again. The crowd built, and in 1991 it was crazy. Steve had notified the local police precinct that we'd be having our annual fund-raiser for Prospect Park, and they agreeably said they'd make sure a squad car would swing by every now and then to help us keep things under control. A huge crowd completely swamped our warehouse and single toilet. Guys were assigned by the girls to pee on the wall outside, while the girls lined up for the toilet. The cops politely looked the other way. I had the brilliant idea of grilling hot dogs inside the warehouse, as it was drizzling outside, and the place quickly filled up with smoke. A homebrewer kept hitting the button to open and close our industrial steel garage door without regard to who was standing underneath it. The drummer from the band whipped the crowd into a frenzy with an acrobatic rendition of the old Cab Calloway song "Minnie the Moocher" ("hidey hidey hidey ho"), leaping from pallet to pallet of beer, swinging the microphone in his hand. It was crazy and slightly frightening.

The party broke up a little before dawn. I swept up the beer-soaked floors, thinking that it was the best party I'd ever been to and that we were lucky no one got killed. It was our last crude warehouse bash, though. In the future, we went straight, with licenses and security and rules.

## Gaining Traction: Initial Signs of Success

There weren't a lot of women in the brewery business 15 years ago. (There still aren't today, for that matter.) One of the few, though, was a pioneer named Diane Fall. She was the U.S. manager for a German brewery named Warsteiner, which at that time was the largest brewery in Germany. Though huge in Germany, Warsteiner was just beginning to make an impression in the United States. Diane's job was to secure and manage a national distributor network. She had earlier worked for Coors in a technical capacity, and was quite knowledgeable.

The Warsteiner brewery had a custom of taking its big distributors on a splashy trip once a year. These distributors—mostly German—would bring their wives and have a great time for four days wherever Warsteiner would take them. In 1991 they were coming to New York City. The only problem was that Warsteiner had no sales in New York City. Diane was used to dealing with larger distributors but came to visit us in Brooklyn and sized us up. We talked and I gave her my usual sales pitch for our company. As we spoke, though, I gradually figured out that she had a very particular deadline. When the delegation of wild and crazy German distributors came to town, they had to be served Warsteiner—in their hotel minibars, and in the bars, restaurants, and clubs they would visit. They would be drinking beer on the bus from the airport and the bus back to the airport. They needed a distributor that could get up and running within a matter of months. Aha, I thought. They need us. It was the first time anybody had actually needed us.

That changed the nature of the negotiations. Now we could be coy. Of course, we wanted to represent Warsteiner, I said. Their expectations, however, seemed quite ambitious. We were willing, but small. An additional truck would help us help them. Could they give us a truck? And what about an extra, dedicated salesperson? Could they pay for that? With a little bit of back-and-forth, we settled on a used truck and half a person (we would pay the other half of the salary). We did our part, and the Warsteiner trip was a rousing success. They drank an astonishing amount of beer while in town—something on the order of a case a day per person. Afterward, we kept the truck.

The initial and tentative steps in taking on other beers accelerated between 1992 and 1994. As a distributor specializing in high-end beers, we became attractive to more and more small breweries. Some moved to us from their existing distributors. Others decided to come into the New York market for the first time, encouraged by our presence. As our selection expanded, we became more legitimate, and thus even more attractive to other brewers. The process snowballed. In October of 1994, *Wine Enthusiast* magazine rated the top 100 beers in the world. When we cross-checked our list with theirs, we discovered that we distributed a strong majority of them. We had become the largest and best-known pure specialty beer distributor in the United States in just three years—though, of course, only specialty brewers noticed.

### Unforeseen Consequences

In retrospect, we were lucky in the first beers we took on. Initial expectations were modest. Their reputations were good. The mix of imported and domestic meant we didn't champion one category over the other—which later gave us an interesting perspective that other American microbreweries didn't share.

Most American micros were (and still are) championing an "America first" beer message, which seemed slightly hypocritical. Most of the early-day founders admired the great beers of Europe enormously. Heck, all of our first beers were modeled after them. Michael Jackson's *World Guide to Beer* (Prentice-Hall, 1977) was our bible. But in the specialty beer category, the imports were seen as direct competition to our new American micros. When the nascent American micro industry got together, all of our legitimate individual "drink local" messages became transformed into an aggregate "drink American" message. It was a lowest-common-denominator type of sales pitch, which ignored that among the crummy Corona-type imports there were some pretty fantastic ones, too.

Almost alone among American micros, then, we developed an economic interest in the broader category of specialty beer—Brooklyn Brewery beers, other American micros, and specialty imports. It forced us to compare our beers not just to the beers next door but to all of the great beers in the world. It made us more ambitious and set the bar higher for our own beers.

There would be other unforeseen consequences of our becoming a distributor. Not only did we become intimate with the great beers of the world, but we came to know their brewers. We were their customer, as their exclusive distributor in New York, and we came to know them in a way quite different from knowing them as a consumer or a competitor. In some cases, it fostered lasting friendships, but in others, relationships became prickly. However, there was always a deeper understanding and appreciation of their business ideas and strategies, which helped inform ours.

A second unforeseen consequence of becoming the main specialty distributor in New York was that we accidentally made it more difficult for other local beers to get started. Either they would be distributed by us or they would have a hard time finding distribution at all. This situation was not entirely intentional. In fact, we successfully distributed a couple of New York beers for several years, only to have them taken away from us.

The first of these was called Harbor Ale. A talented Staten Island homebrewer named Sal Pennaccio had developed Harbor Ale and asked us to become his distributor. For a couple of years we did, and we thought we were doing a pretty good job. Sal thought otherwise. He accused us of favoring our own Brooklyn beers over his and moved to another distributor. His sales promptly declined, which was a source of some satisfaction to us, but the whole episode was a puzzler. Right after that, another New York beer named Saranac took us through almost the exact same scenario. We agreed to take it on, we built sales substantially, and then watched them leave when they too said they felt uncomfortable that we were favoring our own beers over theirs. Saranac's sales took a nosedive after they left us. No other New York beer asked us to distribute them after that.

Were those beers wrong to leave us? Were we wrong to take them on in the first place? As suspicious as they were of our intentions, we were honest in our efforts. In fact, we were trying to give them good advice, based on our growing experience as both a brewer and a distributor. We had developed a philosophy that presented our portfolio to potential customers without favoring any beers, including Brooklyn beers, confident that what was best for the customer would eventually be best for us, too. But regardless of our intentions, and regardless of the facts, our growing domination of distribution in the specialty category seemed to create a substantial barrier to entry for any potential local competitors, an advantage that we enjoyed for the next 10 years.

## THE DILEMMA OF THE BIG SUPPLIER

One brand that I knew we wanted to distribute was Sierra Nevada. They produced a pale ale that was, in my opinion, the finest in the country. The Sierra brewery was selling a little bit of beer back east in 1991 but without a lot of success. I knew that in the two states adjacent to us, Connecticut and New Jersey, the product was available, but just barely. They had not yet appointed any distributor in New York.

I traveled to the college town of Chico, California, in the low foothills of the Sierra Nevada mountains, to see if they were interested in New York and potentially in us. I met briefly with the enigmatic Ken Grossman, who, with a partner, had founded the brewery about 10 years earlier. He was one of the pioneers of the American microbrewery movement, passionate about the brewing process and making great beer. He had no patience for the sales end. He had hired his friend Steve Harrison to handle all sales, marketing, and distributor relations.

Harrison explained to me that he wanted to be in New York but was cautious because of the rough reputation of all the distributors there. His impression was that they were a slightly shady and shiftless lot, and he would rather not be in New York than get caught up in a bad relationship. I gave him my best sales pitch: We were different; we dealt only in specialty beer; we had an upscale customer base; we loved his beer and would sell it with passion. He was noncommittal at our meeting, and I left thinking he was the big fish that got away. But a few months later he called me in New York, and we struck a deal.

Sierra quickly became our best-selling beer, after Brooklyn Brewery products. Its pale ale became something of a phenomenon in New York. The brewery was constantly constrained by capacity, so we sometimes had to allocate beer. In New York, people want what they can't have. It's the velvet rope effect. That we sometimes had to limit customers and make them wait in line made the product even more attractive. Even while Sierra sales in the rest of the East Coast area were modest at best, our local sales were racing ahead. We sold it with terrific enthusiasm. Within two years we became the largest Sierra distributor outside of California, and Sierra became a crucial part of our distributorship.

We were an important distributor for Sierra, at one time representing more than 5 percent of their sales, and they were an even more crucial supplier for us, growing to represent more than a quarter of our sales. Our interdependence fostered a strange love-hate relationship. We were afraid that they might leave us. And if they did, would we go broke, like Pilsner Bottling? If we went broke, how would we pay our always-large outstanding debt? What if they began to think we were favoring our own beer over theirs, like the other breweries had? These were the questions Steve and I asked ourselves, and I'm sure Sierra had their own fears, too, but we managed to keep a solid relationship for nearly 10 years. Eventually, though, our own success, and Sierra's success nearly everywhere else, put a different kind of pressure on the relationship. They wanted to continue to grow, and that meant that they were no longer satisfied to be a "specialty" beer. Their ambitions were now more mainstream. They wanted to be distributed everywhere, in every market, but because we were built as a specialty distributor, this proved a difficult challenge. Ironically, it is one that we also faced with the growth of our own Brooklyn Brewery products.

## AMBASSADORS OF BETTER BEER

Our bundling of beers in the early 1990s came at a favorable time. Other beer distributors still did not appreciate the growing popularity of these wonderful but slightly offbeat beers. Such beers might represent only 1 percent of a large distributor's total sales. However, we loved them, and they represented 100 percent of our sales. We became experts on them. We visited their breweries and talked to their brewers and owners. They came to New York to promote their beers, and we talked to them some more.

Since all we sold was specialty beer, we could also concentrate on selling the category. We knew that if a customer—a store, bar, or restaurant—would switch over from a standard beer list to a specialty list, we would get the lion's share of the new business. Instead of selling an individual beer, then, we could sell the concept, secure in the knowledge that we'd eventually benefit. Typically, we'd get more than half of a specialty list, and all of the other beer distributors would split the rest.

The ability to sell the category instead of an individual beer had a profound effect on our approach. It allowed us to be ambassadors for better beer. Restaurants began looking to us as category experts, not just as salespeople. We could put together wonderfully diverse beer tastings or beer-themed dinners, partly or entirely from our list. Initially, though, we didn't appreciate how large our detour would become. We were just trying to survive.

## LESSON FOUR
### BEING FLEXIBLE IF THE MISSION STATEMENT BECOMES "MISSION IMPOSSIBLE"

A mission statement is meant to be very long term. At no time is it harder to know what will happen in the long term than at the very beginning. Would it be an advantage to have a fixed, immovable goal from the start? Yes and no, but on balance I think not.

If a mission statement is immutable, then what do you do if you can't achieve your goals? Do you bull forward anyway? Quit? Or find a new mission? In the first year of business it likely won't be clear which of these three choices is best. Obviously, sticking with the original mission is everyone's first choice. And no one wants to give up just because it is harder than you thought to achieve what you want (and it is always harder). But what if the choice is give up or adapt? That's a harder choice, and the right answer might not be obvious.

Which is not to say the initial mission statement is not important: For clarity's sake, it is important. Everyone on the initial team needs to be heading in the same direction, after all. But when a small group heads out into the uncharted wilderness, a little flexibility can be crucial. Say you've got a map to the Flying Dutchman gold mine and have done lots of research at the local saloon, talking to the old-timers about trails out that way. But what if the old-timers forgot to mention the river you have to cross? Maybe it wasn't at flood stage when they saw it. (The same river looks different at different seasons.) What if the trail they describe was washed out by landslides last spring? The landscape can change, sometimes quickly and sometimes irrevocably.

Steve and I had experiences highlighting the risks, rewards, and potential ironies of changing direction. Initially, we wanted to brew beer, not distribute it. When we went to the market with our beer, according to our plan, the market told us two things. First, no one actually needed another beer, no matter how good it was. It might be nice, but we would have to expect to swim upriver. Second, specialty brewers (ourselves and all the others) did need a distributor that knew what it was selling, and retail customers wanted a knowledgeable one-stop-shopping source for the niche. When we first discovered our greatest strategic weakness, we also were lucky to discover a great business hole waiting to be filled. We could fill it if we wanted, but did we want to? No matter what a company's mission statement says, the first order of business is to survive. You can't fall in love with your first mission, and if you change it, you can't fall in love with the second one, either. Times change and so will you and your company. ★

Most entrepreneurs will tell you that it is very important to have a clear vision when you start your company. They'll say that you must have a single-minded focus on your objective; that you must relentlessly and optimistically drive toward this objective. But when you take a closer look at their businesses, you often see that they have taken many detours on their way to success. In some cases, the detour even becomes a new business.

When you start a business and begin to get mentioned in the press, hundreds of people come after you with ideas for improving your business, usually by selling you something. It is a heady time. People flatter you. Sometimes they want to be part of what you are doing, and sometimes they want you to join them in a venture. Mostly, they want to sell you something—and they really couldn't care less about whether you need it or not. In retrospect, the choices you make to deviate from that original vision will either make you or break you. Here is a list of the "opportunities" we entertained and rejected in the early years of the company:

- various advertising such as television, radio, transit, and billboard
- building a large brewery in Brooklyn
- building a brewery restaurant in Manhattan
- developing a new line of beers, a bottled water product, or various soft drinks
- buying a building versus using public warehousing
- developing a network of craft beer wholesalers

I stopped answering my phone in the early days of the company because I received literally hundreds of calls weekly from investment bankers who had seen my name in the media. I still get hundreds of calls from television and radio stations, advertising companies, public relations companies, charities, arts groups, and a whole host of not-for-profit organizations.

The road to building a company is filled with tempting detours. Nick Matt, the president of the Matt brewery in Utica where we continue to brew and bottle some of our beers, once said, "The biggest mistakes we have made have come when we got impatient with steady progress."

Many people who knew nothing of the cost of marketing in New York City advised us we should be spending more money on marketing. To them, I often said, "Distribution *is* marketing." The fact is, if you do not have distribution—if your products are not available—then it makes no sense to market your product because people may hear of it through the media, but if they cannot find it then they cannot buy it. We consigned all the good, but impractical advice we received to the "good idea board"—a mythical bulletin board that we posted on the office wall.

One of the advantages that a small company has over a large company is that the small company can move quickly to develop new products or to capitalize on a new idea. Small brewers have developed many new products that have found niches that large brewers would never be able to exploit. Large brewers are looking for national opportunities—and they must move national bureaucracies to seize those opportunities.

However, I think our experience shows that detours should not be taken without a careful reconsideration of a written vision statement. The vision statement should be the polestar of the venture—the place you look to get your bearings when your wagon train gets lost. I think any deviation from the overall vision of a company is perilous.

As Tom explained, we had a clear vision in our original business plan. By 2004, we had largely achieved the objectives of our vision, with the notable exception that we were selling in 10 states instead of just in Brooklyn. But the road to 2004 was anything but straight.

Developing a distribution company for our brands in New York City probably saved our business. But I think we made a fundamental mistake when we did not hammer out a new vision of our company as soon as we went into the distribution business. We should have answered this question immediately: Is the distribution company primarily a vehicle for growing the Brooklyn brand beers or is it a new business in itself? Had we answered that question, we might have mitigated the ups and downs that resulted from some of our mistakes in those early years.

Once Tom and I decided to go into beer distribution, we were essentially running two businesses. We were building a beer brand while hoping to build a brewery in Brooklyn, and running a distribution business. This meant that our very limited resources were being pulled in two very different directions; hence our financial ups and downs. We were faced with questions such as these: How much of each marketing dollar did we invest in the brewery? How much in the distribution company?

By the mid-1990s, more and more of our dollars were going into distribution. One year we spent $50,000 on parking tickets. Tom had developed a theory that craft beer distributors like ours would become viable in many cities across the nation because the big distributors were consolidating and becoming more exclusively focused on the big breweries. Small breweries did not bring volume to a wholesaler, but they brought higher-margin products. Big brewery wholesalers traditionally work on a 25 percent margin, but craft brands may bring margins higher than 30 percent.

In the late 1990s, Anheuser-Busch, Miller, and some imported beer companies institutionalized this relationship by demanding that their distributors sign "equity agreements" that committed them to focusing more on the big breweries. August Busch III declared that he wanted "100 percent share of mind" from his wholesalers. In many markets, this left no alternative for small breweries except small distributors focused on small brands. We opened a second warehouse on Long Island in order to sell more of our Craft Brewers Guild brands. That was the name we gave to our distribution branches in New York and Massachusetts (which we'll talk about more in Chapter 10). We also financially supported small brand distributors in Albany and Syracuse by giving them generous payment terms. Tom's theories gained attention in the beer media. *Modern Brewery Age* magazine interviewed him, and he received many plaudits from distributors who were struggling with the problem of handling small brands.

In 1995, we extended our distribution by buying a struggling craft beer distributor in Boston called International Beverages. This became Craft Brewers Guild—Boston. Eric and Robin Ottaway, sons of my journalist friend David Ottaway, joined the company to run the Boston operation. David had become a major investor in the company early on. Eric was a Harvard MBA who had worked as a consultant for the health care industry. Robin was a graduate of Colby College and had a natural sales personality. At this point, it was clear that our primary focus had become distribution. The Brooklyn Brewery brands were doing well, but most of our company resources were being invested in distribution.

The next year, we also bought the Post Road Brewing Company, a Massachusetts-based contract brewery. The idea behind this move was that we needed a local brand to legitimize the Craft Brewers Guild—Boston that we had just acquired. Brooklyn brands were not enough to carry a distributorship there. This hastened a drain of resources directly from the Brooklyn Brewery. Now our meager marketing dollars were being spent to produce point-of-sale materials for both Brooklyn Brewery and Post Road Brewing Company, which brewed Post Road India Pale Ale, and a seasonal beer, Post Road Snowshoe Ale.

This was a gross departure from our original business plan, and in retrospect, unwise.

Tom liked the distribution business very much and developed a grand vision of what it could be. I liked the way distribution put us in touch with our customers and I liked having big trucks with our logo on them rolling through the streets of New York City, but to me, the heart of the company was more in our brand, Brooklyn Lager beer.

Over the years, I tried to rewrite our mission statement to reconcile this double-barreled mission. The 1992 version fell short of this goal:

The Brooklyn Brewery was established in 1988 to brew fine ales and lagers according to the traditional methods of the world's great brewing nations. Through its distribution company, The Craft Brewers Guild, The Brooklyn Brewery is dedicated to maintaining the highest quality standards for its beers as they flow from the brewery, to our retail customers and finally into each beer drinker's glass.

Eventually, our larger and larger detour into distribution led us to an expensive failed attempt to sell beer directly to consumers through the Internet (see Chapter 6). When this venture (TotalBeer.com) collapsed in 2001, it became clear that our distribution company in Massachusetts was not making money, and in New York we were also struggling. Tom and I agreed that our moves into distribution were taking attention away from the original Brooklyn Brewery brands and mission statement. Furthermore, we agreed that the Craft Brewers Guild was not able to reach parts of the market that could have been receptive. In other words, we discovered that Craft Brewers Guild was directly impeding the growth of the Brooklyn brands.

At a meeting during a conference in Chicago in 2001, Tom, Eric and Robin Ottaway, and I resolved to sell the distribution company and redefine our mission. We sat down and redrafted our mission statement to get our transitional thoughts in line.

### The Vision
A closely held regional brewery, balancing growth and profitability.

### The Mission
To be New York's Brewery by:

- brewing flavorful, traditional beers to win the affection and loyalty of New Yorkers
- developing a brand identity that is treasured by the New York community
- being the most focused and responsive supplier to distributors and retailers
- developing a loyal, highly trained and motivated team of employees excited to work in a fun, fast-paced company

In 2001, with this new mission statement, we were dedicating ourselves to getting out of the distribution business and focusing on building our brand by being the best possible supplier of beer for wholesalers and retailers. We also vowed to be a closely held company and solidified our idea by putting it into our statement. For many years, we had dreamed of going public, but the craft breweries that had gone public in the mid-1990s had not fared so well. With that and many other things in mind, we decided that it would be best for us to focus on building our company with private capital. And even after we started down this different path, it took us the span of two years to eventually sell the distribution company (discussed in Chapter 10).

In 2003, the current vision of the Brooklyn Brewery was developed by the four of us. It reflects the changing events, decisions, and times our company had traversed and from which we had learned, up to the present. It became more specific in scope and offered not only details on the financial and growth-related goals our company intended to fulfill but also our desire to satisfy the customer and create the best possible impact on their quality of life and sense of community:

**Purpose**

The purpose of the Brooklyn Brewery is to brew flavorful beers that enrich the life, tradition and culture of the communities we serve.

**Core Values and Beliefs**

- that we differentiate our beers by adhering to traditional brewing techniques and valuing quality and freshness over volume
- that our beers are rooted in the history of Brooklyn, the New York region and 10,000 years of brewing history and tradition
- that the company must earn respect daily through the integrity of our dealings with employees, customers, suppliers and the communities we serve
- that the brewery should be at the center of communal life in Brooklyn and New York
- that the company should be a fun and rewarding place to work

**Mission**

- to become a 100,000 barrel a year brewery in the next 5–7 years
- to be the #1 craft beer in New York City, the #1 regional brewery on the East Coast and to be among the top three craft beers in every market we enter

The lesson here is that you must have a clear mission when you start a business, and you must revisit and redefine that mission as your company evolves. There must be an understanding of the mission throughout the company. And you must recognize that any deviation from that mission is a huge risk that can make, or break, your company. There will be slight modifications, but the initial mission should always ring true. You should always be able to look up at that polestar.

**Our Grade:** I give us an A for going into the distribution business, but we deserve a D for not clearly defining the scope of our distribution business as the years passed. That resulted in the mission creep (a constant drift from our goals) that cost us lots of money and severely strained my partnership with Tom at various points over the years.

# CHAPTER 5

# Steve Discusses the Keys to Successfully Motivating Employees

## IT STARTS WITH THE PRODUCT

One of the most important attributes of a successful entrepreneur is the ability to attract, and motivate, key employees. I think we had an advantage in this area, and the advantage was beer. Most people would agree that beer is cool. Beer is connected with sociability and good times. Beer has history. Beer is fun. Craft beer—beer made by small breweries dedicated to traditional methods and all-natural ingredients—is part of that revolution against mass-produced products that is currently happening throughout the food industry. Today, consumers are increasingly aware that some products use all sorts of chemical additives to attain the flavor and appearance that big companies have determined the average consumer desires in his or her food. By its very nature, our product and venture tended to attract young, overeducated, talented, and adventurous people, people who were looking for a job that reflected their sense of adventure, of being part of something that was in some small way changing the world. Over the years, we have hired experienced beer salespeople, military academy graduates, people with PhDs, ex-teachers, frustrated writers, people with master's degrees in business administration, and burned-out bankers. We have received resumes from major liquor and beer company executives, disillusioned lawyers, and even doctors, as well as Ivy League graduates from all fields. The product attracts a wide array of personalities.

It seems to me that some people (mostly over the age of 22) need to be able to say they are on their way to becoming lawyers, doctors, or bankers, and others just need a connection to something cool with a community-minded conscience, like the Brooklyn Brewery. Obviously, the product is the draw. It wouldn't be quite the same if Tom and I were making plastic bags.

Looking back on the last 18 years since Tom and I started the company in 1987, I realize that we have managed to keep only one employee for the entire time, Mike Vitale, our vice president for sales. Mike had been my assistant on the foreign desk at *Newsday*. When I started at *Newsday* in 1984, Mike was 21 years old but surprisingly mature for his age. He was a part-time employee at *Newsday* and worked full-time as accounts receivable manager at an electronics firm on Long Island. He was the only 21-year-old guy I ever met who owned a home.

Mike was a talker. He was witty and funny, and he knew when to joke and when to buckle down and get things done. He was the guy who always brought bagels and cream cheese to the newsroom on Saturday morning. Everyone liked Mike. He was the sort of guy who looked like he was going to make a lot of money at whatever he eventually put his mind to.

Mike had a degree in business from the C.W. Post Campus of

Long Island University. When I began talking about starting a brewery, Mike was fascinated. I think I would count Mike as my first convert, even before Tom. He embraced the idea of the Brooklyn Brewery with enthusiasm, and he was more than ready and willing to go to work when the opportunity presented itself.

## SOME PEOPLE GET IT, AND SOME DON'T

With Mike as our first employee, two others quickly came to our company, to make a total of three. I say "came to our company" because both heard about us very early on and walked straight into our first little storefront on Fourth Avenue in Brooklyn to participate. One was an experienced beer salesperson who had been a manager for Coors when they entered the New York market in the mid-1980s. His name was Ed, but we'll call him "the veteran." The other—Ed Ravn—is a six-foot, seven-inch, hard-driving, ambitious man from Long Island who was chafing in his job working for a telemarketing firm. When Ravn first walked into our office and announced he wanted to work with us, we were unable to meet his salary expectations. A week later, he strode into the office and announced he had quit his job and was ready to work on our terms. Ravn clearly needed something more from his job than being one of 100 people in a room soliciting customers over the phone. Like all of us, he was willing to take a pay cut in hopes of gaining greater rewards down the road.

### We Start Working as a Team

It was tough selling beer in the early days of the company. I've learned, after some initial experience, that it takes seven visits to a customer to make a sale. In the early days we did not have draft beer yet, only bottles. A case of Brooklyn Lager beer cost $20—the same as Heineken and other imports. Unlike the big distributors, we charged cash on delivery. Many customers laughed at our audacity in just joining the market and demanding such a level of respect. "Why, that's the same price as Heineken," they would say. We just looked them in the eye and said, "That's right. And our beer is better than Heineken." We were getting lots of press early on by being in Brooklyn, and enough people bought our beer to keep us going.

That team—Mike, Ed, and the veteran—worked very long hours in order to establish our company in those early months. They toiled all day, and then probably two or three times a week they attended promotions at night. Many of the promotions were routine—we raffled off T-shirts at bars that were willing to sell our beer at a discounted price to encourage sampling. Some promotions were more sophisticated and attracted press coverage, such as a baseball opening-day event at a new bar in Brooklyn called the Brooklyn Dodger. From the beginning there was camaraderie among Mike, Ed, the veteran, Tom, and me. It enabled them to keep up their pace and work alongside Tom and me—the founders—with a similar vigor. We became a reliable team, and they were finally a part of something they believed in. And because of their devotion, Tom and I had told all three of them that we were willing to share equity in the company with them.

During that first year in 1988, for instance, Tom and I offered all three men options to buy our personal stock in the company. Tom and I each owned 25 percent of Brooklyn Brewery and we were willing to sell them a total of 10 percent of the company, divided three ways. Vitale and Ravn readily accepted. But the veteran balked. There were two reasons behind the veteran's reluctance to accept the deal. One was related to the deal and one was not. In the 1990s, stock options became a pretty common way of motivating employees. It was pretty clear to most people that a stock option was a good thing. I don't think that was clear in 1988—and certainly it was not clear to the veteran

Dave Monsees of CNN sets up a shot at the Schaefer Brewery with Steve, October 1987.

Steve at the former Otto Huber Brewery in Bushwick, Brooklyn, site of the Brooklyn Brewery's first warehouse.

Our first store-front office, at 230 Fourth Avenue, Brooklyn.

Our first truck.

Fox News shooting Steve and Tom on the occasion of our first delivery from Brooklyn to Manhattan, 1989. (*Courtesy*: Brooklyn Brewery)

The Brooklyn team in 1988. (*Courtesy*: Brooklyn Brewery)

F.X. Matt with Steve and Tom in the Utica brewhouse, 1988. (*Courtesy*: David Tewksbury)

Brewmaster Bill Moeller, F.X. Matt with Steve and Tom at a news conference, 1988. (*Courtesy*: David Tewksbury)

Brooklyn Lager, our first beer.

Our new brewhouse is installed, 1996.

Mayor Rudolph Giuliani, Borough President Howard Golden, and Assemblyman Joe Lentol cut the ribbon on our new brewhouse, May 28, 1996. (*Courtesy*: Jerry Ruotola)

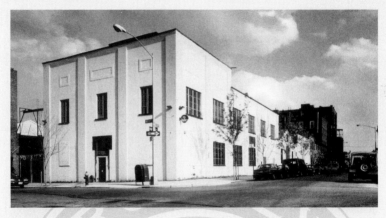

The Brooklyn Brewery, 1996. (*Courtesy*: Paul Warchol)

Brooklyn Brown Ale, our second beer.

The entrance to the Brooklyn Brewery, 2003.

Garrett Oliver, Brewmaster, Brooklyn Brewery. (*Courtesy*: Karl Knoop)

Brooklyn Black Chocolate Stout, the first beer created by Garrett for Brooklyn Brewery.

The Brooklyn team, Christmas 1996. (*Courtesy*: Brooklyn Brewery)

Crowds at the New York Beer Fest at the Brooklyn Bridge, 1993. (*Courtesy*: Brooklyn Brewery)

Steve and Milton Glaser look over new packaging celebrating the fiftieth anniversary of the Brooklyn Dodgers' World Series victory, 2005. (*Courtesy*: Katja Maas)

THE THIRD ANNUAL INTERNATIONAL BEER & FOOD TASTING UNDER THE BROOKLYN BRIDGE SATURDAY & SUNDAY, SEPT. 16-17, 1995 NOON-5 PM

ON THE BROOKLYN WATERFRONT BETWEEN THE RIVER CAFE AND EMPIRE-FULTON FERRY STATE PARK. RAIN OR SHINE!

N.Y. BEER FEST

Tickets: $25 in advance; $35 at door (cash only)

For free tastings of an international array of beers in a souvenir glass. Delectable food from New York's finest restaurants for $1-$5. Free entertainment for the entire family. Limited Tickets.

(212) 307-7171

Information: (718) 855-7882 Ext. 24    Proof I.D. required

Milton Glaser's poster for the New York Beer Fest, 1995.

Robin Ottaway, Steve, Tom, and Eric Ottaway, May 2005. (*Courtesy*: Karl Knoop)

Steve and Borough President Marty Markowitz kick off the "Win a Brooklyn Vacation" promotion, 2005. (*Courtesy*: Kathryn Kirk)

at the time of our offer. He was suspicious of the whole idea. He had it in his head that a stock option could somehow become a liability for him if the company went broke and had to face its creditors. It seemed he was getting bad advice from someone, but I never determined what the advice was or where it was coming from. Also, he did not like the idea that the stock option was going to cost him money if he exercised it.

Tom and I tried to explain to him that he would not have to pay anything for the option unless he wanted to—that it would not make sense for him to exercise the option to buy unless the value of the stock was higher than the price he was paying. But it didn't matter. He did not get it. The other thing that was happening simultaneously with the veteran was that friction was developing between him and the other two employees. He was the only one in our group with experience in the beer business, and because of his background, he expected to be the respected leader of the group. But that was not the overriding dynamic among the three men.

It was becoming clear from the veteran's sales that experience in the mainstream beer industry was not necessarily an advantage in selling our new beer. Within six months, he had exhausted the list of his past "relationships" that he had brought to the table. He had already sold beer to all his old buddies, but overall he was having trouble selling this new product to new customers. Brooklyn Brewery beer did not come with a national brand name and national advertising. There were no neon signs, T-shirts, custom signs, Yankee, Mets, Knicks, Rangers, or Super Bowl tickets. There were many distinctions between our beer and the beer he was experienced with, and he was having trouble getting across the pitch that Brooklyn Lager was made with 100 percent malted barley—no rice or corn; that it was lagered, or cold-stored, for four to six weeks, instead of being made in three weeks like big name brands; that it was naturally carbonated instead of being injected with $CO_2$; and that it was dry-hopped by the addition of hops during the lagering process to give it a flowery aroma.

This was our stock in trade. If you were not comfortable selling our beer on those merits—if you could not get across that Brooklyn Lager was New York's beer (the local beer)—then you had a problem making the sale, let alone the pitch. As Mike and Ed became more adept at selling, friction developed between them and the veteran. The granting of stock options to Mike and Ravn compounded this problem, and eventually the veteran quit the company for another job.

### "Hire Virgins!"

We learned a large lesson from this episode. The lesson was that experience in the mainstream beer industry was not necessarily an asset for our salespeople. It may even have been a detriment for more people than not. This lesson was crystallized for me during a lunch we had in 1989 with the father of our Brooklyn landlord, Tom Fatato. Fatato had gotten rich off the beer business, first as a bootlegger during Prohibition, and later as a legitimate brewer. In 1989, he owned a small brewery in southern New Jersey called the Eastern Brewing Company. He produced a brand called Canadian Ace Malt Liquor, which he said had been Al Capone's brand during Prohibition, and he distributed many brands, including Ballantine Ale and Ballantine India Pale Ale. In 1988, his main brand was not a beer at all, but was Malta, an unfermented malt beverage that was a staple for the Hispanic community in New York.

Fatato was producing a malt liquor called Midnight Dragon for John Ferrulito and Dom Vultaggio, two guys who would get rich years later from Arizona Iced Tea. Fatato was in his 80s, but he came to work every day and he exuded vitality with a thick mane of silver hair. He invited Tom and me to visit his brewery in southern New Jersey with the hope of persuading us to brew our Brooklyn Lager there.

While we were at lunch with several of his executives, Fatato put his arm around my shoulders and said, "Tell them how much you are getting for a box of beer, son."

"$20," I said.

He hugged me closer and boomed, "These guys are on to something."

We talked about how we sold the beer and the sort of sales team we had, and Fatato said, "That's the way to do it: Hire virgins! You'll never get an old-time beer salesman to sell a box of beer for $20! They always want to sell it on price. That is what is killing the beer business."

"Hire virgins!" became the motto of our human resource department from then on. Tom Fatato was a wise man.

### Are You with Us?

So Vitale and Ravn both got stock options that entitled them to about 10 percent of our outstanding stock. But only Mike eventually capitalized on these options. There were several reasons for this. Mike has always been a true believer in the Brooklyn Brewery, and equally important, so has his dad, Gerry Vitale. Gerry invested in our first offering and ended up investing in every offering after that. When things looked bleakest, Gerry was always there with an encouraging word and an offer to invest more money. Like my dad, Gerry had always worked for other people, and I think he liked the idea of his son Mike owning a share of the company he was helping to build.

Ravn worked as hard as any of us, and I think he started out believing in the company as much as any of us. I don't think we would have been able to crack the difficult Manhattan market without his tireless efforts in the beginning. I always found Manhattan to be a forbidding place to sell beer, but Ravn was not intimidated. The saloon owners were the hardest of the hard-boiled. They were used to getting free beer, free trips, and free professional sports tickets from the big international breweries like Anheuser-Busch and Guinness. The big breweries were all under the gun to get a significant presence in Manhattan because they wanted to impress Wall Street and show that they were strong players. We did not offer any freebies. Also, Manhattan was an impossible place to drive a car, let alone park. Parking tickets were $55 a shot, and if your car was towed, it cost $250 to get it back. (Today, the ticket price is $115.) Ravn was undeterred by any of this. He called himself "Scarhead" to describe his ability to absorb rejection. He just kept banging away until he made a sale. Ravn was not afraid of anything.

He was also an entrepreneur in his own right. He had a seasonal business, the Wood Squad, supplying firewood to residents of Manhattan. He bought firewood, rented a truck, and delivered it to assorted apartment buildings. He hired people to help him and paid them a day rate as needed.

He was impatient with the progress of the Brooklyn Brewery in the early years. Every time we raised more money, he was dismayed because he knew this was diluting the value of his options. He did not trust that growth would follow. He wanted profit now, the way the Wood Squad paid him. I think he lost faith in the leadership of Tom and me during the difficult times. He wanted and needed to run his own company and, eventually, he left the Brooklyn Brewery to start his own importing agency, which became very successful in its own right.

From the beginning, Tom and I called these two men—Mike and Ed—"partners," and they wore this title with pride. For many years, they felt they were key parts of the Brooklyn Brewery team, and they were. Both the stock options and the promise of equity in the business had a powerful motivating effect on them. They recognized they were the second tier of management ownership, but they were also proud of their positions and saw them as essential.

In 1991 and 1992, we expanded the distribution company

and did a new round of hiring. These new hires were well educated, and eventually they grew jealous of Vitale and Ravn because they had equity in Brooklyn Brewing. Ownership had motivated our first employees, but it also created expectations in new hires.

In 1994, Tom and I decided to distribute more equity. This time, we granted more stock to Mike and Ed and to six new employees, including a driver, our warehouse manager, and our office manager. These were small stock grants, but they had a significant impact on the motivation of the recipients. Some of the salespeople viewed the stock as compensation for the below-market salaries they were receiving. But both the driver, Tim Buksa, who eventually became a salesperson, and the warehouse manager, Gerald Cogdell, who had worked for many years in a low-paying job for the Fatato family, were extremely grateful. I think some of the salespeople viewed the stock grants to Buksa and Cogdell—working from nonsales positions—as somehow diminishing their own equity, but their attitude was tough luck for them. Tom and I viewed motivated drivers and warehouse laborers to be just as important to our company as great salespeople. If everyone works hard, everyone should be compensated for success.

## ENTERING BEER SCHOOL

After a few years of introducing and selling our lager directly to consumers, we went into the distribution business. The development of our distribution company in 1991–1993 was exciting for us. Tom and I hired six young salespeople, and we began training them in the history and products of the 50 or so breweries that we ended up representing through the Craft Brewers Guild (the name we gave our distribution company in New York and Massachusetts). We held seminars for the whole team on Saturday mornings so they could taste the beers and get to know the product backward and forward. These sessions were an intense study of beer and breweries. We required them to read Michael Jackson's book *The World Guide to Beer* and to watch his television series, *The Beer Hunter*. We played Spin the Bottle Opener, a game in which, when the opener stopped spinning, the person at whom it was pointing had to answer a tricky question about beer. We even gave multiple-choice tests to employees on the histories of the breweries we represented at any given time.

## Companywide Education

While brewing our own beer and distributing for others, we invited the importers and owners of the breweries we represented to attend our weekly sales meetings and talk about how to sell their products. Some of these presentations were quite sophisticated. Joe Lipa, the vice president for sales of Merchant du Vin—East, was selling a portfolio of beers that was the most expensive in the world in 1990. Brooklyn Lager was selling for roughly $5.99 a six-pack then, and Lipa's beers were selling for $12.99 a four-pack. Lipa taught our salespeople to educate customers about a new tier in the beer business—one analogous to the premium varietal wines and single malt scotches that restaurants were then getting into—of which we were a part.

He taught our sales team to size up a restaurant or bar by looking at their whisky and wine selection. If they had a wine list or carried single malt whisky or both, they were great candidates for a beer list that included Merchant du Vin's line of elite beers.

There were many other key educators who raised the bar in the beer world, as well. Don Feinberg, who with his wife, Wendy Littlefield, ran Vanberg & DeWulf, importers of a line of expensive Belgian beers, visited us, and spoke passionately of his initiation into the wonderful world of Belgian beers. He told stories of the breweries his company represented and explained how Belgian beers could be as sophisticated an accompaniment to a fine meal as any French wine.

Similarly, Jeff Coleman, who ran the importing agency for Munich's largest brewery, Paulaner, talked to us about the necessity of good merchandising. Coleman was a journeyman beer salesperson who had experience with many large breweries. He taught us the importance of getting our products on the shelves and in the beer coolers at eye level, where consumers were sure to see them. Thanks to Jeff, Paulaner had the most sophisticated in-store marketing materials, such as hangtags and consumer rebates.

In addition to these guest speakers and onsite education sessions, we invited all our salespeople to the beer dinners we were sponsoring monthly at American Festival Café (now Rock Center Café) in Rockefeller Center, and at Café Centro in Grand Central Terminal in Manhattan. We developed these programs with John Harding, the insightful vice president for marketing of Restaurant Associates (the corporation that owned the restaurants). With each new year, our community outreach and events grew, adding a variety of venues and levels of participation that our employees could enjoy and learn from. The American Festival events featured the American breweries we represented, and the Café Centro events featured the imported breweries. At these events, guest speakers told the stories of their companies and talked about their beers, which were paired with five-course meals. We were aggressively cultivating an atmosphere of participation and experimentation with food and drink. We took our salespeople to the Great American Beer Festival in Denver, where they saw that the Brooklyn Brewery was part of a national movement toward better beer.

Finally, we invited Michael Jackson, author of *The World Guide to Beer,* to New York for special tastings every year. As part of his visit, Michael usually spoke to our salespeople about good beer and answered their questions.

I believe this education program was a tremendous motivating factor for our employees. Education is powerful. It created a background of confidence and mastery within our sales force that may not have been there if we had relied on their selling capabilities alone. We were not just putting them out on the cold streets of New York and telling them to sell these unknown beers; we were giving them the knowledge and the programs they needed to make the sales. Most of our salespeople recognized that they were gaining valuable skills that would enhance their value as salespeople for the Craft Brewers Guild and/or any other company for which they might work in the future.

Today, there are Craft Brewers Guild alumni in many key positions with beer, wine, spirits, and even sake and coffee companies, around the country.

### Sales Incentives: A Powerful Tool

In addition to stock ownership and product education, another important tool that Tom and I used effectively from day one for our Brooklyn beer sales team as it grew is the sales incentive. Paying bonuses for hitting specific goals is a very powerful motivator for a salesperson. Over the years, we have been able to focus our people on specific areas where we want to make gains, and by and large, they have delivered. We enjoyed double-digit growth for the first 15 years of our existence, and I think our sales incentives were a big factor. Today, a starting salesperson at Brooklyn Brewery can expect to make a base pay of $40,000 and earn at least $20,000 in additional pay through incentives. Usually, an incentive program had a companywide goal and a second goal for the territory covered by the salesperson. For instance, the salesperson might get $10,000 if the company reached its goal of 20 percent growth, and an additional $500 for every 1 percent growth in his or her territory. It is important that the sales incentives be attainable to be effective. If you make the goals too tough, no one will believe in the program.

Likewise, executive pay is heavily focused on performance. I like being able to look my employees in the eye and say, "I'm sorry you didn't make as much as you expected to last year, but neither did I." They may or may not believe me, but at least I can say that with conviction because it is true. Really, how many employees can say their success is tied to the company in the same way that the executive manager's success is? Only a few, I'd guess. Credible, attainable sales incentives have been very important to our success, and I think the same is true of many other small companies.

The last round of equity Tom and I distributed was in the form of stock options during the TotalBeer.com enterprise we embarked on in 1999 (see Chapter 6). In this specific round, we granted options at a very high price, expecting to shoot the moon, like every other dot-com of that era. We announced these new stock options at an important company meeting that year. Interestingly, I don't think most of our employees ever had much faith in TotalBeer.com, and few had an expectation of these options ever amounting to much. Unfortunately for TotalBeer.com (as we'll talk about later on), they were right.

In the end, the whole dot-com enterprise had a negative effect on the credibility of our Brooklyn Brewery stock options and grants because it never got off the ground. And with that, there is an important lesson to be learned: Stock options and grants are most effective when the recipient believes he is getting something of value. This seems obvious, but it is not always. For a stock option or grant to be of value, the recipient has to believe in the dream you are selling and work toward the goals at hand to make the dream a reality.

Overall, stock options and grants can be an effective motivator. Currently, in 2005, we are now preparing to grant stock to key employees once again. Having recently sold our distribution company for a tidy sum (which we'll talk about in Chapter 10), it now is clear that the Brooklyn Brewery has value. Many recipients of stock options over the years have earned some money on those options. We went from a high of about 100 employees when we owned distribution companies in New York and Massachusetts to about 32 employees today (after selling these companies—again, see Chapter 10). In the future, when we offer options and grants to motivate and grow our company, we will try to learn from the experience we've had with our various offerings to employees for various reasons over the years, to be sure that the recipients understand, believe in, and appreciate the value of the stock they are taking owner- ship of. Only then is the reward truly a bonus for all.

## LESSON FIVE
## FEELING GOOD IS NO SUBSTITUTE FOR PRUDENT CONTROLS

Tom and I always prided ourselves on being benevolent rulers of our little realm. We never paid ourselves much more than our senior managers, and we always shared equity with key employ- ees. From about 1995 onward, our pay scale was at or above those of comparable companies in the beer industry. Overall, our own salaries were definitely lower than those of most brew- ery and distributor owners in the beer business.

One of the problems all companies face is that employees at all levels want to make more money every year. Of course, it is impossible to meet this expectation unless your yearly growth is exponential. We've grown steadily but have had to balance pay with the ups and downs of our company's expansion. One of the most effective ways we have had of addressing this problem is our annual performance review. My review format consisted of a first section that reviews the activities of an employee in the previous year, a section highlighting the strengths of the employee overall, a section listing the weaknesses of the employee overall, a section outlining the employee's mission for the coming year, and finally, a listing of the employee's pay for the previous two years and base pay and bonus structure for the coming year.

This format has enabled me to manage the expectations of most employees. I don't think anyone I have ever reviewed has ever been entirely happy with his or her review. But I believe that everyone can do a better job, and I think reviews should show how, by offering employees a chance to view a detailed account of where they've come from and where they are going. Through this process, I have been able to address the problem of ever-rising expectations. I have been able to say to the super salesperson who wants to be a manager that he or she does not have what it takes to be a manager . . . yet, at least. (One of the major pitfalls of any company is trying to turn a super salesperson into a manager before he or she is ready.) I have been able to show employees their individual histories and performance records, and say to employees disappointed in the lack of an increase in their base pay that I likewise am not getting an increase in base pay because, frankly, we did not do very well as a company last year—but perhaps a focus on our future targets may help us to succeed in the coming year.

This process is not without pain. I have lost some very good people over the years because they had effectively reached their highest point in our organization. For instance, even if they might have been manager material, I had to let them know that they would have to be patient because I was not going to fire the person above them in order to push them ahead before the time was right.

One particular area of weakness for Tom and me in terms of employment, at least in the first 12 years, was the control of cash. We never really had a good controller until we hired Debra Bascome in 2000. The reason is basically that good controllers are expensive. When we hired Bascome, we began paying her almost twice what we had paid any other controller before because she had big-time experience, with J.Crew and Sunglass Hut, and she knows her business. She has proven to be a consummate self-starter.

In retrospect, we should have paid to hire a good controller years before we did. From 1991 until 2000, we were effectively blind to our day-to-day cash flow and profitability. I think this flaw was apparent to our employees. Early on, we had a controller named Fred, and he was replaced by a Wilma. Mike Vitale, who has an acerbic wit, took to calling them "the Flintstones," referring to the old television series. After we fired Wilma, Mike quipped, "If the next controller is called Barney or Betty (also "Flintstones" characters), I'm quitting."

We always knew how much cash we had, but we did not have a firm idea of how fast we were depleting it. Although our company was small, it was complicated, from an accounting point of view. We essentially had two companies, the brewery and the distributorship, until we sold the distributorship in 2003. The brewery was "selling" beer to the distributorship at a set transfer price, and the distributorship was charging the brewery for certain services such as discounting for special sales and implementing sales incentives and sales programs. The brewery was also selling to distributors outside the Craft Brewers Guild area of New York and Massachusetts. The Craft Brewers Guild was also dealing with 30 other suppliers and representing some of those suppliers in areas outside the New York area. As we added more suppliers and products, accounting for the company became more complicated as the businesses grew from year to year. We hired and fired four controllers over the nine-year period before hiring Debra Bascome.

During those years, when we weren't thinking so clearly about cash flow, we were robbed at gunpoint in our offices of $30,000 cash. We should never have had $30,000 cash in our safe, but we had not been to the bank in a few days. Because of the time of year and know-how of the thieves, the police were certain that the robbers had had the cooperation of one of our employees in planning the robbery. It was the day before Thanksgiving 1995 and the safe was stuffed with cash.

We also lost a trusted manager because of suspected theft

when we discovered that the manager was stealing from our petty cash account. In 1995, we were a $15 million company. Petty cash had gone from being a tin can with $300 in it in 1987 to being a bank account with $10,000 in it. The manager began taking $100 here and $100 there, small amounts that we didn't notice at first, until serious money started to go missing. I have no doubt that the defalcation was as much our fault for not having checks and balances in place (employees who could have monitored these types of transactions and accounts) as it was the fault of the manager.

All in all, we have been very fortunate to attract good employees. We have always provided health insurance, and starting pay for a warehouse job has been well above minimum wage. We do not have a human resources department, so each department does its own hiring. I usually meet with all new employees, but I am not necessarily involved in their actual hiring. Overall, I think we might have avoided some pain if we had had more stringent controls on cash, starting with being more serious about hiring a great controller right away. Perhaps we stayed in the trusting, entrepreneurial mode for a bit too long, instead of transforming ourselves into tough, skeptical managers more quickly. ★

## TOM WEIGHS IN

For our first seven or eight years—between 1988 and about 1995—we thought we couldn't afford market salaries. We usually paid less than larger breweries and distributors for a given position and had to offer something in addition to salary that would make up the difference. We were able to attract very good people, even though our employees could have commanded higher salaries elsewhere. So how did we do it?

Steve points out that beer is different, that it is cool to work for a microbrewery, and I think that was definitely part of it, but there were other elements, too. I think simply being part of a start-up was attractive to some people. Of course, that feeling inevitably faded over time. Then being part of an organization that saw itself as special, and superior in its field, became increasingly important for employees.

A start-up has a lot of organizational disadvantages. It is constantly solving basic problems that more mature companies worked through long ago. On the other hand, it doesn't take basic policies for granted. There is a certain energy in examining everything, all the time. It can be exhausting for managers and confusing for employees, but at least it's fresh. Anyone who thinks they have a good idea—which means just about everyone—feels free to contribute. In a smaller company, complaints and suggestions come directly to the boss, and the boss makes decisions and is responsible for them.

When I worked at Chemical Bank, I felt that policies were set in stone by people way up the ladder whom I would never meet. They worked in a completely different building than I did and might as well have been in a completely different world. As a junior banker, I could see only about three levels up my organization before it got fuzzy. I knew my boss and her boss, and occasionally would meet my boss's boss's boss. I never imagined I could change bank policy or even my division's policy, for that matter. Other people told me what the company goals were. At the Brooklyn Brewery, conversely, employees were constantly telling me and Steve what the goals should be, and we didn't have much choice but to listen. There is no place to hide in a one-room office, and start-ups inherently attract people who want to be listened to.

I never wanted to join the Marines, but I've always admired their cocky "the few, the proud" aura. Everyone wants to think of themselves as special, but not all companies provide their employees with the feeling that they are part of an elite crew. Some don't even try because they are dominated by bullying bosses who see themselves as carrying a sorry organization on their own heroic shoulders. Whenever I hear a manager complain to me that his or her staff is a bunch of idiots, I cringe because it says a lot more about the manager than about the staff.

For our first several years in business, our company was not very good at a lot of basic things, but that didn't stop us from feeling confident. Over time, we got better and our confidence became better justified. When we took pains to train our salespeople, for instance, this had two advantages that became evident over time. First, our training made them more skilled and confident salespeople. We saw that right away. Second, it set us apart from virtually every other beer distributor we competed against. None of our competitors spent nearly as much time and effort training their own salespeople. After a few years, we earned a reputation of really knowing what we were talking about and building a sense of community around our product. Even our competitors acknowledged it. We were the smallest distributor in the market, so it was important for our people to feel that they had an advantage. Like the Marines, they were confident even when outnumbered. We weren't the biggest, but we were the best.

In addition to trying to be better than our competition, we tried to be good by doing good. Both Steve and I wanted our company to stand for something positive. Lots of little things add up: like staying actively connected to the community, keeping all financial transactions aboveboard, and accepting responsibility for our own mistakes while not taking advantage of customer errors. With a positive track record, we attracted better people who wanted to be involved with a better kind of company. In trying to manage a company with integrity, we attracted employees of integrity. It's a virtuous circle, thankfully.

Motivating people is at the heart of leadership. In a start-up, that leadership is intensely personal. Structures, policies, employee handbooks, mission statements, and strategic plans are important, but when there are only a dozen people working together, the personal character of the boss looms overwhelmingly large. When people came to work for the Brooklyn Brewery, they were coming to work for Steve and me. What they saw in our individual characters was probably more important to them than anything written in our employee handbook. Did they trust us when interacting with us? Did they like and respect us? Did they want to drink a beer with us? The character of the workforce and how that workforce interacts can contribute tenfold to the success of a company.

I think that Steve and I have similar personalities in many ways. We're both stubborn, ambitious, articulate, confident, and driven to succeed. Those are qualities that attract some people. (Those same qualities also probably drove others away, to be honest.) And then there are ways that we're different: I'm more analytical and patient, while Steve works well on instinct and has an impulse to action. I think our early employees sensed that we brought those complementary qualities to the table and instinctively trusted our dynamic, as well as trusted us as individuals.

**Our Grade:**  Motivating employees is a challenge that never ends. As the Brooklyn Brewery matured, the nature of that challenge evolved, but as managers, Steve and I never took the challenge or our staff for granted. I think we deserve a grade of B+.

# CHAPTER 6

# Tom Tells the Story of Their Dot-Com Revolution: Fishing for Finance and Failing

In late 1999 and early 2000, the Internet seemed to be shaking up all of American retail trade and challenging long-accepted practices in every industry. Virtually all observers were predicting a huge rise in both business-to-business and business-to-consumer Internet commerce. Consultants like International Data Corporation were predicting tenfold increases in sales, from $5 billion to $50 billion, within just a few years. Forrester Research was estimating that online grocery sales alone would grow fiftyfold, from $200 million in 1998 to over $10 billion in 2003. This was going to be the California gold rush all over again. Opportunity shined like dazzling nuggets in the hills of online business.

You were a better manager than me if the thundering cannons of the Internet revolution didn't keep you awake at night. In January of 2000, the venerable Time Warner (revenues of $27 billion) announced it was being acquired by America Online (revenues of $5 billion) for $162 billion in AOL stock. Did people think that was crazy? Time Warner's shares rose 39 percent the next day. When the merger was completed, the market gave the combined entity a value of $280 billion. You probably could have bought Canada more cheaply.

We became caught up in the fever and were about to make some of our biggest mistakes. A little context will help show how, and why, we went off track. Some of our mistakes came from chasing an illusory big score. Some came from making assumptions about how we could extend our business to implausible extremes. And some, I'm sad to say, came from being stupid.

## RAISING MONEY IS A FULL-TIME JOB

When we started the Brooklyn Brewery I vaguely imagined three stages of financing. First, we'd raise an initial round of private equity; a few years later, we'd find bank financing; then finally, we'd go public and live happily ever after. It was a simple, perhaps simple-minded, view. It didn't work out that way. In fact, in our first 15 years, we had at least six different private equity rounds, one private debt round, and four different bank credit relationships. In other words, we were raising money in one form or another almost constantly.

Here's a chronicle of our early equity financings. We raised our initial $500,000 in 1987 and 1988. We raised another $500,000 in 1990, when we were nearly broke (in fact, technically bankrupt, in that our debts often exceeded our assets) and struggling with our direction. We raised another $500,000 in 1992 as our distribution business began to take hold and expand. Then we raised $1.2 million in 1994 as sales were racing ahead and we began to prepare the construction of the Williamsburg brewery. Only at the very end of this time period (which was six years after our start) did we begin looking for commercial bank financing.

We needed money for different reasons: sometimes because we had lost money the year before, sometimes because growth required additional working capital, and sometimes because we had a specific expansion project to fund. We were able to raise money in these early years because we were growing strongly and could make a good case to investors that we were increasing shareholder value even if we weren't profitable. While growth attracts equity investors, it doesn't necessarily attract a bank. Some entrepreneurs don't understand why, so let me—a former banker—explain. The reason is simple: For a bank, the risk/return ratio is sharply bounded on the upside. No matter how well their borrower does, a bank gets back only its principal plus a modest interest rate. For example, say a bank charges 8 percent for a loan and pays 4 percent for the deposits that fund that loan. Its gross profit is 4 percent. If even 1 loan in 25 goes bad, then that one bad loan wipes out all the gross profit on all 24 good loans. Conversely, an equity investor has no upper bounds on return. One good investment could double in value and make up for one bad investment. Since that can't happen for a commercial bank, it is appropriately risk-averse. It doesn't care about your growth potential. It cares deeply about your potential for going broke and not repaying its principal.

If you've got a business that doesn't have stable cash flow, you don't want a bank looking over your shoulder. It could become skittish if you take even modest risks—risks that make sense for small businesses. The bank may enforce restrictive loan covenants that block what you'd like to do. Worse, if it smells trouble, it will have the power to shut you down to limit its losses. It might decide to pull the plug on your loan and recover a sure 50 cents on the dollar, even as you scream that it's crazy because your company has a bright future shortly down the road. But if you are in that position, it's not really the bank's fault; it's yours, for accepting their risk-averse money. That's why we didn't even look for bank financing until I was sure that we were financially sound.

## THERE'S EQUITY, AND THEN THERE'S VENTURE CAPITAL

When we were planning the Brooklyn Brewery in 1987, the venture capital business was quite small and specialized. That year it invested about $3 billion, almost all of it going to businesses that had some sophisticated intellectual property to exploit. There were a few firms on the East Coast, but the bulk were centered in the Silicon Valley. A normal start-up business in any industry except high-tech would never have thought of venture capital as a potential source of funding back then. A consumer product company like the Brooklyn Brewery, with no intellectual property but our brand and logo, would not have been much of a VC candidate.

Over the next 15 years, the VC industry grew tremendously and is now much more widely known to the general public and to potential entrepreneurs. In 2004, the VC industry pumped nearly $18 billion into various start-ups, mostly still in technology but also in every other industry imaginable. Dreamers in every field these days probably think about the possibility of attracting a VC. The success of venture-backed companies like Starbucks, Costco, and Home Depot are familiar to us all. But except in very special cases, you might want to think again.

## FOUR SOURCES OF FINANCING FOR START-UPS

To put VC financing in perspective, it helps to think about the alternatives. There are four main financing sources for start-ups. The most important, and most often ignored and underappreciated, is *supplier financing*. When suppliers of raw materials or finished goods give a business 30 days to pay, they are lending it money. For a typical small business, these loans are more important than investment equity or bank financing. A successful supplier is a knowledgeable expert in its own industry, acutely sensitive to news about how its various customers are doing. They're not always financially sophisticated, but through long experience, they become pretty effective lenders. Like a bank, they are afraid of losing all of their loan, but unlike a bank, they have good reason to be more lenient. They probably know more about your specific industry than the banker does, and they also have much more upside if the relationship is successful. For example, if you buy $1,000 a month from one supplier, his or her gross profit might be $250 per month, or $3,000 in a year. Lending your business $1,000, which is 30 days' sales, against a potential gross profit of $3,000 a year, might make sense. Cultivating suppliers to earn their trust is crucial to almost every start-up. Of course, any supplier will feel better once a customer establishes at least a modest track record.

The second type of financing for small business is *angel investing*. Angel investors are private investors who put their money into a company as equity, not as debt. This means they are part owners of the business. They are the last to get paid if anything goes wrong, but they share in the upside if the business goes well. This is the primary kind of investor we sought at the Brooklyn Brewery. Some angel investors are quite sophisticated, but in general the company sets the proposed terms of an investment as a take-it-or-leave-it proposition. All the investors are individuals, but usually each one gets the same deal as all the others in a given round of financing. When a founder seeks angel investors, he or she is giving up part of the ownership— potentially a large portion—but in return for sharing the future wealth, the owner receives "friendly" money. There is usually no set due date to repay it, as there would be with debt; there may be no required interest payments (though dividends might accrue or be paid when cash is available); and because the investment is spread among many individuals, the founder usually stays in control.

The third type of financing is *debt*. Classic bank financing, which I did as a commercial lending officer, is the best-known type but actually is not common for start-ups. A classic bank loan has a set term—say, two years—and pays interest each month. It is secured by a general pledge of all assets and probably personal guarantees by the owners as well. At the end of the term, the whole loan is either repaid or rolled over into another loan. Of course, if the business can't repay the loan at the end of the first term, the bank is not likely to extend the loan for a second. Instead, the bank might move to foreclose on any and all assets. There are many variations of bank financing, including loans that are specifically tied to certain assets such as receivables and inventory. There are also small business loans that are made by specialized banks or departments of big banks, sometimes under the auspices of the Small Business Investment Corporation (SBIC). Some are better deals for start-ups than others. But all will have to be repaid within a set period of time, along with interest. So if you choose this type of financing, your business must generate the required cash in the set period of time or risk bankruptcy. Bank financing is cheap, in the sense that it does not dilute the founders' ownership stake. But it represents a ticking clock, and if the clock strikes midnight and you can't repay the loan, it's good night, Mother. Debt can be a good choice for companies with positive cash flow and a forecastable future, but it can be a bad choice for many start-ups.

The fourth type of financing is *venture capital*. The growth of the VC industry has multiplied the different types of funds and the ways they are structured, but most still follow a standard format. Professional managers will put together a fund of, say, $50 million, made up of investments from institutions such as insurance companies and pension funds as well as rich individual investors. They promise to spread their investment across several different companies, for the sake of diversity. But they don't want to have to make too many investments because of the time and money that each requires. Initial due diligence, legal structuring, and ongoing oversight are all costly. So they may declare that their target investment is $5 million with a floor of $2 million, and they are thus looking for approximately 10 investment opportunities. At the end of a set period of time, perhaps 10 years, they will cash out of all their investments and give the money (less substantial fees) back to investors.

## WHEN VENTURE FINANCING IS—OR IS NOT— APPROPRIATE FOR YOU

A venture fund is a very different financier from the first three types. It has a long-term prospective, but a finite life. It seeks the highest return of any investor and is willing to take the greatest risk. It expects that some of its investments will go bankrupt. It needs other investments to return 5 or 10 times the original investment, to make up for the losers and still generate an outstanding overall return. The managers of funds are typically smart, tough financial professionals with extensive experience in one or two specific industries where they concentrate their investments. They want good managers in place and will help them. But they will also structure their investment so that if anything goes wrong—if project targets aren't met or if financial goals slip—they will have the ability to step in and take over. The old managers will be out and new ones brought in. If additional rounds of financing are needed, the VCs can help raise money later, but it can be at a stiff price. Old investors can expect to be diluted heavily if they can't afford to reinvest in the new round.

What kind of investments do VCs seek? First, the investment has to be the right size. Too small is worse than too big: Funds can always share a good big deal with other funds, but a deal that's too small—no matter how potentially good—just won't get looked at. It can't pay enough. Second, the potential returns have to be unusually rich. Just doing better than the stock market isn't nearly good enough. VCs take a lot of risk and expect to at least double market returns, so a company needs to be able to grow like crazy. Third, there has to be a plausible way to cash out once the company has succeeded. An initial public offering (IPO) is the classic exit, but acquisition by a larger company is probably even more common. A VC wants to know that management will head in one of these directions. If you've got a big idea, with fast growth, and are pointing toward either a public offering or being acquired, VC money might be right for you.

### Our VC Hopes Are "Crushed"

In early May of 1994 Steve and I were on the money trail, and this time we were considering venture capital finance. Boosted by the growth of our distribution division in the previous few years, sales were growing quickly and the future looked bright. We thought we'd need a little over a $1 million to finally build our first brewery in Williamsburg, and we also pondered the possibility of a public offering within a few years. Our first three equity rounds had all been with angel investors. We thought perhaps this time—which would be our fourth round— we should consider an institutional investor. Even more than its money, we were interested in an investor that would have the motivation and experience to later take us public so that our shareholders could sell their shares if they wished.

One morning Steve and I took the subway down to the Wall Street district to the offices of Loeb Partners on lower Broadway. We were greeted by Fred Fruitman, a managing partner of the company. We had a bit of history together. Initially introduced by a mutual friend, Fred had followed our company for several years. He'd indicated an interest in investing as early as 1990, but we had never followed up seriously. So long as we were able to finance ourselves with angel money we were leery of bringing in a venture fund, but maybe now the time was right.

I liked Fred. I thought he was smart, engaging, and honest. I viewed him as a financial wolf, but a straightforward one. I knew he'd negotiate hard and be perfectly willing to eat his lunch and ours, too, if we let him. That was the deal, but I thought that if we could negotiate hard in turn and agree on a fair structure now, I'd like to have him on our side as we prepared to go public. I was impressed that he'd been willing to keep in touch with us even though we had essentially blown off his interest for the previous four years. I guess, like any true hunter, Fred had learned the value of patience.

After preliminary meetings with Fruitman, we were introduced to the man who ran Loeb Partners, Tom Kempner (the nephew of John Loeb, who at 92 still came to work every day in an office above Kempner). Kempner's office was dimly lit and he spoke in a gentle, hushed tone. As the meeting went on, Steve and I ended up on the edge of our seats trying to get closer to hear his words. By contrast, Kempner sat comfortably back in his executive chair. The situation was clear: Kempner had the money and we wanted it.

Kempner laid out the essential framework of the deal. Steve and I would gain a larger share of the stock, but Loeb would control the company. Steve and I would have performance goals to meet. If we hit the targets, we would get more stock; if we didn't, we would lose ground. Our original investors could get their money back, but they were not likely to make any profit.

Steve asked how he valued the distribution end of our business. Kempner said he viewed the distribution side as less valuable than the brewery, but he described it as an "anchor to windward." He then explained that in sailing, an anchor to windward was pitched during a storm to steady the ship. He said he felt the distribution company would be worth money, no matter how the brewery fared.

Both Steve and I asked for a better deal for our investors.

They had been in on the ground floor. They had believed in us when we had nothing. They were our family, friends, and colleagues. They deserved some profit, we said. Kempner patiently explained to us the rules of venture capitalism. They invested their money four years ago. You need more money now. I am investing the new money that will enable you to make money. I deserve the upside, and so do you two.

For professional investors, he said, each round of a company's financing might be like betting a round of poker. Either you stayed in with additional money or dropped out and accepted considerable dilution. At the extreme, if you sat out a round you might be wiped out of your entire previous investment. The financial slang for this was being "crammed down," or "crushed." He told us the story of Federal Express, in which anyone who did not invest in something like six rounds was essentially shut out. But those who could afford to stay in for every round eventually did make a lot of money. Our current investors, he implied, could step up or step out.

We knew our investors—nearly all of them personally—and, with a couple of exceptions, they weren't rich. Many of them had already invested in two rounds with us, which was probably one more than they had initially anticipated. Offering them a chance to invest again was one thing; crushing them if they couldn't afford it was another. They weren't professional investors, and both Steve and I felt strongly that we had an obligation to them. For Steve and me personally, Loeb Partners might have offered a very good deal. The next day they gave us a written offer for $1.2 million that we stared at longingly. Then we turned it down.

## THE BREWERY BUBBLE OF 1995–1996

After declining Loeb Partners' offer, we ended up raising that same $1.2 million privately with our largest existing investor.

But within a year of raising the money, it looked like our brewery was going to cost more than we had estimated, and by 1996 we were pondering our financial options again. Within just two years, though, the financial landscape had changed considerably. The building consumer interest in microbreweries had exploded onto the financial pages, and small breweries like ours were becoming Wall Street darlings.

The brewery financial bubble of 1995–1996 would be, in many respects, an excellent preview of the Internet bubble four years down the road, which made our later mistakes in 2000 and 2001 even harder to justify. Our initial experience with irrational financial exuberance came when first-generation microbreweries began to go public in 1995. We watched as colleagues Jim Koch of Boston Beer, Pete Slosberg of Pete's Wicked, and George Hancock of Pyramid took their companies public. What impressed us was not just that they could go public but that very reputable brokerage firms were managing the offerings. The very best firms of the era, including Goldman Sachs and Dean Witter, were peddling their stock.

I will admit to a certain degree of envy when guys I had known for years, as colleagues and competitors, took their companies public. Their investors had a chance to cash out—which I dearly wished for our investors—and the founders were each sitting on stock worth millions of dollars. I longed for that for myself.

Brokerage firms began sniffing around the Brooklyn Brewery as the market for microbrewery stocks heated up. We were smaller as a brewery than the previous companies to go public, but if you added our distribution division revenues to brewery revenues, we weren't far off. Our distribution company gave us a different wrinkle as a potential investment. We weren't a pure brewery play, which for some investors and analysts was a negative. However, it gave an investor a stake in the larger category of specialty beer as well as some vertical integration efficiencies for the brewery itself. It could make a good story for brokers to sell, and several brokers wanted to try.

We met with a half dozen firms that wanted to take us public. Some seemed like real boiler-room operations, quick-buck artists that offered no aftermarket or financial support to investors or the company once the initial offering was completed. Others, like Dean Witter, were quite legitimate and had a depth of experience with other beer companies. In 1996 Steve and I wrestled with what seemed like a genuine opportunity to realize our financial goals.

Two things nagged at us, though, and we hesitated. One was a feeling that we were too small and immature as a company to go public. Did we have the internal financial controls to supply all of the Securities and Exchange Commission (SEC) statements required on a quarterly basis? Were we ready for the intensive daily scrutiny of short-term investors? Were we ready to go from dozens of investors to tens of thousands of investors? The second hesitation was over an issue we found even more troubling. All of the microbreweries going public had announced extremely ambitious growth plans. Some, like Pete's Wicked, were already rolling their brands out across the country. Others, like Pyramid, promised to do so immediately after its offering raised the necessary funds. To go public, it seemed, a company had to promise really dramatic growth. We wondered if Pete's and Pyramid could deliver it. We wondered if we could.

As a distributor, we had a crucial window on the market. We had actually distributed West Coast beers that had come east looking for sales. Sierra Nevada had been an unqualified success, but the experience of several others that followed raised warning flags. We had distributed Mendocino from California, Rogue from Oregon, Grant's from Washington, and Breckenridge Brewing from Colorado, among many others, and it wasn't an easy sell. These were all good beers—some were terrific—but the shelves were getting crowded with good new beers. Outside of their own home markets, only a few could break through from being specialty products into the retail mainstream. We knew that it wasn't our lack of effort as a distributor that was the limiting factor. There were just too many beers and too few taps, and the surging number of new breweries was outpacing the real, but more modest growth in the number of new drinkers of better beer. This dynamic wasn't necessarily a problem unless all the new breweries expected geometric growth. Unfortunately, they did, and the first-generation breweries that were now about 10 years old and were going public promised their new investors that they would be national successes. It would prove a difficult promise to keep.

## SELLING BROOKLYN BEER BEYOND NEW YORK

In addition to our distributing experience, we had some sobering lessons in trying to sell Brooklyn Brewery products outside of our own home market. Within a couple of years of introduction, we had been contacted by distributors from many states. It was amazingly flattering to hear a distributor in Florida or Washington state say that they would like to buy a tractor-trailer load of our beer. In 1989 and 1990, with stars in our eyes and a distributor's fat check in the bank, we sent the beer. And then, as the months passed, we lived through the horror of knowing that our beer was not selling well and was slowly getting older and older in those markets, and there was nothing we could do about it. People were buying dusty bottles of Brooklyn Lager more than a year after we bottled it, thinking they'd been ripped off. In fact, they had been. We hadn't done right by them or by our reputation.

As distributors ourselves, we should have known better. Our beers just didn't have enough recognition that far from home to sell in trailer quantities. Apart from an initial introduction, we couldn't support the distributor with sales promotions or tastings or customer visits like we did in the Northeast or grow-ing foreign markets. We eventually pulled out of the faraway U.S. markets and vowed to restrict distribution to a region closer to home, where we could pay attention and keep our beer fresh. (Even now, 10 years later, our strategy for geographic expansion in the United States is quite conservative.) As other breweries planned ambitious national rollouts to justify their public offerings, our own experience as a brewer and distribu-tor had made us doubly cautious.

## THE DANGEROUS LURE OF FINANCING

The promise of financing can pull even a good business off strat-egy. The lure of going public, especially, pulled many of our colleagues away from a sound, regional focus. For instance, Pyramid Brewing was doing very well in the mid-1990s, enjoyed excellent organic growth, and was guided by a talented manage-ment team. When it raised $34 million in late 1995 on the promise of going national, it quickly spent most of its money in the futile attempt and saw its reputation erode from regional success to national failure. Pyramid's shares went public at $19, and over the next 10 years they lost nearly 90 percent of their value. Pyramid has lately regained some positive momentum and still makes good beer, but the whole episode is a painful re-minder that the business strategy needs to direct the financing and not the other way around. In 1996, we made the right choice. Instead of going public, we raised the money to finish the brewery privately, at an excellent valuation. Unfortunately, it didn't stop us from getting caught up four years later in the next financial frenzy.

### Everyone's Getting Rich in 2000—Why Not Us?

With our brewery built in 1996, we enjoyed several quiet years of solid brewery growth. Our distributorship, however, was slowing down. It had reached the limit of what a specialty distributor could do. We began to rely heavily on other distribution partners to cover chain stores and other off-premise accounts (stores, delis, convenience stores). These were partnerships that would later haunt us as we tried to disentangle our obligations (as discussed in Chapter 10), but at the time they seemed necessary. Meanwhile, the Internet frenzy was building in 1999 and peaking in 2000. We were watching with great interest.

Two dot-com companies—in retrospect, two of the worst possible exemplars—were especially fascinating to me in the year 2000. The first, Webvan.com, had the ambition to revolutionize national grocery sales. Founded by the best and brightest, including the charismatic George Shaheen (former CEO of Andersen Consulting, now known as Accenture), it raised huge amounts of money from sophisticated venture funds like Sequoia Capital, and then raised even more money when it quickly went public. When Webvan placed a $1 billion order with Bechtel to build logistics depots in dozens of major cities across the country for superautomated warehouses, it seemed the opening salvo of a surging retail revolution. The second company was New York–based Kozmo.com. Founded by baby-faced Joseph Park and his roommate, its business strategy came straight from their Gen X insight that it would be really cool to deliver anything to individual apartments that the urban soul could need, morning, noon, or night: ice cream, CDs, cigarettes, books—all the basics of life. These deliveries would be made by bicycle messengers with nicknames like "Spike" and "Buzzkill." Kozmo, too, was able to raise huge amounts of money—over $280 million—for its provocative, if unproven, thesis that you could eventually earn big money by making a lot of small deliveries.

With these companies in our thoughts, we contemplated our situation. Internet commerce was not generally seen as replacing traditional retail stores. But it did seem that Internet commerce would grow and vigorously compete with traditional retailers, and that Internet sales might be especially appropriate for certain specialty goods. These products, like our specialty beers, were sometimes difficult to find at normal stores. Selection at traditional outlets could be quite limited. Nor were merchants particularly knowledgeable about these beers if a customer had a question or wanted a recommendation. And inventory was not always rotated to keep the beers fresh. We sensed that perhaps our business—brewing and distributing specialty beers— just might be one of those due for an Internet shake-up.

With news about Internet ventures flooding the business and public press every day, we looked closely at our own operations. How did we look compared to these new ventures? Was this new sales channel a threat or an opportunity?

We saw that brand-new start-ups without the revenue or infrastructure we had were being valued at premium prices less for their prospects of near-term cash flow than for their potential to shake up the status quo and redefine retailing. We weren't a start-up anymore. We were the classic, old-fashioned bricks-and-mortar operation, but when it came to retailing, we had learned what seemed like an important lesson: Distribution rules. Whether the retailing was bricks and mortar or the new Internet type, physically moving a product was still going to be key. And while most consumer products could easily be shipped by UPS, FedEx, or the U.S. Postal Service, alcoholic beverages mostly could not. State regulations made alcohol very different. Restrictive laws rendered standard third-party UPS-style shipping very difficult, and states like New York also enforced exclusive beer wholesale contracts. That meant that existing exclusive wholesalers, like us, were in an unusually strong position to maintain their primacy, either with the status quo or in creating change. Since we were the little guys in New York distribution, I liked the idea of change. Change represented an opportunity to get bigger. We could be David whacking Goliath.

### An Innovation in Direct-to-Consumer Sales?

As we were contemplating starting up direct-to-consumer Internet sales, we seemed to have a lot of advantages. We had the exclusive New York distribution rights to a huge portfolio of hundreds of terrific specialty beers. It was a truly dominant portfolio, which no other wholesaler could match. We already had a convenient warehouse stocking all of these products for wholesale distribution, so we wouldn't need to invest in additional inventory for retail sales. We'd just make our million-dollar existing inventory work harder and turn over more often. We had skilled drivers who wanted more work and 12 trucks that were busy in the day but idle at night and on weekends. That meant we could deliver at a lower price than potential competitors. We also had a knowledgeable office staff that could troubleshoot customer service issues or delivery problems. Add it all up, we thought, and we were in the catbird seat. We were practically ready to change the beer world. All we needed was a good web site and a marketing campaign.

This seemed to be the logical and perhaps final extension of our long distribution strategy. Over the last few years, growth in our distribution division had slowed down as we bumped up against our limits as a specialty wholesaler knocking on retailers' doors. So why not break through the limits and take the beer directly to the people? It also offered a potential answer to a question that had long puzzled us. How could we get fresh Brooklyn Brewery draft beer out directly to consumers? We thought there was a huge potential market for parties and home draft systems, and as the most prominent local beer, we thought we could sell a lot of kegs. But no one in New York City had ever effectively retailed draft beer. Internet direct retail sales could be our answer, our way of introducing draft sales into the home market. Both the distribution and the brewery sides of our business seemed poised to benefit.

## And While We're Thinking Big . . .

This was not the time for modest, practical dreams. Or even pretty big dreams. The Internet bubble encouraged huge, feverish dreams. So while we were plotting our local vertical integration of brewery–distributor–Internet retailer, we also began to look outside of New York. Why, we wondered, couldn't we duplicate this idea in other states and achieve additional scale economies? We already owned a small distributor in Massachusetts, for instance (our Craft Brewers Guild—Boston). We knew most of the other specialty wholesalers scattered throughout the United States and began considering what the world would look like if 15 or 20 of them would merge. Wouldn't all of us enjoy substantial benefits?

We knew how hard it was to be a small distributor. While having an advantage in focus, we were all at a substantial economic disadvantage in so many other areas. The costs of everything from training staff to delivering beer to collecting accounts receivable are much higher, on a per-case basis or as a percentage of revenue, than for larger distributors. It's hard to make money. It was also difficult to sell out, should you want to, since there were typically few potential buyers. Usually only one or two other local distributors would consider buying a specialty portfolio, making for a buyer's market and poor prices.

What if we created a national specialty beer distributor, though, and took this new company public? What if it could reduce the costs of specialty distribution while improving the national logistics? It would be the first truly national beer distributor of any type, the first legitimate publicly owned distributor, and it could be a platform to enable national Internet sales to consumers as well. There were many complications and individual state requirements to consider, but that was the big idea. And if nothing else, it *was* big.

## ENTER: TOTALBEER.COM!

We split up our ambitions into two phases. In the first phase, we would prove the concept in New York City by putting the logistics in place and promoting the new service with low-key marketing. In the second phase, after we raised a lot of money (we decided that $15 million was a nice round number), we would dramatically expand our marketing within the city and acquire specialty beer distributors in other states.

To finance phase 1, we again raised money privately. The biggest expense would be for our web site. In deciding how much money to budget, we faced a classic dilemma: Should we build a simple web site, suitable only for phase 1, or a much more robust web site that could scale up quickly to the multi-state demands of phase 2? While a modest web site could be built for less than $100,000, the big one would be about $1 million. And then we made a classic mistake. We convinced ourselves that the larger web site and IT platform, which would integrate all the logistics of multiple specialty distributors, were not only necessary but would in themselves help us raise money for phase 2. It would be the showy technological side of what we were doing, and the venture capital funds were looking for technology companies. Without the web site, we decided, we were just a beer company. No one was interested in investing $15 million in a tech-less beer company. So we took the bait, began building the monster web site, and set off down a path that raised the concept-proving costs by a factor of 10. We raised and spent $1 million, convinced that it would help us later raise $15 million in VC funds, which would eventually allow us to go public at a valuation 10 times that.

We put together a team to advance TotalBeer.com. Eric Ottaway, who had been managing our Boston distributorship, moved to the New York area to head up the technology development. Jim Munson, who had managed our New York City distributor's sales force, shifted to become general manager of the new venture. I wrote most of the business plan (my sixth version) and plotted how we would raise the money. Creating the TotalBeer.com team hardened a personality split within the company. We had long had an uneasy marriage of the distributorship and the brewery, with employees identifying more with either one or the other. Now, with money and attention lavished on TotalBeer, a third wheel was being created.

Making the situation worse was a strategic decision to eventually split TotalBeer.com from the brewery. Our concept was to bundle the distributorship and the Internet retailing together as a separate legal entity. The brewery would initially own all of it, but would sell a big stake to a venture capital fund that would position it for an eventual public offering. This idea had some advantages. We would essentially be multiplying the value of the distributorship and then selling it, while keeping a large enough stake for influence. We could keep the brewery private and still offer our original investors a chance to cash out. But against this theoretical advantage was an immediate disadvantage. As we talked up the potential of TotalBeer, employees and managers who weren't involved began to feel left out. If TotalBeer was the exciting new division, everyone else felt slighted.

### Pride before the Fall

I was feeling pretty smart. I had championed the distribution division from the start, ran it for a decade, and now it was going to be our entrée into the big money of the Internet boom. I had won some favorable industry notice. The trade magazine *Beverage Media* called me the "one to watch" in beer distribution for the year 2000. In November of 2000, another trade magazine, *Modern Brewery Age,* put me on the cover and ran a long interview in which I expounded on my theories of where specialty beer distribution was headed. We were called "America's most agile beer company," and I was feeling pretty agile myself.

I decided that the top managers of TotalBeer.com (primarily me, Eric, and Jim, but not Steve, who was busy heading the brewery) should individually receive stock in the new company. Not a lot of stock, and in a pure start-up it would not have been controversial, but as it divided our existing managers into winners and losers, the idea was extremely disruptive. We had several bitter managers' meetings, arguing for hours about whether it was right or not. Steve was furious with me, and I began to get mad at him, too. I felt I had been working harder than he had for a long time, and now I had created this new opportunity. I wasn't taking anything away from him, just claiming a slightly bigger piece of a new pie. I had a lot of excellent justifications for what was essentially a bad decision. TotalBeer wasn't worth a dime yet, and we were already arguing over it.

Strangely, even as Steve and I were arguing in private, we were going out together to try to raise money for TotalBeer. While our other managers, especially Eric and Jim, were excellent at helping make presentations to financiers, it was my old partnership with Steve that I trusted most. We had developed a chemistry about who should answer which question, about how much to talk and how much to listen, and how to shape the spoken and unspoken tone of a meeting. After more than a decade of important meetings together, we had become a very effective team. As I look back, it is interesting to realize that, even as we struggled through one of our most divisive times, the strong foundation of our relationship never changed.

## The Short Life and Unhappy Death of TotalBeer.com

We actually did get TotalBeer.com up and running by the winter of 2000–2001. We had a wonderful web site and promoted our new service every way we could think of. Jim Munson, as the general manager, led the marketing effort and was a tireless and imaginative cheerleader. As we overcame initial hurdles and made our first home deliveries, there was the wonderful, if short-lived, satisfaction of seeing our new business baby come to life. Of course, it was an expensive delivery, but we were optimistic that phase 1 could make money on its own, even while providing the springboard to the major financing of phase 2.

I think we came pretty close to raising the money. We had a slick business plan and an impressive board of advisors, and we were proving the basic concept in the streets every day. Customers liked the service. We met with many venture funds and generated what seemed like serious interest. In our meetings they would ask hard and detailed questions, but we were well prepared. Many of the funds seemed intrigued. One fund associated with a major telecommunication firm said that it would participate in a deal, though it wanted another fund to lead the transaction. We were agonizingly close to landing the big financial fish.

But we were too late. By the spring of 2001, all of the other Internet boom companies were coming to spectacular bust. Kozmo.com and its local competitor, UrbanFetch (even bad ideas were inspiring competitors), originally contracted to deliver our beer in six-packs, but both went broke by April, before they could sell much. The largest residential apartment manager in New York City (Insignia—E.S. Gordon) had agreed to partner with us in promoting TotalBeer.com to their tenants through their own ambitious new web site called EdificeRex.com. We were thrilled at the prospect of efficiently marketing to tens of thousands of upscale renters in a concentrated geographic area, but they pulled the plug on their new venture almost immediately after starting it (at the beginning of the summer) and we lost our most promising marketing partner. Then Webvan went broke in July, having raised and wasted a breathtaking $1 billion in just 18 months, and the already foreboding atmosphere for dot-coms turned funereal. It was the end of an era.

Venture capital firms across the country were desperately trying to salvage any value they could from huge gambles gone bust. No one was looking at new Internet ventures. Our dreams of grand financing for grand expansion were gone. What was left, for a few months, was our industrial-strength TotalBeer.com web site and modest but effective home delivery service. For about a thousand customers who found us, it was a fantastic and well-loved service. Even without much of a marketing budget and even without marketing partners, TotalBeer was operating at more than 50 percent of breakeven and was growing steadily, if not rapidly. Then came September 11, 2001.

All orders came to a halt. No one was thinking about TotalBeer.com, not even us. We closed it down quietly a couple of weeks later, thinking that perhaps we'd start it back up again somewhere down the line, but . . . we never did.

**LESSON SIX**
**CHASING MONEY IS NOT A BUSINESS STRATEGY**

In the economic bubble of 1996, we avoided the mistakes that some of our colleagues made. Did we learn from them? Just four years later we made a series of our own mistakes, most of them avoidable. I'd have to say that lessons learned from making mistakes burn deeper than lessons learned from avoiding mistakes, unfortunately. At any rate, out of the entirety of our experience, good and bad, some important points stick out.

We survived our money mistakes in 2000 and 2001 for a fundamental reason. Though we were chasing money in the form of future VC financing (mistake), we raised enough money before-hand to survive when the VC money didn't come through (sav-ing grace). We never risked the company on outcomes we couldn't control. While TotalBeer.com wasted our time and our shareholders' money, it didn't put the company in jeopardy. I don't believe in "betting the ranch." In any situation I always want at least a couple of options available to me. I'll take a risk—business is all about risk—and sometimes one has to bet heavily on a potential winning hand. But business is not table stakes poker. I'd never want my business to be out of the game if one hand comes up a bust.

### The Verdict on VC and the End of an Idea

I'm humbler now about seeking VC financing. It is a wonderful financing option for large-scale ideas. I think the VC funds, in their willingness and ability to finance high-risk, high-return ideas, are a major reason why the United States has been so innovative in the past 15 years. But trying to shape an idea to attract VC financing (beer company transforms itself into techno-beer company!) is backward. The business strategy itself—its internal logic and demands—should dictate the ap-propriate financing. If it's a fast-growth idea that needs major, agile financing now and wants to go public in a few years, VC funding is right. But there are a lot of good ideas and a lot of good businesses for which VC financing is wrong. Trying to turn a German shepherd into a greyhound is a mistake. In ret-rospect, I'm not even sure I wish we had received venture financing for TotalBeer.com. Getting our hands on the money would have been just the beginning of the struggle, not the end. In hindsight, it might have been better to have wasted only $1 million, not $15 million.

The demise of TotalBeer.com also would lead to the end of our distribution division. When it became clear that we were not going to be an acquirer of beer distributors—that we were not going to be getting bigger—we began to think about becoming a seller instead. Being a medium-size distributor holding on to a couple of brands (such as Brooklyn Brewery and Sierra Nevada) that wanted to get big was a tough prospect. The TotalBeer.com fiasco didn't mean that our distributorship wasn't valuable, but it was beginning to become clear that it would be more valuable to someone else than to us. As Chapter 10 will discuss, we would shortly sell our distribution companies and begin to focus on Brooklyn beer, our core customers, and the community in which we lived, to sell our product. ★

## STEVE WEIGHS IN

From our earliest days, Tom and I were good at raising money. With more and more presentations, "The Tom and Steve Show" got better and better. I think our designer, Milton Glaser, was our most important early convert. We had Glaser's thoughtful emblematic logo stamped on everything we did over the years, and it steadily grew into an icon of Brooklyn's renaissance. Early on, our logo (and what it was born from) validated our venture. We were good and we had good fortune. I think we did well largely because we had a great product to sell: the Brooklyn Brewery. I reiterate that most people would agree that building a brewery is an exciting idea, and Tom and I were always able to sell that idea—first to our family and friends, and later to wealthy, sophisticated investors, including venture capitalists. It definitely wasn't easy, but we raised the money we needed. We were lucky because we knocked on a lot of doors.

I was an early believer in TotalBeer.com. Our customers were always telling us that the specialty beers we distributed were hard to find, that beer stores did not display or explain them very well, and that they often were stale. It seemed to me at the time that the Internet would enable us to find these motivated consumers and deliver these products fresh to their doorsteps. The special nature of the product and its buyers led me to believe there was a market for TotalBeer.com—if not in our regular distribution locations, at least in New York City.

To tell the truth, I was never comfortable with venture capitalist and investment banker types. Milton Glaser called them "money people." Milton makes art. Tom and I make beer. Money people make money. Money is different from art and beer. Art and beer can enrich your life; they can arouse your senses; they can inspire and liberate. Money is not by itself enjoyable. Scrooge McDuck can sit in his vault full of coins and currency, squeeze them in his hands, toss them in the air, and let them cascade over his head, but ultimately money is enjoyable only when you use it to buy something real—such as art or beer.

There is something soul-less about some money people. I'm not condemning all money people. Many successful businesspeople and bankers do wonderful things with their wealth, from charity to philanthropy to offering solid employment opportunities to people. But some seem to check their consciences at the door in their pursuit of the Almighty Dollar. Whenever Tom and I were approached by investment bankers over the years, I always asked one of my journalist friends to check them out in the Nexus network. Once, I discovered that, on the very day we met with him, one of the bankers had been cited and fined by the SEC for improperly boosting the stock price of one of his holdings. Tom and I later recalled that he had been interrupted repeatedly by cell phone calls during our meeting. I recalled him shouting into the phone, "Well, what do they expect us to do—let the price collapse?" It's always important to take note of how people act when they come to you offering great opportunities. Tom and I always tried to learn all we could about potential business partners, and we always asked ourselves, "Do we want to be partners with this person?"

With that said, I became more and more uncomfortable with TotalBeer.com as we pitched it to more and more money people. It seemed to me that we were allowing the bankers to tell us what the plan should be. TotalBeer.com started out as a plan to do home delivery in New York City, but that was not a big enough idea for the money people. They wanted us to have a plan to roll out TotalBeer.com in 15 metropolitan areas. They wanted big ideas, and Tom wanted to give them what they wanted. He revised our plan over and over to fit what the money people told us we needed to show.

When Tom began to talk of spinning off TotalBeer.com, I was deeply dismayed and hurt. I knew that he had his team picked and I was not part of it. In retrospect, he was working harder than I was because he was back in the entrepreneurial stage of an aspect of our original company—he was energized by the possibility of building a dot-com company that would grow much more rapidly than the Brooklyn Brewery. We later learned that many other businesses also had similar ideas about online opportunities at the time. The foundation of the dot-com was our distribution company, the Craft Brewers Guild, and Tom was running the CBG. While he did that, I was running the Brooklyn Brewery. I was still selling and promoting Brooklyn beer, and that seemed very unexciting compared to TotalBeer.com because we had already been doing it for years. The excited feeling that Tom had about TotalBeer.com was in complete opposition to the feeling I had at that time. I became increasingly skeptical of our efforts to raise money for the Internet venture as his planning efforts continued.

I also was suspicious of my own motives. Was I skeptical about TotalBeer.com because I was not on the team, or was I skeptical because it was a bad idea? It probably was a mix of both—but I think it must have been easy for Tom to dismiss my skepticism as sour grapes.

There is a lesson here about the pitfalls of partnerships. If partners divide up the responsibilities of running a business, there are times when one partner will be working harder than the other. There are times when one partner will be growing, professionally and personally, faster than the other. Given our agreement that I would be Mr. Outside and Tom would be Mr. Inside, there were plenty of times when I was getting more attention than Tom. Partnerships repeatedly are tested by such dynamics.

Ultimately, the leadership of the brewery split over TotalBeer.com. Our controller at the time, Joe Dantona (before Debra Bascome), reported to me that some members of the TotalBeer.com team were saying to him, "We are not a beer company; we are an Internet company." Robin Ottaway, who was running our Boston distributorship at the time, joined me in urging a "go slow" approach to TotalBeer.com. Tom, Eric Ottaway, Jim Munson, and the other guys hired to run TotalBeer.com were on one side, and the brewery team and Craft Brewers team were on the other. Eventually, when the cost of the web site ballooned, Munson joined the skeptics on the beer side, opposite the Internet side. Even with this strong split, no one exulted when TotalBeer.com collapsed. It cost us well over $1 million, and besides the monetary loss, relations between Tom and me were severely damaged.

As I wrote in Chapter 4, I think a written vision statement might have helped us address the problems that arose from the development of the Craft Brewers Guild and TotalBeer.com. That is not to say that crafting a vision statement would have been easy in either case, but it would have enabled us to address the monumental shift in vision from the Brooklyn Brewery that each of these distribution ventures represented.

**Our Grade:**  For raising money and dealing with money people who wanted to invest in the Brooklyn Brewery, I give us an A+. For letting TotalBeer.com rule us instead of us ruling it, I give us a D–. Had we raised the $15 million we were looking for, we might well have lost everything we'd built up until that moment.

# CHAPTER 7
# Steve Talks about Building a Brewery in Brooklyn

I think the "edifice complex," or the desire to build and own a building, is a compulsion of many entrepreneurs. In my experience, it is particularly strong for brewers, and many microbrewers have suffered the consequences of overbuilding. Red Hook, in Washington state, built a second brewery in Portsmouth, New Hampshire, that has never come close to capacity. Nor'Wester built several breweries around the country before it collapsed under the debt. Catamount in Vermont, one of the East's pioneers, closed shortly after opening a new brewing facility. Many other breweries are also struggling because they overbuilt. Construction of a new facility is a challenge for any business or individual. Managing a construction project is tricky business as well. Breweries are particularly difficult because they are unique facilities that test local zoning laws and building codes, and it is especially challenging in a high-cost market like New York City.

## LEARNING FROM THE PAST

The only other brewery of our size to have been built in New York in the recent past (say, the last 20 years) was the New Amsterdam brewery. Founder Matthew Reich, now in his 50s, bought an old brewery from Germany and had it shipped to New York City in 1985. It was a stunningly beautiful copper-clad brewhouse, and it was located on the West Side of Manhattan at West 26th Street. Visitors entered the brewery through a doorway into a cavernous restaurant with great, high ceilings. Behind a wall of glass, shining copper brewkettles gleamed behind the bar at the end of the room. Tom and I were green with envy when we saw the elaborate re-creation of the German brewery in the city.

But, inexplicably, at least to the public, the brewery closed barely three years after it was inaugurated in 1985. We were baffled because it had initially seemed like such a success. Eventually, we talked to former employees of New Amsterdam to try to learn what went wrong in the project. They contended that it was a management problem regarding construction of the brewery. The employees said Reich had made a mistake by trying to manage the project on his own instead of hiring a general contractor to manage the teams of major and minor contractors on his job. It was originally budgeted to cost $2.5 million but instead, they claimed, that without the help of a general contractor and cost management, it had ballooned to more than $4 million.

When Matthew Reich and I later became good friends, he told me the numbers were not nearly as bad as his employees had assumed. The budget was $1.9 million, and the actual final cost was $2.5 million. And he assured me that he did have a general contractor. The main problem, he said, was that it was impossible to make money with such a brewery in Manhattan. "It's not just the rent, it's everything," he said. "It's the utilities, labor, transportation in and out of the city. How long do you think it takes to unload a truckload of malted barley in New York City? It takes a lot longer than it does anywhere else."

Reich was a very sharp businessman and one of the pioneers of the microbrewing movement in the 1980s. The closing of his Manhattan brewery was a seminal object lesson for Tom and me. It was clear to us that building a brewery in New York City was not just challenging—it was downright perilous. After learning the details of Reich's experience, Tom and I resolved that we would not undertake such a venture without all the outside expertise we could find.

Fortunately for us, one of our early investors, Stan Mongin, had a lifetime of experience with construction in New York City. Stan was a civil engineer who had just retired as director of facilities for the United Jewish Appeal in New York City. The UJA managed hundreds of buildings in the city. Before working at UJA, Mongin had been the building superintendent at Carnegie Hall. He had overseen the renovation of that venerable concert hall in the 1980s and been responsible for management of hundreds of construction projects. Tom was busy managing the distribution company in 1994, so the job of overseeing the brewery construction fell to me. We hired Stan to be my advisor in the construction of the Brooklyn Brewery.

## THE DRIVE TO BUILD

By 1993, Tom and I were itching to build a brewery. We were producing and selling about 11,000 barrels of beer a year from the Matt brewery in Utica, New York. We felt we needed a brewery somewhere in the city to anchor our claim of being "New York's Brewery." During that time period, I was in talks with Garrett Oliver, our brewmaster, to help us design and build a brewery. Oliver had joined the Brooklyn Brewery team in 1994. He had, at one point, become friends with a British entrepreneur, David Bruce, who had made a small fortune after founding and selling a brewery restaurant chain in England.

Bruce was leading a group of British investors who eventually invested in several American microbreweries: Wynkoop in Denver and the Brew Moon brewery restaurant chain. After a few conversations, Bruce suggested we build a brewery restaurant in New York City instead of a production brewery. By brewing and selling the beer at retail for $5 or more a pint, Bruce claimed the profit margins of a brewery restaurant were astounding. In addition, having an outpost for Brooklyn beer in Manhattan would raise our profile in a quicker fashion than building in our home borough.

Using real estate agents, Bruce helped us scout for buildings in New York and eventually focused on the site of the Village Gate music club on Bleecker Street in Greenwich Village, a club that had been made famous in the 1960s and 1970s hosting jazz concerts by legends like Thelonious Monk. Stan Mongin, our investor and construction advisor, brought in Richard Wolf, a general contractor he knew well, to help us do a feasibility study for a brewery restaurant to determine whether it made sense economically.

There are many famous "important" architectural firms in New York City, but none of the ones we encountered had any experience with the welter of New York City Building Department regulations that concern brewery construction. One of the few architects we found who did have experience was Bennett Fradkin, who had been the architect of the Zip City Brewing Company, a smaller brewery that opened in Manhattan in 1992. After we introduced them all, Fradkin, Wolf, and Mongin collaborated on a feasibility study for Tom and me of a brewery restaurant at the Village Gate site that David Bruce found. This team estimated that it would cost $3 to $4 million to build the project. Milton Glaser, who had worked on many restaurant projects in the city for dozens of clients, had become one of my close advisors. Milton took one look at the plan and said it would cost more like $5 to $6 million, at least. Taking all the specifications and opinions into consideration, Tom and

I abandoned the plan to build in Manhattan, but Bruce invested in the Brooklyn Brewery anyway.

## Finding the Perfect Space

I was sitting in our windowless, gas-heated warehouse office on North 11th Street in Williamsburg on a Friday evening in the fall of 1994, finishing up some work, when Tom, who had left for the weekend, returned to the office.

"I just met the landlord across the street," he said. "Come and look at this building."

It turned out that it wasn't one building but rather three small adjoining buildings with lots of character. There were two floors of about 5,000 square feet each, supported by thick, rough-hewn oak columns; a 5,000-square-foot room with a peaked roof, oak supporting beams, and skylight; and a third room of 5,000 square feet with a 25-foot ceiling supported by steel beams. Having no columns, the latter was perfect for a brewhouse. The buildings were made of red brick. The exterior was coated in crumbling gray stucco, and the interior had 100 years' worth of paint on the walls. It had been a matzo bakery in its most recent incarnation. But it was part of the same complex that housed the warehouse where we stored the Brooklyn beers that were made in Utica and the hundreds of other products we distributed for other breweries. Prior to recent times, in the 1880s, this two-block section of Brooklyn had housed the Hecla Ironworks, a company that made architectural ironwork for the buildings of New York City. Hecla's work is visible today on the facade of the Waldorf-Astoria and St. Regis hotels, and on many other prominent New York landmarks.

After taking the tour, Tom and I both quickly concluded that this could just be the home of our brewery.

After consulting with our advisory team of Wolf and Mongin, we signed a five-year lease with an option to buy the building at $1.1 million. We had two five-year options to extend the lease. The building was then worth about $500,000. The owner,

Hank Harmanoglu, was a Turkish immigrant who had done very well in the poly-bag business. He liked owning real estate and only reluctantly gave us the option to buy. We thought it was important because we believed the neighborhood was going to improve rapidly, partly on the merit of our presence. This was not the prevailing view among industrial property owners, so Harmanoglu accepted our proposal.

Garrett Oliver had been shopping for brewery equipment while we were finalizing our real estate deal, and he felt that we could buy what we needed from a Canadian fabricator for about a half million dollars. Since we were already taking the plunge into building the brewery, we initially thought to make it a simple production brewery and build it as cheaply as possible. We did not think we needed Fradkin for a project on this scale. Mongin consulted Shirley Klein, the former head of the Brooklyn Buildings Department, about a possible architect to handle a bare-bones project, and she recommended a low-cost architect from Queens who sketched out some plans. It quickly became clear to me that I wanted something more than an architect who would basically help us navigate the building codes. If we were going to build a brewery, we wanted a brewery with some character and soul. We didn't want just a "pots and pans" brewery— as our original brewmaster, William Moeller, had described many of the small breweries being built across the country in the 1990s.

## Renovating the Perfect Space

In the spring of 1995, we hired Fradkin to help us develop construction documents for the brewery. Fradkin is a short, mustachioed man in wire-rim glasses who has an extremely deliberate, painstaking manner of explaining even the most obvious details of any situation. At first I was impatient with his laborious manner of laying out what often seemed to me to be self-evident. But I later came to appreciate this quality. Planning and managing construction is a tedious process. There are literally hundreds of simple, small decisions to make almost daily. Mistakes are costly. I think anyone who has ventured into home improvement knows this. Fradkin's manner had the effect of slowing me down and making me face the important details of the project, in turn, probably saving me money in the long run.

Fradkin drew up construction documents for a brewery on the first floor of the building. The documents were submitted to six contractors—all of them midsize contractors with long experience in New York City. We decided on Richard Wolf, who had bid $642,000 for the project. Wolf was not the cheapest of the contractors, but he was favored by Mongin, and I had been impressed with his professionalism during the Village Gate exercise, so I went with his advice.

At the same time, I asked Fradkin to draw up a phase 2 of the project that would develop the second floor of the building as office space for the brewery and our distribution company. Those plans were submitted to three contractors. Wolf bid $371,000. Our largest investor, Jay Hall, had agreed to finance the brewery, but he had not seen the phase 1 and 2 plans. He was expecting a more modest enterprise for a lesser price tag, so we scheduled a meeting with him at our office in Brooklyn.

He arrived with his lawyer Bernard Fultz and his construction manager. We held a climactic meeting in the barren upstairs office of the proposed brewery building. Tom and I had our construction team on our side of the table—Fradkin, Mongin, Wolf, and Oliver. Fradkin deliberately laid out the phase 1 and 2 plans. Hall's advisors asked many questions about the plans and the construction world of New York City. Hall himself said nothing, sitting back and absorbing the information, until the end of the meeting.

His silence had worried us during the presentation. Then he said, "Well, I think you should do the whole thing at once. It will save us a lot of money."

Tom, Garrett, and I were giddy with enthusiasm after the

positive response. We finally were going to get our brewery in Brooklyn.

## Costs Begin to Rise

The first of our weekly job meetings commenced on November 30, 1995. I met each week thereafter with Fradkin; Wolf; Wolf's superintendent, Don Christian; and any subcontractors who were working on the job. In agreement with Wolf, we hired Brooklyn-based subcontractors. These meetings allowed me to understand and manage the project. I was wary of the stories I'd heard about cost overruns from New Amsterdam and other, similar breweries, and even though I was watching closely, it did not take long for the costs to rise.

I approved the first change order (an amendment to the contract that documents an unforseen cost) two weeks after the project began. The engineer working for Fradkin determined that the concrete slab on which the brewery was to be built would have to be buttressed by concrete footings and steel. The wood beams in the crawl space under the slab would not support the brewery's tanks. That would add $20,000 to the cost. *Twenty thousand dollars,* I thought. That is half what I was making in salary that year. I fretted about the added expense. Of course, I wondered if I was being taken for a ride. Shouldn't the engineer and the contractor have foreseen this problem? Why hadn't anyone presented a separate plan for contingencies?

Thank God for Stan Mongin. A veteran of hundreds of construction projects, he had the judgment that I lacked, overall. Stan explained that the discovery of such problems was not unusual, particularly in a renovation project like this. It was reasonable to expect that such issues would arise, he counseled. With his reassurance, I accepted the additional cost. Barely two weeks later, we discovered that the existing floor drains running from the brewery room to the street were insufficient. The cost: $13,000. Then we got a ticket from the city because our sidewalk was badly cracked. New sidewalk: $20,000. Stan had told me to expect maybe a 10 percent rise in the overall project costs. It seemed to me we were going to hit that number in the first month.

Before we had finished construction and Mayor Rudy Giuliani cut the ribbon to open the brewery on May 28, 1996, I approved more than $200,000 in change orders deviating from our original needs. This wasn't even considering the $200,000 that Fradkin and I had rejected in that same time period.

"All the subs are trying to shoot holes in your drawings," Fradkin later explained. "They bid $30,000 for the concrete work in the malt room, knowing that the existing drains will never work and you will have to change the plan. Every now and then, you have to give them the benefit of the doubt. When you are working with old buildings like this, you never know what you will run into."

In retrospect, and knowing what we know now, $200,000, or just under 20 percent, was not a bad cost overrun on a project like ours. We had built an entire brewery for just under $2 million. Of course, we had wanted it to be for less, but we were satisfied. We thought we could make the money back with this facility.

**LESSON SEVEN**
## SOMETIMES YOU STAND ALONE

Starting a business and building a site for that business in New York City present certain problems that would not arise in many other places in the country. As I said before, many of our investors were wary of starting a brewery in Brooklyn, and one of the biggest reasons was the borough's well-earned reputation for being the home of many famous mobsters. As described in Chapter 2, we allayed our investors' fears by hiring an attorney with experience in law enforcement, Nick Scoppetta, who had been deputy mayor for law enforcement under Mayor Lindsay and was the prosecutor in the famous Knapp Commission investigations of the police department that were the basis for the move *Serpico*. But we knew that someday we might have to face this very real problem.

And so we did, just as we were finishing construction of our new brewery in the spring of 1996. The New York *Daily News* wrote a story about our project—the first brewery in Brooklyn since Schaefer and Rheingold closed their doors in 1976. At lunchtime on the day after that story appeared, two big limousines pulled up in front of the construction project, followed by carloads of young men in bulky overcoats. Out of the limos stepped a half dozen union business agents also dressed in bulky overcoats. I was at lunch at the time. The superintendent on our job, Don Christian, a barrel-chested Texan, recalls that the men wanted to speak to the "man in charge."

"I told them they were going to have to talk to Steve Hindy, and he was not here at the moment. Then I said, 'I think he is at lunch,' " recalls Don. "They said, 'No problem, we'll wait.' "

Meantime, all the workers on the job suddenly disappeared like rats off a doomed ship. They just melted away. Our brewmaster, Garrett Oliver, remembers the union men as "straight out of central casting—big overcoats and heavy Brooklynese accents."

"I could not believe they would dress like that," said Oliver.

The men wandered through the construction site for a half hour or so before becoming impatient. They left their business cards with Don and told him to tell me to call them as soon as I got back.

When I returned, Don explained what had happened and gave me a little bemused smile that said, "Well, what are you going to do about this?"

I immediately called Stan Mongin, who said simply that it was not my problem, it was general contractor Richard Wolf's problem.

"Richard has contracts with the unions," said Stan. "He will know how to deal with this."

But when I called Richard, he suggested I handle it.

"This is not a union job," said Richard. "I didn't think anyone would notice. And they would not have noticed if you hadn't gotten that article in the *Daily News*." I insisted that it was Richard's responsibility and not mine. He was the general contractor. His family had been in business in New York for 100 years. Surely he was the man to handle this, not me. Richard agreed to call the contact for the union men.

Two days later, however, I received a phone message from the contact, who headed one of the unions, expressing anger that no one had called him back. I called Richard again, and he insisted that I return the union man's call personally. I felt I needed advice, so I called one of my Brooklyn neighbors, Ed McDonald, who had been a federal prosecutor in charge of the Organized Crime Task Force for the Southern District of New York. Ed had prosecuted many New York mobsters and was now in private practice. A native Brooklyner, Ed had been my son's Little League coach. He also had gained some fame by appearing in the final scenes of the highly successful Martin Scorcese mob movie, *Goodfellas*. In real life, Ed was the prosecutor who turned mobster Henry Hill, played by Ray Liotta in the movie, into a government informant. Ed played himself in *Goodfellas*, and he often was quoted on the mob in the New York media. I was lucky to know him, seeing as my situation was becoming a bit uncomfortable.

I described the situation to Ed and gave him the names of the men who had come to the brewery. He said he would try to do a background check on the names. I told him what Garrett had said about them being out of central casting.

"These guys aren't playacting," said Ed. "These are the real deal. These are the guys they imitate in the movies."

I told him that work on the project had come to a sudden

halt. I said I thought it was Richard Wolf's responsibility, not mine. Ed said he would try to check them out, and then he gave me some chilling advice.

"You can't give these guys the runaround," said Ed. "These are not nice people. You may find your place firebombed, or you may find some of your people beaten up. You must talk to them. These people do not play around."

"Well, what do they want?" I asked.

Ed suggested that they might want "a piece" of the project. He said that typically they might ask for a few no-show jobs. In other words, I would pay them for workers who did not exist. I said I really did not want to go down that road. If they could get that from me, wouldn't they ask for more?

I asked Ed if I should call the Organized Crime Task Force. He said that would be a difficult call. Did I want to be an informer? Did I want to wear a wire? Did I want to risk going into the federal Witness Protection Program? Of course, the answer to all these questions was no. But neither did I want to bribe a bunch of union officials. Ed said I had no choice but to talk to them, and preferably to do it with my contractor at my side.

I called Richard and he reluctantly agreed to meet with the union officials. Meantime, no workers had showed up for a whole week. Wolf said everyone was waiting for us to resolve this problem.

The meeting was set for 11 A.M. on a weekday in April 1996. It was sunny and warm. We were to meet with the boss of the Brooklyn building trades, at the brewery. At 11, however, a limousine pulled up with the boss, the treasurer, and the secretary of the group. They wore dark overcoats over double-knit suits. All had Italian names. Each had two strapping young "assistants," who seemed to have trouble buttoning their shirts at the neck. We talked awkwardly for a few minutes and I suggested I give them a tour of the warehouse until Wolf arrived. I began telling them the story of the Brooklyn Brewery, emphasizing my experiences in two wars in the Middle East and my connections with the media. After 15 minutes, it was clear that Richard was a no-show.

"Well, why don't we go somewhere nearby for lunch," I said with all the enthusiasm I could muster.

"No," said the boss. "We didn't come here to eat lunch. Let's meet in your office."

"My office is too small and it is crowded with people," I said. He was unmoved, so we walked back to our windowless office in the warehouse. It was packed with our administrative staff, and they all gawked at my guests.

"We can't meet here," said the boss. "Too many people."

"Right," I agreed. "Let me take you to lunch."

"No, we don't want lunch," he said. "Let's meet out in your warehouse."

Our gritty 35,000-square-foot warehouse was filled with cases and kegs of our beers and the beers we distributed for other microbrewers. Just outside the chain-link fence that protected access to the office, there was a Pepsi machine, a six-foot table, and four or five dilapidated office chairs where the drivers settled their accounts at the end of the day.

The boss said this was fine, and I volunteered to get more chairs for them.

"No," he said. "At our meetings, the old men sit and the young men stand."

So the boss sat down, along with the secretary. The treasurer—a short, fat guy with a shaved head—remained standing, impatiently, along with the thugs. I could feel the sweat trickling down my underarms and sides, soaking my button-down shirt.

My natural impulse is to sell, so I started telling the story of the company, hoping to evince some sympathy from my stone-faced guests. I told war stories. I told them how Tom and I drove the trucks and delivered our beer in the early days of the company. A couple of times, I was interrupted by questions about some big stories I had covered, such as the assassination of President Sadat of Egypt. I took this to be a good sign, but the guy with the shaved head was not impressed. He had a squeaky voice. I didn't know if he was the model for Joe Pesci or vice versa.

"Yeah, yeah, yeah," he said. "We've heard enough of this bullshit. We're here for one thing: J-O-B-S, jobs. You built this brewery without us. The first brewery in Brooklyn in a long time. That's an insult."

The boss interrupted him and told him to let me tell my story. I proceeded to pour my heart into my story until the boss looked me in the eye and said, "Look, we don't want to hurt you."

I am quite sure the blood drained from my face.

He continued, "I don't mean physical stuff. We don't do that. We have lawyers. If we put a picket around your project, no one will come near it. If we put the word out in Brooklyn, no one will unload your trucks or buy your products."

There is a union-affiliated group in Brooklyn that pickets nonunion jobs and places a 20-foot-tall inflated rat in front of them. I had seen it before but had not paid much attention to the results. What I did know for sure was that no one had showed up at my workplace in a week.

"Well, Mr. Boss, I hope you don't do that. My project is almost complete. I'm on a very tight budget and I think you would be destroying a company that will bring jobs and good-will to Brooklyn."

The Joe Pesci look-alike began a harangue at this point, but the boss cut him off. "We need to meet," he said. It was clear that "we" did not include me. I volunteered to leave the area.

"No," he said. "We'll meet in the warehouse."

As they walked out into the warehouse behind some double-stacked pallets of beer, I pulled up one of the chairs and sat down. The chair I sat in was an office chair that was broken so that you either had to lean fully forward or backward. I leaned back and sighed. My shirt was soaked in sweat. I could hear them shouting at each other out in the warehouse, but they were all talking at once and I could not make out the words. Several times, they laughed.

I thought about the original doubts of our investors about starting a brewery in Brooklyn. I thought about what the boss had said about shutting us down. I wondered what I would do if they asked to put no-shows on my payroll. In that 5 to 10 minutes, the whole history of the company flashed before my eyes. Then they came marching back toward me, with the boss in the lead.

I struggled to sit upright in the broken chair. But the boss was on me before I could right myself. He placed his right hand on the inside of my right thigh, not far from my private parts, which I am quite sure had retreated.

Putting his face close to mine, he said, "We're going to have to hurt you."

I am by nature a bit poker-faced, so I think I stared blankly at him. I am sure I looked scared. Then he grabbed my shoulders and shoved the chair back against the chain-link fence and shouted, "Just kidding."

They all laughed heartily at my discomfort. With the help of the fence, I got the chair upright.

"Look, we're going to leave you alone," he said. "But if you expand this brewery, or build anything new, we have to be in on it."

I quickly nodded.

"And we want you to come to our Christmas party, bring your wife, and take an ad in our journal," he added.

I quickly calculated that an ad, no matter what the cost, was a small price to pay for dodging this bullet.

In fact, I never heard from them again. New York's economy began to turn up later that year, and the building trades have been very busy since. I later learned that all the workers on my job were card-carrying union men who could not get work through the union. After word spread of my meeting, the workers returned to the job. The wages my contractor was paying were comparable to union wages, but the work rules were more flexible. They all said I was right to stand up to the union guys, and they assured me they would not abandon me in the end.

Richard Wolf said he left the union men to me because he thought I stood a better chance of dealing with them than he did. Maybe he was right, but I shudder to think of the other possible outcomes of this confrontation.

The lesson for me was that there are certain challenges in business that only you can face. Sometimes you stand alone. ★

## TOM WEIGHS IN

When we moved our operations to the Brooklyn neighborhood of Williamsburg around the end of 1991, it was a sleepy neighborhood defined in the public's perception as a curious mix of three wildly different ethnic enclaves (Polish, Puerto Rican, and Hasidic Jewish) amid mostly empty industrial buildings. I had looked at over 40 locations in virtually every Brooklyn neighborhood before settling on it. There was a glut of commercial space available in our new neighborhood, nearly all of it available to lease at less than $4 per square foot a year. Now, 15 years later, the streets around the brewery have been completely transformed into an internationally known hipster hotspot, attracting performance artists from Tokyo and young photographers from places as far apart as Berlin and Boise. Real estate values on some blocks are up tenfold. We used to cherish a bar named Teddy's, up the street from us, as the one good place to go. Now we probably have a hundred great brewery customers within walking distance. What caused this remarkable change? In a small way, maybe we did. We were a meaningful part of it, surely.

When we built the brewery, Steve and I were determined that it should be more than just an industrial plant. We wanted a beautiful, welcoming place. Our brewmaster, Garrett Oliver, and other managers were similarly convinced that we could do more than just make beer. We could make the brewery a mutually beneficial center of the community. In his book *The Tipping Point* (Little, Brown, 2000), Malcolm Gladwell describes how relatively few influential people or institutions can have an outsized impact on society. When we opened up our brewery and event hall, we cleaned up our streets, planted trees, and put up a bold statement that we were going to be something special, and we thought the neighborhood could be special, too. I think we were the first large local business in memory to make such an emphatic commitment to its neighborhood. In the fall of 1996 my wife, Gail, curated an art show at the brewery that drew over a thousand people. It was a measure of the potential for explosive local change. A few pioneering art galleries had already started in Williamsburg, but our event hall was by far the largest institutional quality space then available for shows. When the neighborhood galleries had an early art walk the next year, our space was a central meeting point, indicated with maps and directions. We warmed to our role as a catalyst for the community's growth.

Sometimes a business advances by working with a lot of other people in a communal environment. But other times, as Steve points out, the entrepreneur will be tested in a more lonely setting. Steve is the partner you want when a crisis blows in. He sometimes makes snap decisions, and he can display a very quick temper. On occasion I'd get mad at him for making an impetuous mistake in the normal course of business. I discovered, though, that he is at his best when things are really bad. I always felt I could trust his judgment on important issues, in a pressure situation, or if an unexpected setback suddenly loomed. More than once, Steve faced a situation alone that I don't know if I could have handled. Running the gamut from the union guys when we built the brewery to gun-toting robbers and even including a few temporarily enraged customers, he's always proved himself a pretty cool cat. I've sometimes wondered whether his training as a war correspondent made him that way, or if he was attracted to that dangerous job in the first place because it was his nature to be able to deal with the circumstances.

For the first 10 years or so, Steve and I never took vacations at the same time and were rarely both gone from the brewery for more than a day or two. One of us was always there. Having a partner whom I could trust to face the unknown meant that I could at least take a vacation or travel on longer business trips. If I had been on my own, I doubt I would have felt I could leave the business for more than a day at a time.

**Our Grade:** For supervising the construction of a beautiful brewery, for having a cool head, and for letting me go on occasional long vacations, I give Steve an A.

# CHAPTER 8
# Steve Discusses Publicity: The Press Wants You!

## THE AMERICAN DREAM

One of the few advantages that a start-up business has over a well-established business in the same category is that the media are always interested in a new business. There are many reasons for this, but the main reason is that entrepreneurship—starting a business—is at the heart of the American Dream. I think that just about every educated, ambitious American has some dream in his or her heart about starting some sort of business. And in America, the idea that "You can do it!" is hammered into your head from the time you start preschool until the day you finish high school and try to start a business or go to work for someone who has started a business.

In the intensely competitive world of media, there is great respect for entrepreneurship.

Enterprise is at the heart of American journalism. Aggressive reporters are called "enterprising" reporters and they are always looking to outdo other reporters on the staff. Like entrepreneurs, they typically work alone. They want to scoop their colleagues and land a story on that coveted front page. Good reporters identify with entrepreneurs and are attracted to their stories. Editors, who are typically former reporters, also want to see the American Dream validated. And the publisher's heart is warmed by a business success story in his or her newspaper's territory—perhaps one day the entrepreneur will become an advertiser!

Entrepreneurial stories make good reading. It is exciting to read about someone who has left a job working for a big company to try to build his or her own company. It's like watching someone walk a tightrope—you cheer wildly when they make it to the other side, and you feel the thrill in your guts when they topple off the rope and fall into the net below.

Just look at the business pages of your local newspaper. News tends to be a problem for big companies. They have PR firms and company spokespersons to deal with the press. The press is always looking for a good story, and typically a good story for the press is a bad story for a big company. When a big company is doing well—when its quarterly earnings are rising, when its stock price is rising, and its sales are increasing—the CEO is a genius, but when it falters, the CEO is a dope and probably is being paid too much.

But the stories about small companies almost always tend to be positive and in many cases almost celebratory. No one worries about whether the business is hitting its quarterly goals. It is rare that a reporter even asks if the business is making money. Instead, reporters want to know about you. Why did you start this business? What in your background makes this suitable for you? What sort of obstacles have you encountered? Most business stories are really just human interest stories.

## PEOPLE WANT WHAT THEY KNOW

I was a reporter for 15 years before starting the Brooklyn Brewery, and my job was to get my stories in the paper, preferably on the front page. So it was a natural transition, when Tom and I started making and selling beer, for part of my job to be getting the Brooklyn Brewery on the front page. From the day we started our company, the moment we began writing our business plan, I focused on this mission.

Sixteen years ago, I don't think I really knew the difference between marketing and selling. It was all the same to me. We wanted people to buy our products, and we wanted the media to tell the world about our company and our products. Today, I would define marketing as telling the world about your company and products. Selling is inducing your customers to buy your product. Because of the way government regulates beer and other alcoholic beverages, producers rarely are able to sell directly to consumers. Typically, brewers sell to distributors who then sell to retailers who then sell to consumers.

The marketing function is the most important function performed by brewers. They must generate enough curiosity and demand for their products to make them attractive to distributors, retailers, and consumers. Big companies achieve this end by advertising their products on national television and through other big media. Tom and I learned that this is far too expensive for a small company or a start-up company. Small companies have to be much more resourceful to tell the world about their products. We would have to think outside of the normal channels in order to get attention for the Brooklyn Brewery.

## GUERRILLA MARKETING

In retrospect, we were pretty good at marketing Brooklyn Brewery beers. Our marketing strategy was based on what is now known as *guerrilla marketing*. Guerrilla marketing can be done with virtually no money at all because it is aimed at leveraging media coverage of the company. Media coverage is free. Because of the media's attraction to small companies, this can be a very low-cost, high-impact strategy.

For us, marketing started with the name of the company. Tom and I had settled on the name "Brooklyn" for our company and its beers because we believed that "Brooklyn" had meaning far beyond the borders of New York City's most populous borough. We believed that Brooklyn was more than a place. We believed strongly that it was a word tied to a mythical image that was central to the idea of New York City and America. Brooklyn was the hometown of the tough-talking, gritty, but heart-of-gold GI in the World War II movies. Brooklyn was the birthplace, workplace, or adopted hometown of legends: Mae West, Danny Kaye, Dionne Warwick, Norman Mailer, Woody Allen, Barbra Streisand, Mike Tyson, Aaron Copland, Joe Torre, Mos Def, Chuck D., Spike Lee—the list is endless. Brooklyn was the starting point for millions of immigrants coming to America. One in seven people in America can trace their family tree back through Brooklyn. Virtually every country in the world has sons and daughters who end up in Brooklyn. Brooklyn has the largest Jamaican community outside of Jamaica, the largest Russian community outside of Russia, a huge Polish community, a huge Vietnamese community, a big Arab community—that list is endless, too.

My favorite story about the reach of Brooklyn was told by

one of my journalist friends, the late Bill Farrell of the *New York Times*. During the 1982 Israeli siege of Beirut, Bill was arrested by the Palestine Liberation Organization as he was crossing the Israeli lines in Beirut. Bill did not yet have PLO press credentials. A hooded PLO interrogator questioned Bill about his background. Bill told the interrogator he was from Brooklyn. What street? asked the hooded man. Flatbush. What was the name of the baseball team that left Brooklyn? The Dodgers.

Bill said, "You seem to know something about Brooklyn."

"Yes," said the interrogator, "I live there."

Most important, along with being widely recognized and part of many people's personal experience, we believed that Brooklyn was an undervalued name and image. We believed that Brooklyn somehow fit with beer. Brooklyn beer, yes. Brooklyn pinot noir, no. We believed that if we did our jobs well, our little company could become an important force in Brooklyn and New York City and beyond. We believed that we could become a Brooklyn institution—but not just because we called our company "Brooklyn." We hoped to embrace, and become part of, the community of Brooklyn.

We believed that we could be a positive force in Brooklyn by building a company with integrity within its borders. For many years, Brooklyn had been in decline. Many date this decline from the sad day when the Brooklyn Dodgers baseball team—which had played such a historic role in the history of baseball by helping Jackie Robinson to break the color barrier—moved to Los Angeles. During the 1950s, 1960s, and 1970s, thousands of middle-class families fled Brooklyn to the suburbs. Hundreds of the great manufacturing companies that had made Brooklyn a hub of industry closed their warehouses and left for good. Some of this decline in business may have been racially motivated. Poor families, many of them black and Hispanic, replaced the white middle-class families that left Brooklyn. This led to the departure of even more white families. It was called "white flight." In the years to follow, crime, though always present, flourished in many neighborhoods.

In addition to the cultural reasons, many of the manufacturers, including the great breweries, fled Brooklyn because their plants were outdated. They could build more efficient, cheaper facilities in New Jersey, Pennsylvania, and upstate New York. The Port Authority of New York and New Jersey moved most of its important maritime business from the Brooklyn docks to the deeper seaways and docks of Port Elizabeth and Port Newark.

However, one factor that helped us in deciding whether to start our business where we lived was that we believed Brooklyn was on the verge of a renaissance. We knew there were many people like ourselves who wanted to live in New York City but did not want to raise a family in a postage-stamp apartment in Manhattan. We knew that many people like us would be looking for living space in Brooklyn—with its historic brownstone neighborhoods like Park Slope, Brooklyn Heights, and Fort Greene, and rundown former industrial spaces in Red Hook, Williamsburg, and Greenpoint. Many Brooklyn neighborhoods also had great public schools. Already, hundreds of artists were moving into the Williamsburg (where we built our brewery) and Greenpoint neighborhoods from Manhattan.

### Name Recognition

One of the earliest indications that we were on to something with the name "Brooklyn" came in our first year in business. Spike Lee, the successful film director from Brooklyn, used Brooklyn Lager as a prop in his first hit movie, *Do the Right Thing*. When Ossie Davis goes into a Brooklyn deli looking for his favorite beer, Miller High Life, he cannot find it, because the cooler is filled with Brooklyn Lager. The scene identified us with the changing times in Brooklyn. Many beer companies pay big money for such product placement in movies, but we have never paid for it. Our beer has been used in many independent movies including the hits *Smoke* and *Laws of Gravity*. We have also been mentioned in books by mystery writers Robert Parker and Harlan Coben. If your product is part of a culture, the culture reflects it without being paid to advertise it.

Today, Brooklyn is a far different place than it was when we started the Brooklyn Brewery. The two-bedroom apartment that I bought in Park Slope in 1984 for $89,000 now sells for more than $600,000. Within a few blocks of our old apartment, a rundown, sawdust-on-the floors market has been replaced by an upscale D'Agostino Supermarket; a busy Barnes & Noble bookstore has replaced a parking lot. There are great restaurants and fancy boutiques scattered for blocks. Thousands of children of the families that fled Brooklyn decades ago have moved back into its middle-class neighborhoods.

Billions of dollars have been invested in new office space in downtown Brooklyn. Developer Bruce Ratner has purchased the New Jersey Nets basketball team and plans to build them a $400 million arena surrounded by a $2.1 billion commercial and residential complex in downtown Brooklyn. The development was designed by famed architect Frank Gehry. Carnival Cruise Lines even plans to dock in Brooklyn.

After Ratner—flanked by Borough President Marty Markowitz, Mayor Michael Bloomberg, Governor George Pataki, Senator Charles Schumer, and every other politician who could squeeze onto the stage—announced his purchase of the Nets, I fought my way to the stage to congratulate him. "You know, when you guys named that beer Brooklyn, I was the happiest man in town," said Ratner.

Brooklyn has enjoyed a renaissance, and some believe the return of professional sports to the borough will be the capstone of that renaissance. But back in 1988, many people questioned our plans to name a beer after Brooklyn. A March 1988 cover story in *Adweek's Marketing Week* magazine pictured Tom and me sitting on a forklift below the headline "Why Would They Name a Beer After Brooklyn?"

We believed we could be a positive force in Brooklyn if we partnered with many of the classic institutions such as the Brooklyn Academy of Music, the Brooklyn Museum, the Brooklyn Historical Society, and the countless new art galleries, dance and theater groups, writers, filmmakers, and artists who were thronging to Brooklyn for professional opportunities and to raise their families. There was a new creative culture and economy flourishing in Brooklyn. We donated beer to their fund-raising events. We sold them beer at a reduced price for their special events. We joined their boards and helped them raise money. We knew that none of these promotions and partnerships would shine as brightly or reach as many people as a Budweiser ad during the Super Bowl. But we felt that if we lit thousands of little lights, we would eventually reach all the most important people in our immediate market.

We were relying on word of mouth from our customers to spread our story. With a consumer product like beer, there is nothing better than reaching that person in every group of friends who is known as the "expert." We wanted as many beer experts as possible to try and like our beers and to tell their friends about them. And we wanted to reach the creative people in our community, the people who believed in the future of Brooklyn. We didn't do any market research. We just went out and honestly told our story to as many people as we could.

The only market research about the microbrew consumer that I am aware of was done by University of Maryland professor James Robinson in 2001. He concluded that the typical microbrew drinker was better educated and had a higher income than average. Unwittingly at first, we were trying to reach that crowd from day one.

In his study, Robinson also found that microbrews appeal to

younger drinkers. I believe that this is true because younger drinkers are very suspicious of Budweiser ads during the Super Bowl. My own children scoff at ads that target them in a deliberate and heavy-handed way. They seem more interested in niche products that do not have million-dollar advertising budgets. They want to be different. I think this is true of many of our customers. They like Brooklyn Lager because we are not Budweiser or Coors. They like us because we are special. And one of the reasons we are special is that we are part of their community. They can identify with our product.

## Be Ready to Tell Your Story

One of the first public relations problems that we faced was the fact that we were not brewing Brooklyn Lager in Brooklyn, but rather in upstate New York. We overcame this problem by rooting our story in the history of brewing in Brooklyn. Brooklyn has an amazing brewing history. There were 48 breweries in Brooklyn in 1898, the year that the City of Brooklyn was annexed by New York City. The breweries were started by German immigrants who settled in the Eastern District of Long Island—in areas now known as Bushwick, Williamsburg, and Greenpoint. We had the good fortune of finding a fourth-generation German-American brewmaster whose grandfather had brewed in one of those old Brooklyn breweries: Bill Moeller, whom we mentioned in Chapter 2.

Bill Moeller's grandfather's notebooks were the foundation of the recipe for Brooklyn Lager, our first brew. We made no excuses to the media and did not try to hide the fact that we were brewing our beer in Utica, New York. We simply explained that we did not have enough money to build a brewery in Brooklyn, but we pledged to do so when we did have the cash. We were always up front with our strategy, so it was downplayed in most of the first stories about the company.

Our first news story was a great one. One of the potential

investors we were talking to passed our business plan along to Dave Monsees, a seasoned New York City television reporter who was working for CNN. Dave did a wonderful piece about the Brooklyn Brewery that ran all over the world. I can still hear his warm baritone: "Steve Hindy and Tom Potter look up at the old Schaefer Brewery in Brooklyn, and dream . . ."

It was a beautiful feature story that feelingly rendered the history of brewing in Brooklyn with footage of old Brooklyn brewery posters and the ruins of the old Brooklyn breweries. It showed Tom and me making beer in my apartment in Brooklyn and asked this question: "Real lovers of the suds can find beer from just about every country in the world, beer from places like Berlin and Beijing, but why not a beer from the most exotic destination of all—beer from Brooklyn?"

Dave dubbed us the "odd couple of opportunity," and the story gave new impetus to our money-raising efforts. We made copies of his report and showed it to potential investors. That was October 1987, five months before we started selling beer in the streets of New York personally, ourselves.

The CNN piece was the quintessential Brooklyn Brewery story. It is a story Tom and I have told thousands of times since. It is the story I recently told to *The New York Enterprise Report,* a business magazine in New York City. You must learn to tell your story with pride and enthusiasm, even when you are completely tired of telling it—because it is one of the best selling tools you have as an entrepreneur. And the press will never tire of hearing it.

One particular instance when perspective was important was when Tom and I sent out news releases to the local media to attend the unloading of our first official batch of beer on Tuesday, March 29, 1988. We were warehousing our beer in an old brewery building in Bushwick, Brooklyn. The owner of the building was letting us use an ancient forklift to unload the beer.

As we hoisted the first pallet of beer off the gate of the truck, it crashed loudly to the ground. The hydraulic system of the fork-lift had ruptured, spraying hydraulic fluid on everyone nearby and shattering hundreds of bottles of Brooklyn Lager. I held my breath and worried all night long, seeing headlines like "Brooklyn Beer Hits the Streets!" or "Brooklyn Beer Makes a Splash!" But to my amazement, no one wrote about the incident. The next day, all the local papers wrote about the return of brewing to Brooklyn. They showed us proudly delivering beer to our first five accounts. To them, the story was "Brewing Returns to Brooklyn!" They overlooked the negatives because they wanted to tell a good story about Brooklyn.

The Brooklyn borough president, Howard Golden, who never tired of lamenting the loss of the Brooklyn Dodgers baseball team in 1957, told the local press, "If beer is back in Brooklyn, can baseball be far behind?" (It took a while, but Howard proved prescient in his comments. Twelve years later, the Brooklyn Cyclones, a minor league affiliate of the New York Mets, played their first ball game at the newly built Keyspan Park in Coney Island. When they opened in June 2001, it was the first professional baseball game in Brooklyn in 44 years.) We had the good fortune of unwittingly establishing the Brooklyn Brewery at the beginning of an incredibly prosperous run for the borough of Brooklyn—a run that appears likely to climax in the move to Brooklyn of the NBA franchise New Jersey Nets in 2008.

Not only did the early press coverage we gained help us sell into many bars and delis in Brooklyn, it also boosted our confidence, and more important, the confidence of our partners, employees, and investors. Despite all the reports about the public's lack of faith in the media, people are impressed when your company is featured in local papers, radio, or television. It conveys the message that you have made it and you are a success. People begin to listen.

## PUBLICITY AND GROWTH

Emboldened by our early media successes, we undertook more sophisticated publicity stunts. In the first few months of business, we did very well in Brooklyn and began to get calls for our beer in Manhattan. In particular, D'Agostino's, the upscale supermarket chain in the city, was doing well in its Brooklyn stores and inviting us to sell in its Manhattan stores. We decided to "invade" Manhattan—on the 212th anniversary of George Washington's famous retreat from Brooklyn after his bloody loss to the British and Hessian troops. This is one of the great stories of New York history that is not very well known. Washington was routed by the British force in fierce battles in what is now the Prospect Park area where we lived. The Maryland regiment fought a valiant rearguard action against the British while Washington's main force fled across the Gowanus Swamp to Brooklyn Heights, overlooking lower Manhattan. The British massacred the Marylanders and surrounded Washington's force. They were poised to snuff out the insurrection, but they decided to celebrate their victory a bit prematurely.

As the British feasted, Washington had small units light campfires all across Brooklyn Heights. He requisitioned all the privately owned boats in the East River and moved his army to Manhattan under cover of darkness. This brilliant retreat allowed Washington to save his army and, of course, go on to wear the British down and win the Revolutionary War.

Well, the media find it hard to resist an anniversary story—particularly during a slow news month like August. To increase hype, we decided to make our first deliveries to Manhattan by boat from Brooklyn—starting from the prestigious River Café, located on a barge under the Brooklyn Bridge, and ending at the equally prestigious Water Club, located on a boat in the East River. We had a local historian, Everett Ortner (who was one of our investors). We had footage from a short documentary about the "Battle of Brooklyn," and we had a fife and drum to accompany us on the short voyage in a Brooklyn-Manhattan ferryboat provided by a fledgling ferry company that was also looking for media exposure. Impressed by our efforts, the Brooklyn borough president, Howard Golden, joined us, and his media office promoted the event as well.

The Fox News show *Good Day New York* set up its cameras at the River Café and did its entire morning show on the "Battle of Brooklyn." Tom and I were interviewed, along with historian Ortner. The fife and drum played, and Borough President Golden, Tom, and I raised our beers in celebration as we sped across the East River to the Water Club. On the Manhattan side, we were greeted by camera crews from the three main network affiliates and two other independent television stations, correspondents from the all-news radio stations, and a bevy of local papers.

Once you get a few stories in the local or national press, you begin to build a presence in the many databases that reporters consult when they are assigned a story. You can check to see how you are doing by searching for your company with Google or by doing a search on the Lexis and Nexis databases. But beware: This can cut both ways. The good stories are recorded right along with the bad.

Another benefit of the media attention was that the borough president and many other local politicians began to view us as a symbol of Brooklyn's resurgence. We began to be mentioned in Howard Golden's standard stump speech.

Today, we keep a log of all media mentioning the Brooklyn Brewery. We show this log to our distributors and customers when trying to sell them on pushing our products. The 2004 log runs to four single-spaced pages of citations, more than 100 mentions in the media, unquestionably making an impressive compilation.

## Partnering on Events

Another way that we have garnered good media is by partnering with not-for-profit and arts organizations. Every year, we make hundreds of donations to charity groups in New York and other markets where we sell beer. As a result, we have developed a reputation of being a good citizen in our community. This role comes with a responsibility. The more you give, the more requests you receive, and the greater the amount that people end up asking for. For years, I handled these requests myself. Later on, Tom and I hired an events manager to help out because of the volume of requests. Today, we have a committee of salespeople who consider requests from charities and arts organizations in their territories. Because of the nature of the requests, you must be very careful to handle them with sensitivity, as would any business.

Some of these grassroots partnerships have brought us tremendous media exposure. In 1990, we partnered with the producer of the Celebrate Brooklyn summer concert series in Prospect Park, the big public park in Brooklyn, to create the Brooklyn Lager Bandsearch. I was a member of the board of directors of the Fund for the Borough of Brooklyn, which ran the Celebrate Brooklyn series and other arts programs for Brooklyn, largely with funding from the Brooklyn borough president. The Celebrate Brooklyn series ran for about 10 weekends during the summer and featured big-name—but not Top 40—music acts that ran the gamut of styles. Knowing from some of our customers that there was a growing underground music scene in New York, we decided to hold a competition for unsigned bands that did not have contracts with record companies.

Celebrate Brooklyn producer Burl Hash knew of this scene because many local bands clamored for a role in his concert series. Because Celebrate Brooklyn featured music from many genres, we decided to give awards for rock, world beat, and jazz groups. We made up posters announcing the Bandsearch and placed them in clubs and bars that featured original music. The posters solicited tape auditions in each of the three categories. Soon we had hundreds of audition tapes. Burl helped us put together a panel of experts to listen to and judge the tapes. The panel included some record industry scouts and Don Palmer, who worked for the New York State Council on the Arts and wrote for several newspapers. These were credible judges, people for whom you would want to play your music, whether your group was established or unknown.

We picked six finalists in each category. These bands then played at important venues in New York City—the jazz finalists at the Knitting Factory in Soho, the world beat finalists at SOB's (Sounds of Brazil), and the rock bands at the Cat Club. Getting a gig at one of these clubs was a breakthrough for many of the bands. They played on a Monday night before sellout crowds. The bands were happy because they were playing at important clubs, and the clubs were happy because we were filling their rooms with crowds on a traditionally slow Monday night. Of course, we were also happy because the crowds were drinking a lot of our beer.

When I introduced the bands, I explained my theory that Brooklyn Brewery, which was largely unknown, felt a kinship with the bands, which also were largely unknown. I said that the Bandsearch was an effort to introduce both the beer and the bands to New York. This struck a chord with everyone. We chose a winning band in each category. The winner received a check for $1,000 and the chance to open for one of the big-name acts at the Celebrate Brooklyn concert series.

After the first year, Burl developed a partnership with the local affiliate of National Public Radio. This got Celebrate Brooklyn and the Brooklyn Lager Bandsearch free mentions on the radio, which eventually led to NPR's broadcasting the winning concerts on national radio—fantastic exposure for the Brooklyn Brewery and the winners.

We did the Bandsearch for three years before we burned out.

We were doing this promotion on a shoestring budget. We were selling and delivering beer by day and being music promoters by night, among many other things. It was exhausting work, and every year the price of the promotion escalated. The clubs wanted lower and lower prices for our beer, the bands wanted more and more perks, and we had to pay for professional recording of the winners' concerts for NPR. Of course, it was a great bargain in the big scheme of things, but it was taking its toll on us.

Tom and I developed a good relationship with Celebrate Brooklyn and we convinced the producers that our beer should be sold at the concerts. We sold the beer for them and gave them much of the profit. This relationship lasted for close to 10 years—until Burl moved on and the big breweries noticed that Brooklyn Brewery was making inroads in the local beer market in ways they hadn't thought of. Then Budweiser offered twice as much as we were contributing to Celebrate Brooklyn. Sponsorship of the event ever since has alternated between Budweiser and Heineken, and each year it goes to the highest bidder.

At first, I was disappointed about losing the relationship with Celebrate Brooklyn, but I soon realized that there were many similar opportunities in New York. Brooklyn Brewery had local knowledge that Budweiser did not have, and we had the ability to move quickly to capitalize on such opportunities. Budweiser had a corporate marketing bureaucracy to contend with, making us much quicker out of the gate.

## Networking for Opportunities

The relationship with Celebrate Brooklyn was developed through my service on the board of the Fund for the Borough of Brooklyn, a not-for-profit organization. It mutually benefited the Brooklyn Brewery and the fund. I had a similar relationship with the American Institute of Wine and Food. In 1989, I was invited to be on the board of AIWF by Matthew Reich, the New

York chapter chair of AIWF and the founder of New Amsterdam Brewery. Matthew had sold New Amsterdam and was looking for help in running a successful AIWF beer and food event he inaugurated in 1989.

The format of the event was simple and based on wine events that were very popular in New York City. American microbreweries were beginning to enter the New York market at the time and were looking for opportunities to showcase their products and get people to sample them. At the AIWF event, known as the AIWF Beer and Food Tasting, we paired microbreweries with New York restaurants. Each restaurant made tasting portions of dishes that paired with two beers from a microbrewery.

This idea developed at a propitious time for the Brooklyn Brewery. We were just deciding to begin distributing other breweries' products through our Craft Brewers Guild distribution company. The AIWF event was a perfect way to promote the new line of beers we were distributing. I eagerly embraced the role of chairing the AIWF's beer and food tastings. Over the next five years, we held these events at Bridgewater's catering hall at the South Street Seaport. We routinely sold out 1,200 tickets at $25 each and $30 at the door. (By the end of the run in 1994, tickets were $35 and $40.) The Beer and Food Tasting became the biggest fund-raiser for the AIWF. In later years, we did two events, one for American microbreweries and one for imported beers.

We learned much from working with the AIWF, and we made great contacts in the restaurant world. The AIWF board of directors was dominated by wine professionals. It seemed to me that the way we were selling Brooklyn Lager had much more in common with the way wine from small wineries is sold than with the way beer is sold. Small wineries had no marketing money. They relied on salespeople who could tell the story of their products. They relied on waiters and sommeliers who could appreciate the story behind their products and tell it to consumers. They needed to educate their customers about particular wines and the differences between them. We were in a similar place with our beers.

In 1991, David Rosengarten, a food and wine writer who taught at the Windows on the World Wine School at the top of the World Trade Center, approached me about doing a "beer dinner" at Windows. The dinner would be similar to a wine dinner—we would pair a beer with each course of a five-course dinner. The dinner was a huge success. We drew more than 60 people on a night when we were competing with the NCAA basketball championships. The menu was not sauerkraut and hot dogs. It was a sophisticated five-course meal:

*WINDOWS ON THE WORLD*
*GLOBAL BEER NIGHT*
MONDAY, APRIL 6, 1992

*Reception*
*Hors d'Oeuvres*
*Pinkus Weizen (Germany)*
*Grant's Weizen (U.S.)*
*Brooklyn Lager (U.S.)*
*Jenlain (France)*
*Sierra Nevada Pale Ale (U.S.)*
*Orval Trappist Ale (Belgium)*

*Dinner*
*Angel Hair Pasta in Cream Sauce with Duck Confit*
*Warsteiner Pilsner (Germany)*
*New York Harbor Ale (U.S.)*
*Tournedos of Beef Tenderloin in Shallot Red Wine Sauce*
*Samuel Smith's Nut Brown Ale (Britain)*

*Brooklyn Brown Ale (U.S.)*
*Montrachet with Mesclun Salad*
*Lindeman's Framboise (Belgium)*

*Dessert*
*Chocolate Cake with Raspberry Coulis*
*Samichlaus (Switzerland)*
*Catamount Porter (U.S.)*

Over the next 10 years, we did hundreds of such dinners at fancy restaurants in New York City and other, similar markets where we were selling beer. It was a great way to promote the beers we were selling. In the very civilized setting of a fine dinner, people were much more likely to listen to our stories about our beers. And the food enabled the guests to keep their heads— and us to keep their attention—longer than in a straight beer tasting. Without food, beer and wine tastings tend to dissolve into social events after the third or fourth taste.

### When Publicity Equals Education

Educating the public about beer has been and continues to be key to our company. Tom and I required all our salespeople to read the books of Michael Jackson, the British journalist who is the world's authority on beer. At our weekly sales meetings, we used to play a version of spin the bottle in which the chosen person would have to answer a question about beer. We had weekly multiple choice tests about beer. We brought Jackson to New York and did a series of beer tastings in 1990. The most interesting was held at the blues club Tramps in New York City. The owner listed the event, held on a Monday, as "British Beer Authority MICHAEL JACKSON LIVE!" in his regular advertisement in the *Village Voice*. We sold 300 tickets and got many important retailers to attend. Jackson led the group through 12 beers. The crowd got noisy as we got into the fifth or sixth beer, but I didn't hear anyone complaining that it was not the other Michael Jackson.

Tom and I have continued to do events with Michael over the years. We just completed a series of tastings that led to participants receiving an MBA (Master's in Beer Appreciation) for attending five tastings that encompassed beers representing all the world's main beer styles. We held a class every year for five years from 1998 to 2002. We have continued to do beer dinners and tastings whenever possible. In similar fashion, our current brewmaster, Garrett Oliver, wrote a book about pairing beer and food, called *The Brewmaster's Table* (Ecco, 2003), showing the integral relationship between these two subjects.

The dinners have always been a great marketing vehicle for our company. The AIWF event was a great marketing opportunity for new breweries entering the New York market, but it was limited by the size of the venue. It was clear that we could sell many more tickets if we had a larger venue.

In 1992, the Democratic National Convention was held in New York City. One of the big parties was staged under massive tents in the cobblestone esplanade under the Brooklyn Bridge in Brooklyn. I saw a photo of this event in a local newspaper and started thinking about the possibility of doing a beer and food tasting at that location. The area under the bridge is often used for publicity photos. It has an incredible view of lower Manhattan. At sunset, the sun falls behind the New York skyline. When the lights of the New York skyline become brighter than the sky, the effect is magical. It is one of the great views of New York City.

I approached Nanette Rainone, president of the Fund for the Borough of Brooklyn, about the possibility of developing a beer and food tasting under the Brooklyn Bridge, grouping American and foreign breweries. I told her I thought it could be a great moneymaker for the fund. Nanette and Borough

President Golden helped secure approvals for the event from the welter of city and state bureaucracies that had jurisdiction over the property: the Department of Transportation, Ports and Terminals, the New York City Parks Department, the New York State Department of Parks, the New York State Police, the New York City Police Department, and the New York City Fire Department.

We called the festival New York Beer Fest—The International Beer and Food Tasting because we wanted it to be a New York City event, not a Brooklyn event. We wanted to grab all the real estate we could and create an event that would compare to the Great American Beer Tasting, the granddaddy of all beer festivals, held every year in Denver. Milton Glaser did a terrific logo for the event, scheduled for early September. The first year, we tented the entire cobblestone esplanade under the Brooklyn Bridge. We had a separate tent where we provided child care because from the beginning we wanted this event to attract families, not just beer enthusiasts. We were careful to design an event that would produce a tasting, not a beer bust. The ticket price was high—$30 in advance and $40 at the gate—to discourage the idea that it was an all-you-can-drink sort of event. We had two sessions in one day and drew about 3,500 paying customers. There were more than 50 breweries serving their products. The event went off well; it was more a tasting than a beer bust, just as we had hoped. It was a financial success for the fund, but not an overwhelming one. The fixed costs—for the tents, for portable toilets, for security, for live music, and for parking—were high.

The next year, we made it bigger and did sessions over two days. We pitched a large tent in the park next to the esplanade, and we had an outdoor stage. We drew more than 5,000 people, and some of the breweries even ran out of beer. The third year, we drew about 8,000 people. It was growing into a fantastic event. We had worked many of the kinks from the first two beer fests out of our execution. But then, the state parks commissioner suddenly decided she did not want beer served in her park after all. The borough president weighed in on our side, but it was no use—the New York Beer Fest under the Brooklyn Bridge was dead.

We were somewhat ambivalent about this development. On the one hand, the AIWF event and the New York Beer Fest had enabled us to showcase the many small breweries that we were distributing in metro New York. One the other hand, many of our distributor competitors had also gotten into the festival and their breweries tried to outdo ours by giving away keychains, T-shirts, glassware, and other paraphernalia. The breweries we represented—mostly small, family-owned companies from Europe—could not afford to hand out freebies. Also, at that time we were just completing our new brewery in the up-and-coming Williamsburg neighborhood. If the New York Beer Fest could be held in the street in front of our brewery instead, and be limited to the breweries that we represented, we would be able to promote our suppliers and our new brewery alone. So we quietly folded the tents of the New York Beer Fest and started promoting the Brooklyn Beer Fest at the Brooklyn Brewery. Still, I feel some regret that the New York Beer Fest was not allowed to continue. It was the perfect embodiment of the sort of beer culture that we were trying to promote in New York City. It was a wonderful celebration of the world's breweries that was fit for young and old alike, for families as well as for singles. I still hope a festival of that nature can be revived at some point for the city's sake.

## A PLACE TO CALL OUR OWN

When we opened our new brewery on May 28, 1996, Mayor Rudy Giuliani was on hand to cut the ribbon and celebrate the return of brewing to Brooklyn. The mayor did us a big favor by planning his daily news briefing during the visit to the brewery. More than 80 reporters, photographers, and camera crews came out for the event. This was probably the biggest media event we ever staged. Giuliani, who had a very combative relationship with the media, pulled me to his side as he spoke and said, "I want you all to look at this man. He used to be a reporter, but now he is making an honest living." The assembled media took this ribbing well, and Giuliani invited them into the brewery, where he served them draft beer, explaining that his family had owned a saloon when he was younger, so he knew how to pour beer. It also happened that May 28 was Giuliani's birthday, so we presented him with a large cake and sang "Happy Birthday" to him.

### Great Minds Think Alike

In recent years, we have partnered with the International Slow Food Movement to stage several high-profile events. Slow Food was started about 20 years ago by an Italian journalist and a group of people outraged by the spread of American-style fast food in Italy and in Europe as a whole. Slow Food advocates a return to traditional farming and animal husbandry and to traditional methods of preparing food for the table. This philosophy perfectly matches the philosophy of the Brooklyn Brewery and the American microbrewery movement.

Our brewmaster, Garrett Oliver, got involved with the Slow Food Movement when it came to America. He was on the original board of Slow Food USA, along with such food industry luminaries as Alice Waters of the prestigious Chez Panisse restaurant in San Francisco. I was invited to be a judge on the panel choosing the International Slow Food Awards. In 2002, we went to Bologna, Italy, to attend the conference that presented the Slow Food Awards. The winner was a humble beekeeper from an obscure village in rural Turkey who had championed the raising of local bees while all his competitors had fallen to competition with imported honey. The winner had borrowed a suit—reportedly the only suit in his village—to come to Italy for the awards. He had never flown on an airplane before in his life. When he was given the award, his only comment, through a translator, was, "This is not possible."

And we thought starting a brewery in Brooklyn was difficult! After the Bologna ceremonies, we went to Turin, Italy, for the Salone del Gusto, the international exhibition of food producers and preparers who subscribe to the Slow Food philosophy. It is an astounding gathering of artisan food producers—tiny producers of traditional cheeses, game, vegetables, fruits, breads, wines, beers, liquors, oils, vinegars, and all manner of prepared foods. It was nourishing just being in the presence of so many like-minded people.

One of the biggest hits of the Salone was a group of barbecue experts from North Carolina, led by a former airline pilot named Jim "Trim" Tabb from Tryon, North Carolina. Jim and his team prepared dry-rubbed slow-cooked barbecue, Carolina-style. Wearing red rubber gloves, he pulled the pork right off the bones and threw it onto platters for the patrons to sample. The Europeans were dazzled by the flavors. Garrett introduced himself to Jim, and we later discussed the possibility of bringing Jim and his buddies to Brooklyn to do an event for the nascent Slow Food USA.

Jim readily agreed, and the Brooklyn Pigfest was born. Jim and three other barbecue champs, Kevin Cowan from South Carolina, Bill Eason from North Carolina, and Jerry Eliott from Maryland, towed their big barbecue rigs up to Brooklyn for the event. Right after September 11, 2001, we were a bit nervous about their driving across the Verrazano Bridge into New York City with the strange-looking contraptions behind their six-wheeled pickup trucks. But they passed over the heavily guarded bridges without incident. We also were nervous about cooking barbecue over wood fires in New York City without the proper permits. But the Brooklyn Brewery had great relationships with the local police and fire departments. We informed them of our plans, and no one raised any objections.

The Brooklyn Pigfest has been one of our most successful events. The inaugural event was covered by the *New York Times,* the New York *Daily News,* the *New York Post, TimeOut New York,* and many local TV stations. In addition, Rita Braver of CBS News made it the lead of a story she had been working about Slow Food coming to America. Her piece appeared on Charles Osgood's *CBS Sunday Morning.* The *Daily News* story pictured the North Carolinians raising their state flag over their barbecue rigs in the Brooklyn Brewery parking lot. The barbecue champs could not believe the reception they were getting in New York City!

In 2000, we did a fun promotion, called The Art of Fine Beer Contest, aimed at one of our core customer bases, the creative community. An old college friend of mine, Dave Mason, is an antiques dealer. Dave sent me a batch of German beer coasters that had sketches on their blank sides done by the famed illustrator James Montgomery Flagg, best known for his "Uncle Sam Wants You!" posters from World War II. Flagg had done the sketches in one of the German bars in the Upper East Side Yorkville neighborhood. Dave suggested that the Brooklyn Brewery do a contest for the best painting or drawing on the flip side of a Brooklyn Brewery bar coaster.

At the same time, Jim Munson, our vice president of sales, had met David Lehman, editor of the Scribner's annual Best American Poetry series. David was urging us to do something related to poetry. So I decided to do the Art of Fine Beer Contest and offer prizes for the best painting, drawing, or poem executed on a Brooklyn Brewery bar coaster. We made posters explaining the contest and circulated them in bars where artists hung out—mostly in Brooklyn and Manhattan. Like the Bandsearch judges, the judges for this contest were people that visual artists and poets would want to have reviewing their work. Judges of the visual art were Milton Glaser, our designer; Charlotta Kotik, the curator of contemporary art at the Brooklyn Museum; Joe Amrhein, the owner of Pierogi 2000, one of the most successful small galleries in Williamsburg; and Bruce Ferguson, then president of the New York Academy of Art (now dean of the School of Art at Columbia University). Judges for the poetry prize were David Lehman; Robert Pollito, chairman of the graduate arts program at the New School University; and William Wadsworth, from the Academy of American Poetry.

The entrants created wonderfully ingenious art and poetry. Again, we received tremendous coverage in the local press and also in several literary magazines.

All of these promotions were carried out with shoestring contributions from the Brooklyn Brewery. We handled most of them with Brooklyn Brewery staff. Most were financially beneficial for our not-for-profit organization partners alone. We did not make money from any of them, but we did garner invaluable media coverage and public exposure for our products. One pitfall is that these promotions all seemed to cost us more and more money as the years went on. When your not-for-profit partners see a successful event with a high ticket price, they inevitably want more of a return each year, regardless of the fact that you created and nurtured the event for them. As a result of our experience, I tend to think of such promotional events as having a life span of about three years. If you push it beyond that, you begin to need a new angle.

Another pitfall is that our giant competitors often wanted to take over events that proved successful, as was the case with the Celebrate Brooklyn series. Sometimes, however, a not-for-profit partner will stick with you. For example, for years we supported the Brooklyn Botanic Garden's Chili Pepper Festival, a wonderful autumn event that celebrates the use of peppers in cooking. A few years ago, Budweiser went to Judy Zuk, president of the garden, and offered $10,000 to be the exclusive beer at the festival. Judy said she would be happy to take Bud's money, but she wanted to serve Brooklyn Beer at the event also. Reluctantly, they agreed, but suggested that Budweiser would have exclusive rights to any signage at the event. Judy refused. Bud gave her the money anyway and shared the limelight with Brooklyn Brewery.

One of the most successful partnerships we have is with PS1, an alternative art space in Long Island City, Queens, which was bought by the Museum of Modern Art several years ago. PS1 is located in the former Public School #1, the first elementary school in Queens—a beautiful old brownstone building that occupies an entire block in a commercial/industrial/residential neighborhood. PS1 is MOMA's showcase for new and emerging artists. Every summer, PS1 does a 10-week series called the Warm Up in the outdoor space that once was a children's playground. There are 10 one-day events, running throughout June, July, and August. An artist is commissioned to create an environment for the yard. One year, a beach theme was developed. There were large areas of white sand and beach chairs. There were pools of cool water, showers, and saunas. Participants wore light summer clothes and swimsuits.

Food and beer are sold in the yard each year. A team of Brooklyn Brewery employees gets one-day beer-selling permits for each of the events. PS1 buys the beer from the Brooklyn Brewery at a special price, and they sell it at the events. PS1 collects all the money by selling beer tokens. PS1 also pays the brewery staff, who often make generous tips from their customers.

There is no problem getting volunteers to work at this event. PS1 attracts a very young, hip, and beautiful crowd of people. The beer sales net PS1 more than $100,000 every year. The international brewing giants—Budweiser, Heineken, and Inbev—

have tried to supplant us at PS1 with generous offers of money—but none of them have the capability to serve the beer and make the event happen the way we do. True to my rule of thumb about such events, the more PS1 makes on the event, the more they want from us. But so far, the relationship has proved valuable to us both.

## A COMMUNITY-MINDED BUSINESS

We take our role in the community seriously. We often allow community groups to hold meetings in the event space at the brewery. Recently, several public hearings on a proposed rezoning plan for the Williamsburg and Greenpoint neighborhoods were held at the brewery. Most of our events make donations to local charities and causes.

After the attacks on the World Trade Center on September 11, 2001, our trucks ferried food from many of our restaurant customers to the relief workers at the site in lower Manhattan. Some of our employees volunteered to help clean up the wreckage. The attacks were a blow to the New York economy and to our company. In addition to the devastation to human life and the area surrounding the towers, we lost about 25 customers in the immediate vicinity of the site. Many more customers were out of business for weeks because the lower part of the city was off-limits to all but residents. For our efforts, we received a commendation from the New York City Fire Department. No one at the Brooklyn Brewery questioned our efforts to help after the attack. We all believed it was clearly an extension of our role in the community.

### When It Feels Right to Advertise

In 2004, we did our first big-time media advertising, in the form of ads on the New York Yankees radio network. These ads, read by me, were simple and told the story of the Brooklyn Brewery and our beers. We did them because we had sold our distribution business to a big distributor who reaches 100 percent of the market, compared to the 25 percent that we had been reaching, and we felt that we had to tell our story to the rest of the market to have a chance at getting sell-through when we were placed in new stores. The ads were costly ($100,000 plus), and I am not sure how effective they were. The only immediate and measurable effect was that they impressed and motivated the distributor's sales force. That was not a small accomplishment. The transition from self-distribution to the new distributor went well, but not great.

The ads worried me. I was afraid that big-time advertising would alienate that core contingent of consumers who liked our beers because we were not Budweiser and did not use Budweiser's tactics. We are at an interesting crossroads now that we've expanded our distribution, because we need to reach more of the market, but we do not want to do anything to jeopardize our relationship with our core customers. We still insist that our salespeople stay in direct contact with our best customers, even though the distributor's sales representative is now their primary contact.

In 2005, we went back to our guerrilla marketing roots, with a statewide New York sweepstakes for people to win a Brooklyn vacation. The contest is being promoted in supermarkets and bars around the state. Ten lucky winners will enjoy a Brooklyn vacation in August 2005. Each winner and five friends will get a limousine to visit the brewery for a VIP tour, travel to Coney Island for lunch at Nathan's Famous original hot dog stand, attend a Brooklyn Cyclones baseball game, and then ride Coney Island's famous Cyclone roller coaster and Deno's Wonder Wheel ferris wheel.

I announced the event in March 2005 with Borough President Marty Markowitz by my side, and it was covered by major newspapers, radio, and television. Our upstate New York distributors embraced the plan, and we hope to expand it to other states in the future. JetBlue Airlines is flying winners from upstate New York to New York City. All our partners in the promotion volunteered their services.

We also developed a special label for Brooklyn Pennant Ale '55 commemorating the fiftieth anniversary of the Brooklyn Dodgers' World Series victory. We have pledged $1 for every case of Brooklyn Pennant Ale '55 and $5 for every keg we sell in 2005 to Mayor Michael Bloomberg's Fund to Advance New York City. We expect the contribution to be about $50,000. The fund is erecting a monument to Dodger great Jackie Robinson, the African American player who broke the color barrier in baseball, and Pee Wee Reese, the white teammate who supported Robinson during a tense moment in Cincinnati.

## LESSON EIGHT
## A NEWS RELEASE CAN GO A LONG WAY

Many companies spend a lot of money on public relations firms. And generally speaking, it is money well spent. Good press goes a long way toward creating an image for your company. If you are uncomfortable dealing with the press, a small public relations firm may be the answer for you. But I believe there is a treasure trove of goodwill in the press toward start-up companies. You can unlock that treasure if you know how to write a simple news release.

The first requirement for a news release is that you must have a story to tell. The news release gets your story in front of an editor at a newspaper or an assignment editor at a radio or television station. The editor will decide whether your story gets in the paper or on the evening newscast. You don't have to send them a polished story. Just tell them who, what, when, and where. You simply need to get the story in front of the editor.

An example is the news release we did recently when we

decided to start buying our electricity from a company that operates windmills in upstate New York. We were contacted by Community Energy Corporation in the spring of 2003 about switching to wind energy. They explained that we would still get our electricity from New York City's utility, ConEdison. But ConEd would buy the electricity from Community Energy, which would deliver it through the ConEd grid. Wind power would cost more than regular power by about 10 or 15 percent. This had immediate appeal for us because we had been involved for several years in our community's effort to block plans to build a huge power plant just down the street from us on the East River. I had always felt slightly guilty about our opposition because we are a big user of energy and New York City needs more capacity. The opposition clearly had a NIMBY (not in my backyard) flavor. No one wants a power plant in their backyard.

By switching to wind power, we could proclaim our independence from fossil fuel power generators. We could demonstrate that there were ways of getting clean, sustainable power without building new power plants. We mulled this idea over for several months, and then in August 2003 the lights went out in New York City and much of the Northeast when the massive network of generators and transmission lines that supplied the region failed.

The lights were out in parts of Brooklyn for more than 24 hours. Unfortunately, the Williamsburg neighborhood where our brewery is located was one of the last to have its power restored. Our conditioning tanks, where the beer is fermented and conditioned, are cooled by an electric-powered glycol system. They are usually kept lower than 40 degrees. We had no backup power. August is one of the hottest months of the year in New York City. If the temperature in those tanks rose above 60 degrees, we faced the possibility of losing thousands of gallons of beer. Garrett circulated cool water through the system to keep the tanks cool. But there was little else he could do.

Lucky for us, there is a lot of beer in each of those tanks—more than 100 kegs' worth—so they maintained their temperature and did not spoil. But it was a nerve-wracking experience.

Shortly thereafter, we decided to switch to wind power. It was largely a symbolic gesture. Wind power would not protect us against another blackout, but it would make a statement that Brooklyn Brewery understood that something has to be done about our dependence on fossil fuel energy sources. Yes, wind power costs more than conventional power, but it is the right thing to do (along with buying a gasoline generator to back us up in the event of another blackout).

We crafted a news release to announce that we would be buying 100 percent of our electricity from Community Energy. We sent it out to all local media and beer industry media. Community Energy sent it out to their list. The new Brooklyn borough president, Marty Markowitz, learned of our effort and gave us a quote to include in our release. We renamed our annual September beer fest the "Brooklyn Windfest" and scheduled a media announcement at the event. Here is a copy of the release:

BROOKLYN BREWERY GOES 100%
WINDPOWER IN NEW YORK CITY

BROOKLYN (Aug. 29, 2003)—The Brooklyn Brewery Corp. announced today that it would buy wind-generated electricity for its New York City facility.

The company's Brooklyn plant will be 100% wind-powered, supplied with NewWind Energy™, a product of Community Energy Inc. (CEI), a leading marketer/developer of wind-generated electricity. NewWind Energy™ is produced from windmills in Fenner, New York, in upstate Madison County. The five-year wind power purchase represents the first brewery in the Eastern U.S. to convert to wind power.

"It is no secret that The Brooklyn Brewery is opposed to plans to develop another goliath-sized power plant on the Brooklyn waterfront," said brewery president Steve Hindy. "We wanted to demonstrate that there are viable, clean alternatives to building another polluting power plant. We also wanted to take a significant step in demonstrating a needed reduction in dependence on Middle East oil.

"Windpower costs a bit more, but we think it makes sense to invest in new sources of energy. The recent blackout was a wake up call—everyone has to be more conscious of their use of energy."

Brooklyn Borough President Marty Markowitz issued a statement saying: "This is Brooklyn at its best. The Brooklyn Brewery is committed to this innovative, environmentally friendly way of powering its facility. I hope other businesses realize that there are other clean, safe and affordable energy options that will help all of us conserve energy and protect our environment."

Compared to the average generation mix in New York's power pool, Brooklyn Brewery's commitment of 284,960 kilowatt hours per year is equivalent to the reduction of more than 335 thousand pounds of carbon dioxide ($CO_2$) that would be emitted into the atmosphere annually. The $CO_2$ reduction is equivalent to the amount removed from the air by 22,000 trees, or the amount emitted by cars driven over 290,000 miles annually. In addition, the switchover will reduce emissions of sulfur dioxide by an estimated 1,593 pounds and nitrogen oxides by 564 pounds annually.

Brent Alderfer, President of CEI, said: "Brooklyn Brewery is leading the way to clean energy for New York City. This means New York-based electric power with no fuel and no pollution. The more customers that follow Brooklyn Brewery's lead, the more wind farms come on-line in New York."

The Brewery and CEI will celebrate this historic commitment in a 1–5pm "Windfest at the Brewery" on September 13, featuring a model of the Fenner windmills, a DJ and of course Brooklyn's fine beers. Admission is $20. Tickets can be purchased by calling the brewery at 718-486-7422 Ext. 1. Food, by Waterfront Alehouse, is extra. Community Energy will be signing up residential wind energy customers at the event. New customers will receive a $20 rebate on their electric bill, covering the cost of admission to the Windfest.

CONTACTS: Steve Hindy, 718-486-7422 x104; Brent Beerly, CEI, 215-778-3898

Some local papers used the news release as written, but the New York *Daily News* did its own story, with live quotes from everyone involved, under the headline "There's Wind In Their Ales." Several local television stations covered the event at the brewery, and some did their own pieces at the brewery, quoting me and the borough president. This has proved to be a story with legs. Several European and Asian newspapers have interviewed us about our commitment to wind power. We have gotten many more stories in media with special interest in environmental issues and have become one of the rallying points for environmental groups in the New York region. We participated in a media event in 2004 in Manhattan when a large new skyscraper in Times Square decided to buy 10 percent of its power from Community Energy. A similar event is planned in Brooklyn for the many other companies that have subscribed to wind power.

This is a fairly sophisticated news release. It tells people the basics of who, what, when, where, and why. But it also includes quotes from the Brooklyn Brewery, Community Energy, and the borough president, which add credibility to the release, although they are not absolutely necessary. I have done much simpler releases that got similar results. The important thing is to be concise and use language that is accessible and positive. Don't try to make it too complicated. ★

## TOM WEIGHS IN

In business school, I double-majored in finance and marketing. Initially, marketing seemed to come more easily to me than finance. Marketing made intuitive sense. It seemed a shorter reach for a numbers-avoiding former college English major like me.

Though my business school marketing classes were excellent, they seemed (when we started the Brooklyn Brewery) to have little relevance for a small business. How does a tiny start-up think about sophisticated concepts like market segmentation, focus groups, multivariate market research analysis, and product life cycles?

For a niche consumer product business, the founders typically start by looking around and saying, "Okay, the market segment will be people like us." We know what we like. Our focus group will be our friends. Our research will consist of asking them questions. We'll find out what they like, too. The product cycle will start when we raise our money, and last as long as we can keep pushing it forward. Let's go!

That about sums up what Steve and I did. It wasn't very sophisticated, but it worked well enough to get us started. As the years went by, however, I gradually came to believe that all of those seemingly academic marketing concepts were actually pretty useful in the real world. I just didn't know how to use them at first. I found myself constantly analyzing whether a good marketing idea was the right idea for us, and the measuring sticks for our ideas were those basic theories I had learned in business school. Did the idea play to our competitive advantages? Did it strengthen our position within our market segment? What was the goal, and how measurable were the results? We came up with a lot of marketing ideas, many of them good ideas, but more often than not, they weren't right for the Brooklyn Brewery. We consigned them to the "good-ideas board." It helped to have the theoretical framework I learned back then to sift through ideas as they came up.

One marketing field that I don't recall being covered at all in business school, though, is promotion and public relations. In the 1980s, it was seen as more or less the bastard child of marketing, the realm of hustlers and self-serving rogues. I think business schools are more comfortable analyzing process-driven innovators like Henry Ford than promotional geniuses like P.T. Barnum or Edward L. Bernays. Perhaps promotion is too creative to yield easily to analysis: At its best, it is closer, in its daring spirit, to performance art than to sales programming.

Yet promotion—several big events, and hundreds of smaller ones—was probably more important in shaping the image of the Brooklyn Brewery than anything else. And our promotional genius was Steve. He didn't come up with all of the ideas (we had a lot of talented people working with us), but he generated many of them and shaped the rest with a team. He set the tone early on with events that put our little company on the map before we had a brand identity. He had a terrific feel for what might intrigue an assignment editor and what would not when it came to getting our story in the news. His background as a genuine foreign correspondent for the Associated Press resonated with the press and gave him instant credibility when he talked with reporters. I think every local reporter, even one covering the small business beat, secretly dreams of being a dashing foreign correspondent. Steve had done what some of them dreamed of doing in journalism, and now he was doing what they might dream of doing afterward, in starting his own business—especially a brewery!

I would have said you were crazy if you had told me back when we started our company in the late 1980s that we would receive generous coverage on CNN, all local broadcast and cable television stations, all local and regional newspapers including multiple features in the *New York Times,* the *Wall Street Journal,* the *Washington Post, Time* magazine, *Gourmet, Food & Wine, Fortune, Forbes, Inc,* National Public Radio, and the dozens of others I'm probably forgetting. Once the coverage started, it snowballed. We quickly found that *being* a story made us a story.

Observers of the Brooklyn Brewery often assumed that the great press coverage we received was because Steve, as a former reporter, had special contacts, but that wasn't really it. What Steve had was a gift for creating and shaping events that the press would cover. And once the press came, he could tell our story with authority. Even those of us without his background or his special touch can learn from his example. For a small company without a big marketing budget, imagination and a bit of daring can be a great equalizer.

**Our Grade:** For shaping the positive image of the brewery through imaginative and attention-grabbing events without paid advertising or much prior experience, I give us an A+.

# CHAPTER 9

# Steve Reveals How the Revolution Kills Its Leaders First

There is a contradiction at the heart of entrepreneurship that I think every entrepreneur should understand at the outset: The skills and personality that enable a person to conceive and start a company are not necessarily the same skills that will enable that person to manage and institutionalize a maturing company.

As both brewers and distributors of other brewers' beers, Tom and I had a ringside seat to watch the development of the microbrewing industry in the eastern United States in the 1990s. New York City has always been a harsh environment for microbrewers, and we have watched many well-financed start-ups fail for many different reasons. Nothing is more heartbreaking than watching a company go under because the founder is unable to develop and manage his or her business. As Tom would always say when he did presentations, usually to the media, about the

Brooklyn Brewery, "When you are building a small business, you can be boasting about your accomplishments one day, and fighting for your life the next because there are literally hundreds of pitfalls out there that can sink you at any time."

## THE PIONEER (WITH THE ARROWS IN HIS BACK)

Matthew Reich, the founder of New Amsterdam Brewery, was one of the visionaries of the microbrewing business. He pioneered the idea of *contract brewing*—contracting with an existing brewery to produce a beer for you. He sold approximately 15,000 barrels of beer a year in 1987, the year Tom and I started our business. Since a microbrewer is defined as a brewer producing fewer than 15,000 barrels of beer a year, Reich had in five years graduated to becoming a regional brewer before we were even out of the gate.

It later appeared to us that Reich had built too grand a brewery in Manhattan, and indeed, Reich now says that the brewery he tried to build could never have made money because of the inherent costs of doing business in Manhattan. But according to Reich, it was not the brewery that did him in, but rather the success of the venture firm that backed his enterprise. He said the venture firm he used had hit the jackpot with one of its investments, making a half-billion dollars on a small investment in a railroad. Shortly after that, the firm closed its doors and refused to extend further financing to New Amsterdam. Saddled with debt that he could not service, Reich was ultimately forced to sell the company to pay the banks. This is not one of the problems that a successful business owner sees coming. Who could have ever anticipated that the success of the very venture firm that backed him would end up being the end of his business?

When Tom and I first started out in business, a reporter for *Manhattan Inc.*, a local magazine, was writing a story about us.

The reporter called me just before publication to say that she had asked Reich for a comment on our venture. His comment: "I hope they fall flat on their faces. They have stolen every idea I ever had."

I don't like the word *stolen,* but I have freely admitted to Reich that Tom and I certainly went to school on his project, and it had a tremendous impact on the way we ran our business and made some of our decisions. We contract brewed our first beers, and we set ourselves up as a limited partnership like Reich. Others went to school on New Amsterdam, too. The most successful of all the microbrewers, Jim Koch of Samuel Adams, agrees that it was Reich who pioneered the idea of contract brewing, which enabled Samuel Adams to attain its meteoric growth in the first 10 years of its business. The rule of thumb here is that if you are a business owner, you can be sure that people will go to school on your business, too—with a vengeance.

I think Reich's problem with the venture firm was unusual. A more typical problem is exemplified by pioneers like Bill Newman of Albany Amber Beer and Nat Collins with his Woodstock Brewing Company in Kingston, New York. Tom and I were so impressed with Nat's microbrew that we actually invested in his company in 1995. Nat is a former building contractor (and Olympic swimmer) who caught the microbrewing bug. He built his small brewery from the ground up and started making a great ale. Nat was a dynamo. He would get up in the morning, brew a batch of beer, harvest another batch in the afternoon, rack it into kegs, and deliver the beer to his customers in the afternoon and evening. He was builder, brewer, salesperson, distributor, and promoter—all packed into a burly, 5-foot, 8-inch frame. He always had a smile on his face and never had a bad word to say about anyone. I used to call Nat "Superman" when I introduced him at beer dinners in New York City in the mid-1990s.

## THE ONE-MAN BAND

Nat exemplified the optimism and confidence that characterized the microbrewing business in the 1990s. We all were enjoying double-digit growth, and we all thought it was going to continue forever. People were drinking less beer, it was true, but they were drinking better beer, like the beer Woodstock Brewing Company and Brooklyn Brewery were producing. It was a euphoric time. It seemed that every day we heard of a new brewery starting up somewhere in the country. We all thought we had the big guys on the run.

Only later, when Nat partnered with a local businessman and his brand began to wane, could I reflect on what had happened. I think Nat's problem was that he had never been able to raise the capital necessary to bring more people into his business. One man or woman can't do everything alone. The beer business is about quality, which Nat's brewery clearly had, but it also is about volume. One person can only reach a certain number of customers. I don't know what that number is . . . maybe it is 100. But 50 customers will not sustain a brewery. You need 2, 3, or even 10 times that to cover the expenses of a 25-barrel brewery like Nat's, pay your bills, and try to make a little money for yourself. Ultimately, there are many cases demonstrating that, 9 times out of 10, you can't do it all by yourself and expect to grow.

Milton Glaser, our designer, impressed me because he told us at the outset that he would personally be designing every bit of material his company created for us. Milton works with a small staff of fewer than 10 people. At any given time, he has dozens of projects under way for all levels and styles of markets and businesses. His company is named Milton Glaser Inc., which sounds like a real corporate sort of business, in the way that Martha Stewart Omnimedia does. With his success, he could easily expand his office and increase the number of employees, so I once asked him how he had settled on the size of his company.

"Years ago, I thought I wanted to build an empire," he said. "I wanted a big office with lots of designers. But when I had the big office and all the designers, I realized that I was no longer involved in the creation of the work, which is what I love. I was more like the director of personnel. I decided to scale things back and find a size that would enable me to be involved in every project."

That decision has made Milton a successful, and happy, businessman.

Nat Collins seemed to want to have his hand in every aspect of Woodstock Brewing Company. But he never developed the organization. Microbreweries do not have to keep growing forever, but like any business, they need to achieve a certain size to make money. For example, David Geary, of DL Geary Brewing Company in Portland, Maine, has maintained his volume at around 20,000 barrels for years and managed to keep his business going. Geary's success seems to rely heavily on the loyalty of customers in his home market.

The Brooklyn Brewery started in a position similar to that of Nat Collins and Woodstock Brewing Company. We contracted with the Matt Brewing Company to make our beer, but we sold every bottle ourselves in the beginning. We were five people at the outset, and there was no training program for us to go through, no "beer school." We just told our guys to get out there and sell the beer to whomever would buy it. We sold and promoted and solved problems all day long. If a customer had a problem with a foamy keg, we took our tool kit and tried to adjust the draft beer system. If a customer forgot to order for a weekend, we put a keg in our car and made the delivery—no matter what day it was. When one of our drivers got hurt in a car accident, I took over his route for almost three months, delivering our beer all over Brooklyn.

In Thomas Wolfe's story "Only the Dead Know Brooklyn," there is a line that people are fond of quoting: "It would take a guy a lifetime to get to know Brooklyn, and when he did, he'd be dead." I think I disproved that theory in those three months, delivering our product to every reach of Brooklyn. Nevertheless, entrepreneurship will kill you if you let it.

Tom and I have participated in every aspect of the business, from brewing and delivery to sales and managing cash flow. We have grown our business by hiring additional employees and allowing them to do their jobs. We have learned that we cannot micromanage all our employees. At night, we did T-shirt give-away promotions in smoky bars. During the day, we put on suits and did beer dinners in fancy restaurants. We did co-promotion events such as running the Brooklyn Lager Bandsearch and the Beer Festival under the Brooklyn Bridge. And with our hands in so many pots, our direct involvement in selling the product—whether to customers, media, or the community—has always been integral. No one could sell Brooklyn Lager like Tom or I could, so in theory at least, one of us had to be involved in every sale along the way.

## HIGH ANXIETY AND A FORCED LESSON

Our company hit a financial low point in 1991. We were really struggling to sell enough beer to pay our bills. We went without pay for two months. We made it a point to pay our employees, but we did not pay ourselves. Both of us dug some holes of debt at that time that would haunt us for many years to come. That same year, my former employer, *Newsday*, asked me to come back to the paper to work on the first Gulf War. Tom and I discussed this option—taking our financial situation into account—and we reluctantly agreed it was the right thing to do.

### Delegating Authority

When I returned to *Newsday*, I was working a shift that started at 4 P.M., so I was able to be at the brewery most mornings, but

I could no longer handle many of the important customers I had personally dealt with from the beginning. Problems instantly arose as my favorite customers, people who were used to personal service from a cofounder of the company, discovered they could no longer get the individual attention I had given them before 1991. And the result was that they cut back on their orders. Unfortunately, these customers also refused to do the in-store promotions they had done with me and Tom since 1988. When I went to see them about this, they accused Brooklyn Brewery of betraying them after they had helped us to build our brand. They felt neglected, and they acted on that feeling. It got messy. But unlike in prior years, I now had a full-time job to tend to in order to bring home a paycheck, and this job started at 4 P.M. every day. The reality was that I just had to walk away at a certain point and trust my new employees to deal with our disgruntled customers. We would try to give them the same attention we'd always offered; it would just be coming from a new member of our brewery family. The transition, therefore, was somewhat complicated but necessary.

In retrospect, this was probably a good thing. It helped me understand that if Brooklyn Brewery was going to grow, I had to learn to work through and leverage its salespeople. I could not personally handle every account forever, and neither could Tom. We lost sales in my favorite accounts because it was difficult to win them back, but we gained overall because two salespeople can cover twice the territory of one. From this particular growth experience I learned to step back and look at the bigger picture no matter how much I initially tried to grapple with the changes.

### Help Getting the Word Out

Our experience in the marketing arena was similar. Until 1991, I personally managed all the marketing we were doing. But that year, Tom had to run the Brooklyn Lager Bandsearch and handle contacts with the media that I could not field from my desk at *Newsday*.

It is difficult for entrepreneurs to accept the realization that they might someday no longer be vital to the success of their own companies, but it is a reality that all entrepreneurs should work to create.

When I returned to the company full-time in 1992, after a year of multitasking, I had a different view of my role at the Brooklyn Brewery. I was very self-consciously trying to mentor and work through the company salespeople rather than rushing out of the office to solve every problem on my own. This gave me more time to devote to setting up and presenting beer dinners and tastings, among other things. Ultimately, this use of my time was much more satisfying and productive.

I did a beer dinner every couple of weeks for the next two years, and I became quite proud of my presentations over that time. I was able to keep a dining room full of people, usually 50 to 100, entertained for the two hours or so it took to present a five-course meal with seven beers. I began to hone my speaking skills at these productions. I started to recognize which lines would get a laugh, and I sharpened my presentation. One of our salespeople, Jim Munson, went to school on my dinners—taking note of style, content, and what worked—and soon began scheduling his own presentations.

Munson was a graduate of Williams College, an English major like Tom and me, and he quickly developed a very entertaining style of presenting beers and beer dinners. I felt some pangs of jealousy as I watched him doing solid productions at fancy New York City restaurants. But I knew in my mind that this was a good thing because it meant we could reach twice as many people.

## Becoming a True Manager

In the business world, the entrepreneur and manager roles are analogous to those of reporter and editor in the journalism world. A reporter is out there digging for stories, which are the lifeblood—and the fun part—of journalism. Some good reporters go on to become good editors, but many do not. A good editor doesn't just deal with content but battles with other editors to get his or her reporters' work into the paper. A good editor must be willing to nurture reporters to enable them to go out and get great stories. But the stories appear under the bylines of the reporters, not the editor, so the reporters get the glory. Some reporters who become editors never let go of that desire for glory. They never give their reporters everything they have; consequently, the reporters who work for them never develop as fully as they might.

For a period of about six years, from 1988 to 1994, I had been the primary public face of the brewery. But it was clear that we were going to need more than one face if we were to spread our story more widely, especially by word of mouth. When looking for someone to help get the word out, Munson was my first disciple. I overcame my jealousy that he was mirroring my presentations out of my belief that the Brooklyn Brewery needed Munson to help it expand. In effect, we needed all the Munsons we could find. Interestingly, some of the other senior managers also became jealous of Munson because they saw him slowly assuming the role that, up to then, only I had played. When I noticed this response, I told them that Brooklyn Brewery needed "all the stars it could find" and that they could be stars, too.

The next breakthrough on my journey from entrepreneur to manager came when Tom and I hired Garrett Oliver to be our brewmaster in 1994. The first time we met, I recognized Oliver as a very strong-minded, flamboyant man (see Chapter 2). He has been a student, lover, and champion of beer for many years, and has visited most of the classic breweries of Britain, Belgium, and Germany. Once we hired him, he quickly became one of those stars I had hoped for. And I immediately realized—perhaps because of my experiences with Munson and similar talented individuals—that I would have to further curb my ego to accommodate him.

## Making Room for the Brewmaster

Garrett's talents became very apparent to me at the Great American Beer Festival in Denver in 1994. An independent film-maker was doing interviews with all the pioneers of the current microbrewing movement at the festival. During his round of interviews, he asked Oliver and me if we would sit for an on-camera discussion and talk about our company and our beers. As the camera started rolling, I began to tell the story of how Tom and I had started the Brooklyn Brewery, but within minutes Oliver elegantly took over the show. Although Tom and I had originally developed the recipe for Brooklyn Lager, and Brooklyn Brown Ale had been based on my early homebrewing recipes, Oliver spoke with proprietary passion about both beers. In the months after joining the Brooklyn Brewery, he had tweaked the recipes of both these beers, making them his own. During the interview, I was very impressed by his presentation of our product and as a spokesperson for our brand. The camera was clearly drawn to him. If I could have disappeared, I would have. To this day, I defy anyone to try to get between Garrett Oliver and a rolling camera.

It was clear to me from that moment that Oliver was much better at talking to that camera than I was. His opening line was lifted from the John Belushi/Dan Aykroyd movie *The Blues Brothers:* He claimed to be "on a mission from God." He spoke eloquently of the mysteries of yeast, malted barley, and hops. Later, when he gave tours of the brewery, he plunged his hands into the grain and shoved it into the faces of his audience. He vigorously crushed the hop flowers between his hands and urged his listeners to smell their flowery aroma. He grabbed their attention. He wanted them to smell and taste and feel the beauty of the simple, sensuous ingredients that go into beer.

Soon after he joined the company, I urged Oliver to collaborate with Timothy Harper, a former AP national writer, on a book about beer. They published *The Good Beer Book* (Berkley Books) in 1997, and it established Oliver as a beer authority. Soon the *New York Times* was calling him "one of America's foremost authorities on beer." Because of his genuine passion, he has won equally genuine attention. In 2003, Oliver published his second book, *The Brewmaster's Table,* which firmly cemented his position as an authority on beer. I am pleased to say that from day one he has always highlighted his role as brewmaster of the Brooklyn Brewery. In addition to his books and interviews, he has appeared on *Emeril Live* and *Martha Stewart Living,* and on NBC with Al Roker.

Our brewery in Brooklyn must be one of the most photographed in the world because of its accessible location in a city of millions. There are camera crews at the Brooklyn Brewery in Williamsburg virtually every week of the year. This offers the perfect forum for all of us to talk to the media about our business, whether we are discussing our products, special events, or our many community-based initiatives. Oliver's personality has translated well to the media, and he now routinely speaks at beer festivals and all manner of events around the world.

As for me, I still get my share of attention from the media. Tom and I are the founders of the Brooklyn Brewery, and no one can take that fact away from us. But nowadays, I tend to pass most of the television appearances on to Garrett Oliver because I know he is the best at presenting our company on camera.

About the same time, I also ceded the day-to-day management of sales for the Brooklyn Brewery to Jim Munson, who ran the overall sales for the distributorship, and Mike Vitale, one of our three original employees, who ran the overall sales for the brewery. (These were always two distinct roles. The distributorship sold all the beers we distributed; the smaller brewery sales force focused on the sales of Brooklyn Brewery products.) Tom divided the managerial aspects between us. Munson reported directly to Tom, and Mike to me. Ed Ravn, second of our three original employees, was responsible for all out-of-state sales, and he also reported to me. Among the five of us and our sales representatives, the number of whom shrank and grew throughout the years, we had selling covered.

## PROMISES, PROMISES

The development of a sales department with real managers who wield real power over a team and assume responsibility for profit and loss is a key indicator of whether a company has made the transition from entrepreneurship to successfully managed enterprise. Over the years, I learned the aspects of this transition from watching the sales operations of breweries that we represented. More than a few of the breweries whose products we helped to distribute were constantly turning over their sales managers. It seemed that the founders would come to our Craft Brewers Guild sales meeting three or four times a year to introduce new sales managers as the primary contact for their companies. You could almost see our salespeople trying not to roll their eyes when the rookie sales managers, most of whom lived outside the city, appeared before them and pledged to work five days a month in the New York City market in order to support our sales efforts.

As I have noted, New York City is a cold place to sell beer—to sell anything, for that matter. The customers who buy our beer to sell to consumers are very busy people, with their own supermarkets, restaurants, and bars to run, and they don't have much time to spend with salespeople. They are tough and abrasive. One of the lessons we learned right away is that some owners, buyers, and managers even seem to take pleasure in tormenting salespeople. These people deal with a demanding public every day of the week, and thus take their own doses of abuse. A salesperson who walks through the door is an easy target for an exasperated owner, buyer, or manager who has been taking it all day and now has a chance to dish it out. There are dozens, even hundreds, of beer brands that get sold to these buyers every year. In their fast-paced environment, who has time to listen to all the sales pitches?

Truck drivers are often treated even worse. I know this from personal experience. Once, I was delivering beer to a deli in Brooklyn Heights. I pulled up right at noon, when there was a line of customers at the cash register. I signaled to the owner that I had her Brooklyn Beer delivery. She said, "Okay, go ahead." I opened the metal trapdoors to the basement, piled my cases on the sidewalk, and started walking them down the steps into the storage area. After the first load, I walked up the steps and felt a slap on the side of my head. "Don't open doors," the owner scolded. "Don't open doors." After berating me, she forced me to take the beer back out of the basement and wait until she had checked out her lunch crowd before I could make my delivery. And this is only one of many incidents I could recount.

So when a fresh-faced sales manager blows in from the suburbs or from Vermont and commits to being in the market one day a week, or one day a month, no one who has actually worked in this region is impressed. That sales manager will either prove himself or herself in the coming weeks or fail. Some of the breweries we represented went through six or more sales managers. Looking back, you could predict the success or failure of the company by evaluating the performance of the sales representation they put in the market. Developing a disciplined sales force that does what it says it will do is essential to the success of a brewery. We required our salespeople to make 20 to 25 calls per day, including three cold calls, on new customers, and report on the results. And we constantly told them that if they couldn't deliver on a promise, they shouldn't make it.

## SO WHAT DO I DO BESIDES MANAGE?

So what is my biggest role today, you ask? Well, today I deal directly with the general manager of the brewery, Eric Ottaway, and the sales manager, Robin Ottaway, on a daily basis. Eric schedules meetings of our operating committee about every two weeks. The operating committee includes Eric, Robin, and me; our brewmaster, Garrett Oliver; the controller, Debra Bascome; and our VP for sales, Mike Vitale. At these meetings, we exchange information about what we are doing and discuss any pressing issues that have arisen in the previous weeks.

In general, I try to stay out of the day-to-day workings of the administrative and operations side of things, including the sales organization. In other words, I try not to micromanage the company's distinct parts and trust our employees to do their own jobs. I have lunch with Oliver every week or so, and I look at Debra Bascome's tax filings. Bascome also gives me weekly reports about our cash position and monthly reports on our profit and loss and expenses, by department. I look at the big picture and oversee the financial flow and sense of the company's work.

I do try to get out into the market with at least one of our brewery salespeople or a sales manager from the distributor once a week. I also visit some key customers every week or so to ask how our distributor is doing and get feedback about our beers and our marketing efforts. When I go into the market and stop over with customers, I try to stay out of their day-to-day issues. I do not make any deals with the customers I'm visiting unless I clear it with the salesperson for that area first. When I make my rounds, I find that customers appreciate having direct contact with the president and founder of the company. Many remember when I was selling them the beer myself and delivering it to their doorstep from the back of my own truck.

The only area that I continue to micromanage is marketing. Brooklyn Brewery is a fairly high-profile company for its size, and we get pitched by ad firms, public relations firms, and marketing firms on a daily basis. Because we have been effective at guerrilla marketing, I have never entrusted our marketing to anyone else. Milton Glaser (who developed our logo) and Tom and I have written every slogan we have ever had. Milton alone has done all the artwork for us. Looking back on our marketing tactics of the past 15 years, I think we have made a pretty good team, one that is constantly pushing the envelope. Conversely, all the material we have seen from outside ad firms smelled too much like traditional advertising. I believe that advertising can be effective, but I don't think that traditional advertising is an area where Brooklyn Brewery can shine. It seems to me that if Brooklyn Brewery is spending X on advertising, and Samuel Adams is spending 10X, and Budweiser is spending 1,000X, then Brooklyn Brewery looks like a speck on Budweiser's behind. Why play in that game? Traditional advertising just won't win us the attention we deserve against the dollars of the big competitors.

### Recent Innovations

In 2005, we embarked on the first consumer-focused program we have ever done: the Brooklyn Vacation, the purpose of which is to expand our presence in supermarkets and stores. Supermarkets like promotions that offer prizes to their customers, and they guarantee that we will have displays in all their stores. This gets us into stores that have not carried our beer before. Maybe someday, Milton and I will run out of ideas and then we may have to farm out the marketing to innovative ad firms, but until that day we continue to churn out our own successful programs, continually creating new markets for our products.

## LESSON NINE
## HIRING AND FIRING

In his book *Jack: Straight from the Gut* (Warner Books, 2001), well-known CEO Jack Welch, of General Electric, recommends that the bottom 10 percent of any organization be fired every year to keep people on their toes and bring in new blood. I doubt that Welch insisted on an exact number of firings, but after reading about it, I thought there might be something to this rule of thumb.

In the early days of the Brooklyn Brewery, we rarely fired anyone. We were too busy selling beer and solving problems to worry much about the intricacies of personnel. Some people left the company because they clearly did not want to work as hard as we did. We also let some people go when they were caught stealing from the company. In most cases, stealing and driving while intoxicated were the only two infractions that led to summary dismissal. In other cases, we let some drivers and salespeople go because they mistreated our customers, and there were also a few times when we had to let people go because we did not have the money to pay them.

Of course, no one in our company liked firing people. But once the company reached a certain size—about 30 employees—we began to let people go on a fairly regular basis. With the growth of the company, we established annual performance reviews (discussed in Chapter 5), and these reviews inevitably began to show that some people were not living up to expectations in their position. I know this sounds harsh, but after a dozen or so years of leading a company, I became much more confident about firing people because I knew that, in many cases, you are doing someone a favor when you let them go.

The other side of this coin is the problem of attracting too many overqualified people because of the allure of the product we are making and selling. All in all, we have had a fairly stable cadre of senior managers. It occasionally becomes clear that a middle-level manager has reached as high a level as he or she can in the company. When this happens, the employee can develop a simmering resentment toward the senior staff and might become alienated from the social life of the company, necessitating some heart-to-heart talks. My only regret about many past firings is that I did not give those employees the attention they needed earlier, possibly saving them some unnecessary grief.

In such cases, we often did not fire people outright. In the course of discussions with these employees, the reality of the situation would surface and we would ask them to resign, assuring them that we would give them good recommendations for the future. Without exception, these employees took our offer and went on to good jobs. In some instances, they even started their own companies.

At our high point, we had about 100 employees between New York and Boston. Even for a company of this size, Welch's 10 percent rule is still an important idea. When considering performance, employees at any company should prove that they deserve to work there and be evaluated at regular intervals to determine whether they are living up to the manager's expectations of their position. Most important, the company should be a fulfilling experience for the employees. If this is not the case, they are better off somewhere else. Employee job satisfaction adds to the growth of the company and in turn creates more opportunities for employees. The relationship between employer and employees is symbiotic and should be reviewed regularly because the health of this relationship is a major determinant of the success of a company. ★

Let me admit it up front: I'm no Jack Welch. I don't have his amazing record of success, I haven't created billions of dollars of shareholder value, and I'll never run the largest corporation in the world. I'm not as dynamic as he is and not as smart. So why listen to me rather than him? Well, you're probably no Jack Welch, either. Maybe you're more like me.

Everyone who starts a company for the first time wrestles with internal demons. Like a brand-new teacher in front of a classroom, you struggle with how you see yourself and how others see you. You wonder: *Is anyone paying attention to me? Do they respect me? Or are they giggling at me?* You reach out mentally to role models, stealing bits and pieces from people you admire until you can develop your own management style and skills that are effective for you. Depending on your personality and the skills you start with, Jack Welch might not be the right role model.

Leaving the corporate world and starting a company stripped me of all exterior management support. There were no policies at the Brooklyn Brewery until Steve and I created them. There was no financial system, no back office, no sales programming, no nothing; and in creating them, we created ourselves as managers. It is an entirely different process and a more personally revealing one than becoming a manager at an existing company. Some things about myself I learned quickly; some things only over time.

I found out that my first instincts were often wrong. Like a new teacher, perhaps, I did not appreciate the importance of daily discipline. I thought that if I worked very hard myself and set as high an example as I could, I was being a good manager. Wrong. What the company needed was more structure and less sloppy love. Over time, Steve and I grasped that providing discipline actually helped us create the positive work environment we wanted.

At first I also thought I could do anything and everything. For instance, I created all of our original office procedures and set up, programmed, and ran our first three automated accounting packages. Even when our company grew larger and more complex, I didn't want to waste money on hiring a real controller or chief financial officer because I thought I could do it better than anyone we would hire. In a backward way I proved myself right: I was making the mistake of being so cheap that we kept hiring people who didn't have the skills to do a great job. We'd call the person a "controller," but I kept thinking of him or her as just assisting me. Naturally, we kept being frustrated and disappointed. We kept getting lousy financials until we finally hired a real professional. I learned.

I eventually figured out that as a manager I could do anything, but I couldn't do everything. Not well enough. And I also learned that working hard and setting a good example are necessary but not nearly sufficient. Without an environment of smart discipline, a good example means little.

I hate firing people. I always have and always will. I don't think I'd want to work at a company where a certain percentage of people are routinely fired, and I don't want to run a company that way. That's not the kind of motivation I want to build a culture around. So I'm no Jack Welch. I most admire CEOs like the former Procter & Gamble chief John Pepper, a legendary nice guy who was also able to make smart and tough decisions. That style better suits my own personality (or at least the way I'd like to see myself). Sometimes my own managers criticized me for being too nice, and there was some truth in it, but I believe you've got to be true to yourself. I found a way to make it work, eventually.

I have learned the hard way that avoiding or delaying firing someone inevitably makes everything worse for the individual and for the company. Often I felt guilty because I found myself firing people for reasons that were more my fault than theirs—or that were no one's fault. Perhaps I had approved their hiring even though they weren't really suited for the job. Or they were given a job that was poorly defined or poorly supported. Or the company had just moved on, passing their skill set by and leaving them awkwardly out of place. No matter the circumstances, and even if the ultimate fault was my own, the good of the company still required fast action. That was a tough lesson. I think Steve grasped it much earlier than I did.

**Our Grade:** Steve and I each had a lot to learn as managers. I initially thought I would be a natural but instead found myself on a long learning curve. As Steve noted, an entrepreneur's take-charge skills might not be those suited for running a mature corporation where intelligent delegation is key. And the reverse is also true. I found that management skills I had initially learned in business school and in a corporate setting didn't always translate in a start-up situation. Both Steve and I took some self-inflicted wounds, but we survived and adapted. I give us both a B for honorable hard work and improvement.

# CHAPTER 10

# Tom Talks about Cashing Out and Reinventing The Business, Again

Building the total of our distribution operations took 10 years of hard but exciting work. Then we spent another 5 years of harder work trying to keep them running. Finally, we spent 2 of the hardest years of all, in 2002 and 2003, trying to sell them. We were ultimately successful—at a level beyond anything we could have dreamed of when we started the company—but there were times during the process when I thought we could lose all we had painstakingly built.

## WE CASH OUT . . . EVENTUALLY

Why sell the distributorships? By 2002 they had come to represent two-thirds of our total revenue. But they were also a dead end. We could no longer grow them, and they were slowing the development of Brooklyn Brewery products. The distributorships were a lot more valuable to sell than to hold, so Steve and I and our other managers decided it was time to reinvent our company, again.

The end of TotalBeer.com in 2001 marked the beginning of the end of our distribution operations in New York and Massachusetts. The dream of using our distributors to sell specialty beers directly to consumers and to consolidate other specialty beer distributors into one powerful unit offered at least a theoretical growth path. With the death of TotalBeer.com, we lacked a strategic reason to keep the distributorship. We couldn't imagine a growth path for it that we believed in, and having it stay the same size wasn't viable, either.

In Massachusetts, our distributorship (CBG) was simply too small. We weren't able to put together a portfolio of beers with critical market mass, and we were losing money every month. Between 1997 and 2000, our two on-site managers, Eric and Robin Ottaway, worked feverishly. Account by account, they built the brands we carried as we bought additional brand rights to try to add volume, but the results were indifferent. They also kept expenses as low as possible by doing as much of the work themselves as they could, but we just couldn't break even. In late 2000, Eric came to New York to help with TotalBeer.com and Robin was left to run the division in Massachusetts on his own. By the end of 2001, it had become clear that we were not going to succeed.

In New York, the distribution economics were more complex. We weren't losing money on distribution, but we weren't making much, either. Our two biggest brands—Brooklyn Brewery and Sierra Nevada—were both doing fine in bars and restaurants but were not well distributed in stores, where we felt the bulk of future growth would come. Lack of store growth was a real problem, and because of a contract entered into in 1996, we were stymied in our attempts to address it.

Most of the beer distributors servicing New York in 1987, around the time we started the Brooklyn Brewery, were out of business by 2002. In those 15 years, many had gone broke and disappeared and the rest had consolidated with larger companies. We were an exception: a new distributor that had grown. Our focus was on an expensive product line sold to what is termed *on-premise* accounts, meaning customers like bars, restaurants, and hotels, where the consumption takes place on the premises. We had successfully mined our niche and grew to fill it. There was one other beer distributor called S.K.I. that was also an exception. S.K.I. had started at about the same time we did and also grew while focusing on a niche: the exact opposite market from ours. For a while we were complementary partners, but we then became troubled, sometimes bitter, adversaries. Our experience was a cautionary reminder that in business, as in romance, it can be easier to get into a relationship than out of it.

## TIES THAT BIND: OUR CONTRACT WITH S.K.I.

S.K.I. was originally started by three partners. One was Spanish, one was Korean, and one was Italian—hence the initials in the name. Small business segments are often divided by ethnicity in New York, and the S.K.I. partners were a direct ethnic match for most small store and deli owners. When the Spanish partner quit early on, the remaining two partners built the business. Ralph Mauriello was the outside partner, the primary voice of the company, who dealt with suppliers and key customers. He was a hard-knocks sort of guy but keenly intelligent. If they gave SAT scores for street smarts, Ralph would have aced the test. Charlie Kim was the inside guy, who ran the office, directed the sales staff, and organized the deliveries. A former Army Ranger who had reportedly led two missions to rescue MIAs in Vietnam, he was a handsome, quiet guy who commanded respect within his company. Both Ralph and Charlie had also been successful soda truck route drivers before creating their own company.

When Steve and I looked at S.K.I., we saw a weird mirror image of ourselves. They were like us, but in reverse. While we were upscale, they were down and dirty. We only sold expensive beers and only bought directly from breweries that we represented exclusively. S.K.I. bought most of its beer from other, larger local distributors and made a living reselling Bud, Coors Light, and Heineken at a thin profit margin. We sold mostly to on-premise customers like restaurants and bars. They sold mostly to off-premise customers like stores and delis. We had a college-educated sales staff who were well paid and received full benefits. They hired hardworking immigrants, paid them modestly, and offered few benefits. We prided ourselves on promoting and building brands. They prided themselves on reaching a wide number of stores and moving boxes.

Despite our vast differences, we were each successful at what we did. But we each had struggled in the other's turf and were concerned that our suppliers wanted solutions both on-premise and off-premise. Unless both of us provided better solutions, these suppliers might move to one of the large distributors. For instance, Sierra Nevada, our largest outside supplier, had warned us several times that they expected us to do better in stores. A working partnership between our two mirror-image companies seemed to make perfect sense.

In 1996 we struck a deal and signed a contract appointing S.K.I. as our official subdistributor, dividing up the market and pooling our strengths. Initially, S.K.I. probably benefited more than we did. We handed over about a million dollars a year in existing store sales to them—albeit, this was low-margin business for us. We also arranged for some of their first chain-store authorizations by insisting to upscale local chains like D'Agostino's and Gristedes that they could buy Brooklyn Lager and Sierra Pale Ale only from S.K.I. Their subdistribution contract with us gave them their first well-respected brands on an exclusive basis and represented an important market validation. They did not pay for the business they received from us, but we reserved the right to buy back all our rights at any time in the future at a set price of $2 per case. As long as they increased our business, they couldn't lose.

For the next several years, the arrangement worked. S.K.I. increased the sales of our beers. We passed off-premise leads to them and they passed on-premise leads to us, but gradually our paths diverged, as S.K.I. decided to pursue our part of the market as well. Not content to be half of the equation, they wanted to become a full-service distributor serving both off-premise and on-premise customers. They solicited a series of secondary breweries that we did not want to represent and began to sell these beers to on-premise accounts in competition with our products. At first it was just an annoyance. Steve and I argued that they were diverting their attention away from building long-term brands with us. We thought they had a "flavor of the month" sales mentality, flitting from new brand to new brand instead of choosing a few suppliers to build around for the long term. It seemed to us that S.K.I. always had a new brand that was hot— it was on fire!—and a previous hot brand that they didn't want to talk about anymore.

By the year 2000, after four years of working together, S.K.I. had gone from being a help to being a drag. More and more of our suppliers complained that they were no longer growing off-premise and that they couldn't get basic sales and promotion information from S.K.I. Our two companies weren't working well together and each was suspicious of the other's motives. A possible answer seemed to be to merge our distribution company with theirs and break through the barriers. Steve and I talked with Ralph and Charlie and we all agreed that it was theoretically the right thing to do. But Ralph and Charlie insisted that they would have to run the combined company and do things their way.

We had a culture clash. We didn't think their rough-and-ready ways would work with our customers, and they didn't think our high-society ways would work with theirs. They said we should just concentrate on the brewery and let them worry about the distribution side. We couldn't agree on the relative value of our distribution business (which was all-exclusive and high-margin) and theirs (which was larger, but mostly lower-margin). Things became increasingly antagonistic and tense.

## An Alliance That Wasn't

While we were struggling with our S.K.I. partnership within New York City, we were also concerned that we were spread too thin in the suburbs. Consolidation was leaving fewer distributors in New York, and the remaining ones were getting larger. The market was always changing, and it was getting tougher. Our main distribution competitors were 10 to 20 times our size and offered broad geographic coverage to suppliers. It was my thought that we could forge market alliances with other complementary distributors in order to offer a stronger, integrated group able to compete with our larger rivals, without actually merging. We could standardize our internal information systems, compile aggregate information across the allies, and offer suppliers an integrated solution for the complete market area.

The logic of this plan was strong enough to actually bring our company together with S.K.I. and three other suburban distributors to strike a deal in early 2001. We all agreed to a specific information platform, mutual roles, and sharing of existing brands across our territories to work together to win new brands for what we called our "alliance." We sold our suburban brand rights to our new partners at a good price and were settling in to concentrate on New York City and make it all work. I even had cautious hopes that the new arrangements might improve our tense relationship with S.K.I.—but these hopes didn't last long.

One of our alliance partners gained the rights to distribute Yuengling Brewery beers, which held enormous promise in New York, and decided that they couldn't, or wouldn't, share these rights with the rest of the Alliance. Instead, they used the brand to come into New York City on their own and began looking for additional brands to bundle with Yuengling. Instead of a partner, we found ourselves with another direct rival. With that, another attempted formula to keep our distributorship competitive proved flawed. An alliance to cooperate, no matter how seemingly logical, isn't always strong enough to withstand the contrary self-interest of one of its members.

## ALCOHOL FRANCHISE LAWS

Government regulations can have a huge effect on a competitive marketplace. When regulations change, markets change. Unlike other consumer products, alcoholic beverages are closely regulated by the states. Other products are ruled by the Commerce Clause of the U.S. Constitution, which prohibits states from interfering with interstate trade. The reason alcohol is different stems from a historical anomaly. The temperance movement won a constitutional amendment banning all alcohol sales in the United States in 1919. The resulting period of prohibition proved beneficial only to moonshiners, bootleggers, and organized crime. When President Franklin Roosevelt engineered the constitutional repeal of the amendment in 1933, he had to bargain for votes in the Senate. The price of support from certain parochial-minded senators was language that specifically gave to states the right to regulate alcohol production, taxation, and distribution.

What followed was a confusing patchwork of wildly different regulations from state to state. Almost all states are alike, however, in that they impose on beer distributors certain obligations including collecting taxes and registering individual brands. Some states also regulate the relationships between distributors and their brewery suppliers. These laws, called *franchise* laws, trump ordinary commercial contracts. As a result, they can make it difficult for a supplier to leave a distributor, no matter what a contract might say. Breweries hate franchise laws. Distributors love them. Since we were both brewer and distributor, we had distinctly mixed feelings.

When we started distributing in 1988, New York State had little franchise protection. Brands came and went freely, according to contracts if a contract had been signed, but often without any written agreements. This freedom worked to our advantage early on. We were attractive to specialty brands and they moved from other distributors to come to us. In 1996, however, the New York legislature passed a moderate franchise law and then strengthened it in the year 2000. This law stated that if any of our current suppliers left us for another distributor, we would likely be compensated, but it also said that if any brand wanted to move to us, we'd have to pay for it. Since we were one of the smallest distributors in New York, we were among those least able to buy new brands. The law made our then-current portfolio of distribution rights more valuable, but it also made us less likely to grow through acquisition. With this in mind, the biggest questions for us were: Did the newly strengthened franchise law also apply to S.K.I., our subdistributor? Did it render our contract with them worthless? Were we stuck?

## Looking in the Mirror, and Deciding to Sell

By the fall of 2001 we had closed TotalBeer.com and, in the aftermath of the WTC terrorist attacks, faced an extremely difficult business environment. New York's economy had begun to go into a tailspin even before the attacks, but afterward the decline was sharp and brutal. We were concerned that hundreds of our restaurant customers, especially ones that had started in the late 1990s (when the economy had boomed) and those located in downtown Manhattan (surrounded by a devastated infrastructure) would now go broke. We hoped they wouldn't take us with them. (In fact, the city's economy recovered rapidly and then boomed again under Mayor Michael Bloomberg.)

There's nothing like the prospect of hanging to focus the mind, as Benjamin Franklin said. A crisis at hand stimulates decision making like nothing else. When one is fighting to save the business, it's a lot easier to jettison old favorite theories, out-dated conceptions, and vague future possibilities. We looked at ourselves in the mirror and stared pretty hard.

In November 2001, Steve and I were joined by Eric and Robin Ottaway in Chicago at a brewers' function. Away from our daily operations and with time to talk, we huddled and chewed over the company's future. It seemed clear to us that our future was with the brewery, not distribution. We decided to sell the Massachusetts distributorship as soon as possible, at what-ever price we could get. We also decided we would seek buyers for the New York distributorship, though only for the right price. We had invested a lot in it and thought it should prove valuable if we could shake free of our ties to S.K.I. And then we would become what we had originally intended and never been: a brewery, period. And hopefully, a well-financed one, too.

## FINDING THE RIGHT BUYER

In selling the New York distributorship, we were interested in three things: first, getting the best price; second, moving the Brooklyn Brewery beers to the distributor that could best grow it for decades to come; and finally, for each of our other suppli-ers to be able to go to whatever new distributor they preferred. Balancing the three goals would not be easy.

There were four potential buyers for our distribution busi-ness. Our first choice was a company called Phoenix Beehive, which was the Heineken, Guinness, and Miller distributor in New York. They had a declared strategy of handling fewer brands but focusing on them. Our modest dealings with them previously had been very positive, and we thought they could give Brooklyn Brewery the best attention. A second possibility was a huge company, the largest stand-alone beer distributor in the country. They had a broad and deep portfolio already, and the market muscle to throw behind whatever brands they chose. A third possibility was a disciplined Budweiser distributor currently selling only in Brooklyn, but interested in expanding their footprint by representing specialty beers throughout the city. A fourth choice was our former alliance partner, now coming into the city with Yuengling and perhaps needing brands to bundle with it.

Tentative inquiries with Phoenix Beehive at first were quite positive, raising our hopes. But shortly after that, they turned us down, politely but without further explanation. We were puzzled, but determined to press on with the other possibilities.

The problem that the potential buyers saw with us was our subdistribution contract with S.K.I. The new franchise law was written vaguely enough so that no one could be certain whether it applied to subdistributors or not, and if so, what it meant to a prime distributor like us. Everyone wanted us to clean up our contract before committing to a purchase. The problem was that S.K.I. didn't want to clear it up. They wanted to keep the status quo. We moved to terminate them, giving notice under our signed contract, and their lawyers fired back, claiming that the contract was no longer valid and that if we tried to terminate it they would be entitled not only to market compensation but treble damages as well. It was an extreme threat, but if the intent was to intimidate us, it worked.

## Stalemate

We found ourselves in an uncomfortable position. We could sell all of our distribution rights that S.K.I. didn't have a claim on—which meant everything outside of New York City and all on-premise business inside New York City—but S.K.I. threatened to ruin us if we sold any off-premise rights. Their position was that our original contract, which allowed us to buy back all of our rights from S.K.I. at $2 per case, was now invalid. When we asked what price they thought was fair, Ralph Mauriello said that they wouldn't sell it for less than $30 per case. We offered to buy them out for $6 per case. We thought splitting the proceeds (we hoped to get $12 per case from a buyer) was fair, especially since we had originally given them a strong base of business for free. But Ralph wouldn't budge. He said he didn't want to sell the business anyway, that S.K.I. needed it. The only answer, he hinted, was for us to sell our business to them.

One night, trying to bridge the gap, Ralph and Charlie invited us to the famous restaurant Rao's, in Spanish Harlem. A reservation at gangster-chic Rao's is almost impossible to land, and we appreciated that Ralph had pulled some serious strings. When we sat down, he was in an expansive mood and regaled us with stories of the favors different people had done over the years to get a Rao's table and also with stories of the shady, underworld types he had grown up with in his old Italian neighborhood. When we edged around to discussing how we might resolve our stalemate, though, the good feelings quickly evaporated. Soon Steve was shouting at Ralph, and Charlie and I were trying to keep ourselves between them. When we left, our goodbyes were stilted and the East Harlem night seemed pretty dark.

### The Search for an Enlightened Buyer

Of our two distributorships, in Massachusetts and in New York, the Massachusetts operation was easier to sell because our expectations were lower. We initially generated a fair amount of interest and were hopeful that we could achieve a good price that might justify our years of work and operating losses. We met with one large distributor that seemed inclined to buy it, and even seemed in agreement with us on value. Our hopes soared, and then they stopped talking to us. A few weeks later we discovered the reason: They themselves had just received an offer to be acquired. In a period of consolidation, things shift quickly. At the end of 2002, we finally sold our Massachusetts business at a modest price that was paid out over time. We didn't get much money, though we had stopped our financial bleeding and all of the brands including Brooklyn were at least placed in a good home. It was a reminder that selling into a turbulent market where there are only a few potential buyers is selling into a crapshoot. One week the offering price might be good. The next week there might be no offers at any price.

We made no progress in 2002 in selling our New York distributorship. The economy was terrible, sales were slow, and S.K.I. wasn't giving an inch. In early 2003, we had extensive conversations with potential buyers, and with the help of our ace lawyer, Steve Gersh, hit on the concept of a two-stage sale. We offered to sell our on-premise business first, which would give us the financial war chest to reach a settlement with S.K.I. We promised to sell our off-premise business as soon as we could get a release from S.K.I. The potential buyers considered the idea seriously, but backed off, fearing that if we didn't accomplish what we promised, they would be stuck with half a business.

In the summer of 2003, a year after Phoenix Beehive had mysteriously turned us down, we received a call indicating they might now be interested. Cautious, Steve and I visited their owner. He received us graciously and explained what had happened. A year earlier they had asked approval from one of their existing major suppliers to purchase us, and they had been turned down. Now, however, that supplier was willing to approve. We were thrilled. But what about our S.K.I. dilemma?

The owner was inclined to trust us. He directed his lawyers to draw up the two-stage purchase contract and included commonsense protections against our failure. But he didn't insist on draconian contingencies or elaborate restrictions. Sometimes against the advice of his lawyers, he gave us the flexibility we needed to pursue an intelligent campaign to extract ourselves from our S.K.I. contract. We quickly agreed on price, with little haggling on either side. He also offered to buy the distribution rights for all of our other beers, but agreed to let them go to any other distributor if those breweries preferred. It was exactly what we had hoped for, and fought for, for so long. By the fall of 2003, we had signed our contract with Phoenix Beehive, the buyer that had been our original first choice and whose amicable negotiations had given us some breathing room to start dealing with S.K.I.

## ANTICIPATING THE SALE AND GETTING IN FRONT OF RUMORS

Some secrets are hard to keep, and when a company or a division of a company is for sale, alert managers and employees sniff it out. No matter how careful the principals' negotiating might be, the process is itself a bit unnatural. Doors may be shut instead of open. Regular appointments have to be skipped. Decisions that normally would be easy to make become more difficult as business calculations begin to include buyer motivation as well as seller self-interest. Customers hear rumors from salespeople, and pass them on with relish and enthusiasm. Employees want to know what is going on.

At an afternoon company meeting in 2002, we had told our employees that our distributorship was indeed up for sale. We decided that we weren't going to be able to keep the process secret for long. More than half of our employees worked in the distribution division, and most would end up losing their jobs with us. All would be interviewed by the buyer and surely many would get hired, but there were no individual guarantees. Telling employees there are no guarantees is not what any manager wants to stand up and say.

However, the truth wasn't as bad as the rumors and uncertainty. When all other beer distributors in New York had sold out or gone broke—which had happened frequently—the employees would typically find out on a Friday that the company was closing its doors. Don't come in on Monday. Period. We could tell our employees, truthfully, that we would give everyone four weeks' notice. We would offer a severance plan that was generous for a small company, and unheard of in our industry. And we would help everyone who wanted help in getting a new job, with the eventual buyer or elsewhere in the industry.

When we signed our contract with Phoenix Beehive, it was time to talk to our employees again. In early September 2003, we had the sad responsibility of breaking the news that we had sold the distributorship. I stood up in front of the tense and mostly silent crowd gathered in the brewery and did my best to present it honestly.

"Over the last year you have all heard a lot of rumors. I'm here to tell you that this time, they are true."

I went on for about half an hour, explaining the situation and answering questions. It was the hardest presentation I'd ever had to make. I'd practiced it in my head dozens of times and all through the previous sleepless night. How do you tell people that they will likely be fired, but to please stick with us for a few more months? Since our sale was two-part, we were entering an awkward interim period. Until we received a release from S.K.I., we were still a distributor, but we didn't know exactly how long that would be. Employee morale would be more than difficult to maintain in that time.

I was hoping that Steve and I had earned the credibility and respect of everyone and that they'd trust us now. We knew nearly everyone personally, but still there were doubts in my mind. After 17 years, a company changes, inevitably, and the intimacy and group commitment that adhered to us as a start-up had evolved into something else. When you're the boss, it's tough to really know what people think of you. What they say is not as much a measure as what they do, and we were about to find out what they'd do.

After the main meeting we broke up into smaller groups: the warehouse crew and drivers, the sales staff, the administrative

staff, and the brewing crew. Only the brewers were largely unaf-
fected—for everyone else, big changes were coming. Amazingly,
as I held my breath over the next few weeks, no one quit. We
didn't lose a single employee. Everyone was willing to keep
working in order to receive the severance pay and retention
bonuses we would eventually pay, as promised.

## Our First Lawsuit

In all of our years in business, we had never sued, or even
threatened to sue, anyone. But now we were faced with a situation unlike any we had faced before. We couldn't go forward on
the second half of the deal with Beehive without an agreement
with S.K.I., and they had no incentive to do anything. They
seemed to prefer an unresolved status quo to any resolution. So
for the first time, we hired lawyers for the purpose of litigation
and prepared to go to battle.

Our strategy was to sue not for damages but simply for a
declaratory judgment. We wanted a judge to decide: Did we or
did we not have the right to enforce our contract and take back
our rights at the agreed price? And if the contract didn't govern,
then what were S.K.I.'s subdistribution rights worth? Preparing
for litigation is extremely time consuming and extremely expensive. For a month, we helped our lawyers draft the litigation documents and quickly ran up a six-figure legal bill in the process.
The only thing more expensive than preparing for litigation, we
were warned, was actually going to court. We hoped we wouldn't
have to. We hoped that merely filing in court and demonstrating
that we were deadly serious about needing a resolution would be
the spur we needed.

We filed in New York Supreme Court on Thursday, October
9. Three days later, the biggest convention in the beer world
would start in Las Vegas. I would be there and so would S.K.I.,
Beehive, all the other New York distributors, and nearly all of
our suppliers. People would be talking about the court filing. If

a resolution could come, I thought, perhaps it would come when we were all in one place at one time. If it didn't come, there would surely be sparks.

## FACING REALITY, TOGETHER

On the morning of Sunday, October 12, I found Charlie from S.K.I. on the convention floor alone, without his partner, Ralph. Earlier, all my negotiations had been with Ralph. Lately, I had begun to think that Charlie was the key, since Ralph wasn't budging. I said hello and asked him if we could meet to talk privately later that day. He was noncommittal, but I gave him my cell phone number and urged him to call. He called about 4:30 P.M. We agreed to meet in front of Le Café at the Paris Hotel.

When we met, we spoke for a few minutes, awkwardly, about the convention. Then I shut up and waited. Finally Charlie started to speak. He said he hadn't been as involved as Ralph in the talks with us, or with his lawyers, but he had followed it very closely. He said that Ralph had hoped to eventually attract our suppliers to come to them, but that it didn't seem to be working out. Originally S.K.I. hoped to get some money from us and distribution rights from some of our suppliers to replace any lost cases. But now it looked like it was just going to be the money.

He said it would be hard to replace the lost business, and that S.K.I. would consequently lose money the next year. He could fire a few people, he said, but not enough to make up for the lost gross profit. He was speaking from the heart, and I was listening.

Then he said that when we gave them the papers a few days before, initiating the court case, Ralph was very angry. We should have given them more time. Now that we had done that, they would have even more lawyer's fees. Who was going to pay for that? Originally he had told Ralph they should settle for $12 a case. But now, he told Ralph, they should hold out for much more.

I told Charlie that Ralph had never stated a dollar amount. Not since a year earlier, when he had put out the $30-a-case fig-ure, which was crazy. I said we didn't want to have to go to court. It was expensive for us, too. But I reminded him that it was S.K.I. that had threatened to sue us for the last two years. All the legal threats had come from their side. And Ralph had never responded at all to our $6-a-case offer.

I said the $6 was not a final offer. We had been waiting and waiting for a counteroffer—any counteroffer. It was not our intent to put them into any situation where they thought their best bet was to go to court. We had tried to wait for Ralph, but he never responded.

Charlie said he didn't know why Ralph had never responded with a figure, and at that moment I sensed that he was groping for a face-saving way to initiate an honest negotiation. I wanted to grab this instant of fragile promise, without accidentally crushing it.

I carefully said that regardless of the past, we all wanted to look forward and do the right thing before running up steep legal fees and going to court, where no one could be sure what would happen. He didn't say anything, but I could tell he was listening carefully.

My offer was this: I couldn't get any settlement approved by Steve and my board that gave S.K.I. more than we were getting. It was just a nonstarter. We were willing to do more than a fifty-fifty split, but there was no way we would voluntarily give S.K.I. more than 100 percent. I reminded him that we had given them a lot of business to start with, and Charlie acknowledged that was so. I continued: What if we give you $12 a case for the number of cases by which you have grown the brands? He thought about the proposal for a moment, but then dismissed it and went back to his arguments about how hard it was going to be for S.K.I. to lose these cases and the legal fees that they had already paid. He said it would have to be $12 a case from case one.

Finally. I had an actual proposal from S.K.I. that I could live with, down from their only previous offer of $30 a case. As simple as it was, it was the breakthrough we had waited for and agonized over for more than two years.

"Charlie," I said, "ask Ralph if he'll agree to that. If you ask Ralph, I'll ask Steve." In fact, I knew Steve would say yes. It was the price we had privately prepared for.

Charlie hesitated for a long moment, thinking. "Okay," he said finally. "I'll ask him."

"Ask him now," I said. "Right now. Call him on his cell phone. If he goes for it, I'll call Steve."

I was aching to shake hands on a deal right now, but Charlie shook his head no. He would speak with Ralph tomorrow, in private, to agree on something simple, an agreement an ordinary person could understand, and he hoped to do it fast. I liked the sound of that.

Charlie said he'd call me four days later, after talking with Ralph and probably his lawyers, and that if we agreed on $12 a case, maybe we could even sign something Friday. I said okay, though I thought that was too optimistic. In reality, I just wanted to encourage the idea that moving fast was best for everyone.

We shook hands and parted, and I raced off for my next meeting. My head was reeling. I couldn't be sure that we had a deal with S.K.I., but my hopes were soaring. Charlie was an honorable guy, in his own way, and I was confident that this was a big step toward settling.

### How to Survive a Meeting from Hell

During our standoff with S.K.I., our suppliers were stuck. They wanted to move on, we wanted them to move on, but until we broke the S.K.I. logjam, we couldn't afford to let them go or we risked losing everything. It was excruciating, and our biggest supplier, Sierra Nevada, was running out of patience. Their national sales manager, Steve Oliver, had summoned me to his hotel suite to talk.

I went up to the eighth floor of the Paris Hotel, where Ollie held court. His staff was there and so was the entire senior management of the distributor they wanted to move to. There were nine people in the room, and eight of them were mad at me.

Ollie began the conversation politely but insisted that he needed to hear from me now that they could move. When would I have the release from S.K.I.?

I told him that I had just had a meeting with Charlie and that I thought it was the first productive meeting in two years. I acknowledged that I could offer no guarantees, but I thought we'd made important progress. Ralph and Charlie had been very disappointed not to get any supplier approvals, but even negative answers at least moved the process along. And I said that our going to court might have focused everyone's attention on the urgency of getting an agreement done.

For a moment, the mood lightened as a result of the first good news in months, but then the senior manager from the distributor ripped into me.

"This is all bullshit," he said. He had seen our lawsuit, and his lawyers had seen it, and they all said it was crap. He said that we had made this bed with S.K.I. and now we had to lie in it. We needed to pay S.K.I. whatever they wanted to get them out. That was the only way. He said he'd talked to all the suppliers, and they all said that we'd screwed them the last two years and they were ready to revolt. He'd talked to Jack Joyce at Rogue, for instance, who said he was sick of Tom Potter and Steve Hindy. Rogue was ready to terminate us right now, and other suppliers would follow.

Oliver from Sierra broke in to say that Sierra had been supportive of us in the past, but they really needed an answer, and they needed it right now.

I was doing the best I could by trying to protect the Brooklyn Brewery and still work for the best interests of suppliers like Sierra. I noted that whatever power the franchise law gave S.K.I., a subdistributor, it should offer to me, the legitimate contracted prime distributor. People like Jack Joyce could say what they wanted, but Jack never bothered to inform himself about anything that was actually going on in New York.

Realistically, S.K.I. had not given us a response until just prior to this meeting with the suppliers. The suppliers were quick to tell me to settle with S.K.I., but it takes two to negotiate, and in my opinion, S.K.I. was the party that needed to move.

In an amazing and sustained burst of profanity, the senior manager from the distributor started to ridicule everything I'd just said. His face turned red and he became apoplectic as he dismissed it all as utter nonsense. His voice got louder and coarser as he commanded the room, while his own managers and the Sierra crew listened and said nothing. He was a big man who was used to being boss and getting his way.

I'd never been in that position before. It was eight against one, and I just had to take it. The hotel room was large, but seemed to be getting smaller and smaller around me as the big man's voice rose and his anger boiled over. I kept telling myself to keep my cool, to not get mad, to not respond in kind. His anger didn't change any of the facts. It was just another fact to note, to file away.

Finally he demanded that we sell Rogue and other, smaller brands to him right then. S.K.I. didn't have much of a claim on them, he said, and if they tried to go to court, we'd learn about their legal strategy.

That idea didn't make sense to me. I told him we finally had a real chance at a deal with S.K.I. and needed to move as quickly as possible to get an answer; we needed to keep our eyes on the big picture.

That was it. The senior manager went into a rage. I was talking shit, he said. And when I tried to speak again, he just cut me off. He didn't want to hear anything more from me because what I was saying wasn't what he wanted to hear. He indicated to his managers that it was time to go, and they all followed him out of the room. A couple of them shook hands with me, silently and awkwardly. I wondered if they saw this kind of performance often from their boss.

When they left, three-quarters of the tension left the room with them. With only the Sierra Nevada guys remaining, I told them I would work fast to move things forward. I asked them to remember that we had announced our deal with Beehive only four weeks earlier, and that S.K.I. had to be convinced that it couldn't get brands before it would even talk about price.

The Sierra managers seemed bemused by what had just transpired. They were in an understandable hurry to settle their future, but their future was presumably going to be with this distributor, who had just blown up in front of a room full of his colleagues. It must have been a little sobering for them to watch.

Oliver said quietly that he hoped it would work out soon. He said the distributor crew was actually going to the Sierra Nevada brewery the next day to meet with his boss. That was very bad news for me. Ollie said they had arranged to go, since Las Vegas was so close to California. The good thing was that the meeting was to be in the morning, Ollie said, so hopefully the distributor's big man would not have started drinking yet. Coming from Ollie, a famous drinker, I thought the remark was pretty ironic.

### Leaving Las Vegas, Again

I went back downstairs and felt completely out of equilibrium. Maybe I had made a deal with S.K.I., and maybe not. Maybe I had held off Sierra and the other distributor and bought us some more time, and maybe not. I felt I had done the absolute best I could do. I just didn't know whether it was enough.

I ran into Kim Jordan, the owner of the New Belgium Brewery. I've always respected her and her brewery. It's among the very best of the American regional breweries and has a progressive ethic that I admire. I was grateful for her company for a few minutes and for a chance to share a cup of coffee, though I was so distracted I doubt my conversation made much sense.

Two years before, in 2001, we had both been in Las Vegas, at this same annual convention, when the World Trade Center was attacked. All of the small and regional brewers had huddled together in the immediate aftermath, glad for our little community, needing to pool our strength in the confusion. All the airports were shut down. I ended up getting a ride in the back of a beer delivery van to California, where I would spend a few days with my frightened mother until the airports opened again and I could get to New York. I remembered leaving Las Vegas then, sitting on cases of beer, driving through the desert night looking out into the very dark sky, listening to wild speculation on the radio. Weirdly, I felt almost as disoriented now as I had then. And I was just as glad to have a friend to talk to in Kim.

In my last hours at this Las Vegas conference, I got a lot of funny looks. Some of our suppliers—other brewers I had known for years—seemed to be avoiding me. I got it. The Brooklyn Brewery may have been the good guys when we were introducing their beers into the New York market, but now we were just another jerk of a distributor tying them up in legal wrangles that were none of their concern. To be fair, it shouldn't have been their concern, but I just had to believe that things would eventually work out.

## CLOSING THE DEAL

Back in New York, I waited for the call from Charlie. I kept imagining reasons why S.K.I. would change its mind. I wanted to play cool, but finally I couldn't wait any longer. Thursday afternoon I called over to S.K.I. Ralph picked up the line. I told him that Charlie and I had agreed to talk today.

"Do we have a deal?" I asked.

"I don't know," Ralph said. "Do we?" He didn't want to commit until he heard that my side had committed.

"I've got a deal if you've got a deal," I said.

"You've got a deal?"

"I've got a deal."

"Then I guess we've got a deal," he said.

"At $12 a case?" I asked, just to make sure.

"At $12 a case," he confirmed.

It was like someone had lifted a truck off my back, I was so relieved.

The release from S.K.I. opened up the floodgates, and the sale of distribution rights could begin. More than one of the distributors involved quickly proposed to us that we sell them all of our rights even without supplier approvals. They would pay us in full and indemnify us against legal liability. They thought that the brewers, especially the smaller ones and brewers from far away, wouldn't fight a forced assignment. We just repeated what we had said from the beginning: that we wanted to get paid, but we wanted every brewery to end up wherever they wanted to go. We weren't going to sell any of them down the river.

The last-minute legal maneuverings were amazing. It seemed like every distributor and every brewery had some particular issue they wanted addressed in the assignment agreement.

Deals get exponentially more complicated as the parties involved add law firms. The best scenario is when one firm represents one client and drafts internal documents. With direction and careful vigilance, it takes only twice as long as you'd think. With two law firms representing two negotiating parties, everything takes at least four times as long. When you go to three firms, I think it's about 16 times more complicated! And four firms—well, no one has ever accomplished a deal involving four firms, so no one knows.

Was it time for all of us to meet in the same room? Preparing for a complicated legal closing is like docking a boat. As you near the dock, you wait and assess the distance. At some point, you've got to jump with a rope in your hand. Wait too long, and you crash. Jump too soon, and you are cold and wet.

When we were nearly finished, momentum slowed. Each of the most-involved companies was hearing from its lawyers that the other guys' lawyers were holding things up. In order to make the final push, we all agreed to meet in person and not leave until we had the deal completed. So with all of us on the phone to our lawyers at the same time and in the same room together, we cut through the welter of fingerpointing that was stalling us.

As the evening wore on, a rhythm developed. We would agree on how to proceed, direct our lawyers, and then wait. The lawyers would draft furiously and perhaps an hour later exchange documents by e-mail. Then they'd each review the work the others had done and call us to explain it and get further direction for the next step.

Finally Steve Gersh, our lawyer and longtime advisor, told me it was done. Wire transfers followed shortly. After 15 years of building the distributorships, and another 2 trying to sell them, we had cashed out. We had sold them for about $10 million, after adding up all the pieces. Of course, we didn't net nearly that much; we had to pay S.K.I., and we had a lot of other costs as well. But considering that the distribution activities hadn't even been part of our original business plan, we had done pretty well. We sold off what had originally been an ancillary part of our business for enough money to put the brewery on an exceptionally sound footing, while keeping the brewery itself and placing it with an excellent distributor in our home market.

After years of agony, we were deeply satisfied.

## LESSON TEN
# ONLY YOU WILL KNOW WHEN IT'S TIME TO SELL

Buy low, sell high. It's a pretty simple idea. But for a company founder like me, the calculation can get complicated.

An entrepreneur usually seems to buy low, in that he or she is creating something of value from scratch. After a few years, though, the buy-in includes sweat, blood, and emotion. The personal investment can be tremendous even if there wasn't a lot of initial cash involved. As the entrepreneur's sweat equity grows, his or her sense of a fair selling price might go up, too. Only the market will determine what the company is worth if sold. But the entrepreneur might have a different idea of what it's worth to keep.

And therein lies a potential danger, if there is a considerable gap between the objective and the perceived value. If the founder is the sole owner, perhaps it doesn't matter. The psychic value the owner gets from being the owner is real, after all, and who's to say if that's more important than selling the business at the right time and getting the maximum financial value. But when there are investors involved, the founders need to step back and remember that they are working for others, and their choosing the right time to sell can be crucial.

Steve and I always felt a tremendous obligation to our investors. When we solicited other people's money, it became a heavy burden. A company's financing starts a chain of fiduciary responsibility that sits squarely on the founder's shoulders, though not everyone feels the burden the same way. Steve and I once had lunch with Buffalo Bill Owens in the 1990s. Bill had started the first brewpub in California in 1983 and has been active in the industry ever since. He cheerfully acknowledged that he was not in business to satisfy the investors. Though I kind of admired his devil-may-care position, I still can't really relate to Bill's attitude. Giving our investors' money back, with a positive return, consumed my life for the better part of 17 years. If you're like me, it's even harder to lose someone else's money than to lose your own.

When Steve and I sold our distributorship, it was like we were selling my baby. I felt I had championed its creation, run it during the glory years, and nursed it through a lot of hard times. But the truth was, it was worth a lot more to someone else than to us, moneywise. For the business, and for our investors, the time was right to sell it.

A couple of months after we sold our distributorships, the Ottaway family approached me about selling them my voting shares, too. Steve and I still held all of the voting shares, 50 percent each, and the Ottaway family was by far the largest holder of the nonvoting shares. Without the distribution operations, the new company would be much smaller, and it didn't particularly need me. We had a lot of good managers and a lot of money in the bank. Was this personally the right time for me to sell? I had to think about what was really important to me.

I asked the Ottaways if they would tender an offer to buy out all of our small investors, too, which was asking a lot. It could potentially triple the cost to them, as opposed to simply buying me out alone. But if they would offer to buy out everyone that Steve and I had brought into the company, I said, I was willing to sell. I didn't want to leave the company without giving our investors an opportunity for a similarly positive exit.

It is difficult—almost impossible—to negotiate with friends. After eight years of working with Eric and Robin Ottaway and coming to respect them tremendously, the last thing I wanted was a protracted negotiation with them. Price wasn't really an issue. The Ottaways knew the company as well as I did, and we generally agreed on its value. The sticking point regarded the cost of buying everyone out.

After some contemplation, they agreed to do it all. It was a huge landmark for the company and for all of our small investors, but once agreed upon, it didn't take long to complete the transaction.

Thanks to the Ottaways, we offered our investors a much-appreciated conclusion. Our original investors did well, making over four times their initial investment—not as good as some other investment opportunities, but it was certainly better than most other companies in our industry could provide. Investors who came in later got less (returns on the last round were pretty modest, to be honest), but at least everyone made money, and for an entrepreneur like me, that is what makes for a *very* happy ending. ★

## STEVE WEIGHS IN

The sale of our distribution businesses was a very stressful experience for all of us and for the breweries we represented. Distribution is a vital concern for all breweries, and it is paramount for a start-up brewery. Start-ups depend on their distributor for their very existence. The trend in the beer distribution business is toward consolidation of distributors into larger and larger companies. These companies need to be large to deal with the powerful multinational breweries they represent. Small companies like ours, and the hundreds of other small breweries that have appeared in the last 25 years, are like ants playing on a large field with elephants.

Before Prohibition, and for many years after, the brewing industry effectively controlled its distribution networks. There were no franchise laws. If a brewer did not like the job the distributor was doing, the brewer would simply leave that distributor for another. Distributors lived in fear of the breweries they represented. Today, the pendulum has swung in the other direction: Small brewers live in fear of their distributors.

Consequently, our negotiations with potential buyers were extremely perilous. All of the distributors we bargained with had big-time law firms backing them up. Unlike us, they did not fret about legal fees. For them, legal expenses are a way of life. Big, expensive lawsuits are common in the beer distribution business. Legal expenses are more than covered by the tremendous profits the distributors make selling beer. And the franchise laws assure the distributors that any brewer leaving them will have to pay if the distributor grants them that privilege. In many states, a brewer has no right to change distributors without the consent of the distributor.

In some states, such as New Jersey, there are laws exempting small breweries from these franchise laws. Through their trade association, small brewers are working to gain exemptions like this in other states. But New Jersey distributors are working to close this loophole, and distributors in other states have shown no interest in exempting brewers from their franchise laws.

The good news for small brewers is that many big distributors have begun to see the value in representing small brands. American craft breweries and microbreweries sell at premium prices and bring higher profits to distributors. In addition, small breweries are growing rapidly, while the mainstream beer industry has been growing little in the past few decades. Small breweries, like imported beers, bring excitement to the beer business, and many distributors have begun to see their value.

During our effort to sell the distribution companies, we kept our lines of communication open with all the potential buyers. We knew they wanted our brands, even though no one was in a particular hurry to make a deal with us. Eventually, all the talking paid off. Our new distributors in Massachusetts and New York are doing a great job getting our product to market for us.

**Our Grade:**  Neither the Brooklyn Brewery nor the 30 or so breweries and importers we represented in New York would ever have gotten a foothold in New York or Massachusetts without the efforts of our distribution team and Craft Brewers Guild. For selling our distribution businesses at full value, I give us an A+.

# CHAPTER 11

# Tom Wants to Know If You Have What It Takes

## ARE YOU AN ENTREPRENEUR?

I remember sitting at my mother's kitchen table a few years back with a questionnaire from her Sunday newspaper.

"Are you an Entrepreneur?" it asked. *You bet I am,* I thought. Picking through the survey, I was pretty sure I'd know the right answers.

"What position would you play on a football team?" Quarterback, obviously. Well, not always. Sometimes I'd get stuck playing wide receiver. Hmm. Are receivers entrepreneurial?

"Do people close to you look to you for leadership?" They certainly do. Except for my wife, of course. And my mom.

"Are you decisive?" Absolutely. Most of the time, anyway, except when it was better to be cautious. Decisiveness can be overrated. Look before you leap is my motto. Sometimes discretion really is the better part of valor.

As I completed the 20 questions, I began to think it was a pretty lame exercise. I knew what the "right" answers were supposed to be. Hey, I can take a test. But I thought: These are the wrong questions. Whoever wrote them doesn't know what an entrepreneur actually does. They clearly weren't written by someone who had struggled to make Friday payrolls. They just recycled stereotypes about what an entrepreneur was supposed to be.

### Don't Believe the Hype

There's a standard image of an entrepreneur in the popular imagination. Here in the United States it's a largely positive, heroic conception. The entrepreneur is a brave, solitary figure who struggles alone against the forces of mediocrity. He is David fighting corporate Goliaths. He can be brusque and overbearing, but that's how he gets things done. He's a bit of an oddball, but those high school heartaches merely fueled his ambition to show them all . . .

I don't buy it. I think there are many different kinds of entrepreneurs, and the movie stereotype doesn't work. There may be certain personality traits that help a potential entrepreneur, and a person's background may hold clues to entrepreneurial potential, but there are a lot of potential winning combinations.

If you're playing poker, it helps to start with a couple of aces in your hand. But if you don't have an ace, are you out? Nope. A bunch of little cards can beat a couple of big ones. It's all in how they're put together. It's the same with starting a business. You look at what you've got, you look at what you'll need, and then you figure out if you can fill in your hand.

### What's in Your Cupboard?

Every person has strengths and weaknesses. It's hard to be honest with yourself about your own shortcomings, but if you are going to start a business, you'd better look in the mirror. When we work for other people, we get used to camouflaging our weak areas. Even if we can admit to weakness in our honest, private moments (perhaps you're thinking: *I'm not a very good public speaker,* or *I hate working under pressure,* and *Am I the only one in the office who doesn't understand how this stupid phone system works?*), we aren't encouraged to admit it. The incentives of working for others lead us to cover our rear ends. And when we make excuses to others, there can be a natural tendency to start believing those excuses ourselves.

When it's *your* company, the incentives shift. Not that you will publicly proclaim your shortcomings; in fact, there may be more pressure than ever to appear omnipotent. Your employees, vendors, and stakeholders all want you to reassure them every day that you've got it figured out. But even as you struggle to appear on top of things, you will be privately, intensely, acutely aware of your own shortcomings. You will agonize over your mistakes and curse your own weaknesses.

To minimize the self-inflicted agony, be honest with yourself up front. Open your personal cupboard and take stock of what you've got and what you don't. For instance, I knew I was no salesperson. I don't have what it takes. I hate rejection, I get impatient with indecision, I'm shy in many social situations, I don't like to introduce myself, I have a lousy memory for names, I think it's rude to be pushy, and I can't even remember jokes. I knew a long time ago that if I ever started a business, I'd need some help on the sales side.

If you can honestly face your own weaknesses, there are two ways to improve your chances.

First, you can work on them. Every now and then you can turn it completely around. My first semester at business school I discovered I was a natural at marketing. The concepts came easily to me and made intuitive sense. Conversely, finance seemed strange. I struggled to understand accounting. But I knew that if I ever wanted to own my own business I'd want to master accounting, so I kept working at it. I ended up double-majoring in marketing and finance, and purposefully chose a finance-based job with a great training program when I graduated. I made myself into an expert.

Second, you can find a partner who's got what you don't. You don't need to have every skill in the book. For me, that meant partnering with someone like Steve, who covered my weaknesses on the sales side. You do need to be strong at something so you've got something to offer. But then you can recruit, or be recruited, for the team.

Steve had a lot of skills that I didn't have. I had skills he didn't have. We put them together and were much stronger together than either of us would have been apart.

## MISTER INSIDE AND MISTER OUTSIDE

Steve was the right guy to be the public face of the Brooklyn Brewery. He had better sales skills and he had a better personal story. In fact, he had an outstanding, romantic story that directly related to our business. He was a dashing former foreign correspondent who had learned to homebrew in the Middle East, and now he was turning that dream into a reality. I, however, was a gray-flannel former banker who had always wanted to start a business. Which was a more interesting angle for newspapers? For potential customers? Steve had a great story to tell and was also gifted at converting that story into positive attention and actual sales. I figured that my most important contribution to our story line was to stay out of the way.

Nevertheless, I had a lot to contribute to actually creating and running the business. When it came to setting up our office and managing almost everything in it—daily billing, accounts payable, legal work, weekly payroll, whatever—I figured it was my job.

This rough separation of roles into Mr. Outside and Mr. Inside is common with two partners. It allows both to be fully active and work hard without tripping over each other. It is easy for other employees to recognize who is in charge of what decision. It's a commonsense, workable arrangement that lets two partners complement each other and give the business their best.

When we chose our titles it reinforced this separate-but-equal division of management roles. Steve became our president; that's a title that customers, the press, and the public associate with being the boss. He was the outside boss. I became our CEO; that's a title that banks, suppliers, and other businesspeople associate with being the boss. I was the inside boss. So both of us were bosses, each in our own world.

But even simple arrangements have complications. The truth was, our separation of roles was never neat. We ended up talking over almost everything of importance. Steve had a lot to say about office policies. I had a lot to say about sales strategies. Sometimes we had sharp disagreements, and we had to hammer them out in private. Our roles became even messier when our distribution business became prominent. We tried to readjust, with Steve mostly running the brewery side and me mostly running the distribution side, while keeping our general outside and inside roles, but it was not always a brilliant success.

At one point we sensed we were struggling. In 1995, we hired a consulting company to analyze our business and our management roles. Maybe we shouldn't have been surprised at his report, but I admit that it startled me when he reported that even our senior people didn't know exactly whom they were working for. When managers or employees had questions, they would simply calculate which one of us was more likely to give them the answer they wanted, and ask accordingly. (Just like you did with Mom and Dad when you were a kid.)

We took the consultant's report to heart and clarified our roles. For a while, at least, we improved the situation. But in truth, the separate-but-equal arrangement is a dynamic that never loses its tension. At its best, it can be a creative tension that doubles imaginative energy while providing useful checks and balances. But maintaining trust and communication is hard work, and when either breaks down, the business is particularly vulnerable.

When two strong-willed partners come together, there's a temptation for each to think that his or her own role is the most important. I'm sure Steve would sometimes think, *Without me, there would be no sales.* And I admit that at times I'd think, *Without me, there would be no business.*

As Mr. Inside, I sometimes found it hard to see Steve become the public face of our company. I remember a chamber of commerce event we hosted one night at the brewery. My wife had joined us, and the three of us were sitting together when the speaker up at the podium introduced Steve as the founder and owner and thanked him for his generous hospitality. Gail glared as the crowd applauded Steve, and he and I both felt uncomfortable. Steve was usually quite fair about sharing credit, but a lot of people just assumed that Steve, Mr. Outside, owned the brewery. It was a natural result of the roles we had chosen. I just had to tell myself: whatever is best for the business.

## HAVE YOU EVER ACHIEVED ANYTHING?

Forget about those Sunday supplement questionnaires. I've got a simpler test to take to see whether you've got what it takes to be an entrepreneur. Have you ever really achieved? At anything?

In my opinion, past achievement is the best predictor of future achievement. Simple as that—and the field does not have to be related to your current endeavor. It's the attitude that counts, more than any specific knowledge. Business experience is good, but experience in business is not the same thing as success in business. I'd rather gamble on someone who has had success at anything—sports, the arts, community work—than someone who has toiled in business for a while without distinction.

The best qualification for being a good entrepreneurial boss might simply be a record of being a really good employee. Learning how to work with other people and for other people, to succeed as part of someone else's team, can be great training when it's time to start your own business. Often, people think it's the reverse: that if you're a crummy and difficult employee, you should probably work for yourself. It's part of the myth of the heroic but prickly entrepreneur. Frankly, I doubt it. If you're really prickly, it's far better to plague someone else than to plague yourself. And it's certainly more comforting to blame someone else when things go wrong.

## HAVE YOU EVER MANAGED ANYONE?

Some people are natural candidates for starting their own business. Their leadership skills are recognized early on by peers and authority figures alike. She is president of her high school class. He's captain of the swim team. She organized the school's first Toys for Tots drive last Christmas. This type of leadership is distinct from raw success. The class president does not always have the best grades; the team's captain is not always the team's most valuable player. Although leadership is distinct from success, it is nevertheless a great clue to future success. The ability to manage people, in any setting, is a crucial asset to the potential entrepreneur.

There's a lively debate about whether leaders are born or made. But there can be no doubt that practicing leadership and management skills improves them. I think there is such a thing as a late-blooming leader—someone who was not class president or Girl Scout troop leader who nonetheless becomes a successful businessperson—but that late bloomer probably had chances, and instinctively took them, to gain management experience and improve his or her skills. Perhaps later in life he or she became a supervisor at work, a leader in a community group, or president of the school's PTA.

You do not want your first business to be your first management experience. Whether you learn management skills early or late is less important than that you have learned, and practiced, them. Managing people under pressure is very difficult, and there is no substitute for on-the-job experience. If you've never really run anything, never managed people, you're probably not ready to start your own business. Get some experience on someone else's nickel first.

## ARE YOU DRIVEN BY THE IDEA OR THE EMOTION?

What kind of people start their own business? There are many different types of entrepreneurs. I think Steve and I represent two different, but quite common, ones. The first type, like Steve, is idea or product driven. This person is pulled into starting a particular business because he or she has learned it, or some corner of it, and decides to squeeze in among the existing players. This type might work for one of the big companies or, like Steve, might be a hobbyist who dreams of going pro. The product-driven entrepreneur identifies an opportunity. The question is, can he or she create a business out of the idea?

The second type of entrepreneur, like me, is emotionally driven. This person is the purposeful entrepreneur who wants to own a company for its own sake and is constantly searching for the right idea. I was perceived as a winner in my own organization (the former Chemical Bank, now part of JPMorgan Chase). If I'd just stuck around for another 15 years, I might well have become an executive vice president. But I'd go home and think, *What's this all about? Why am I working for these guys? I'd rather run my own small company than become an executive vice president of someone else's big company.* And why should I wait? The question for me was: Could I find an idea?

I felt I lived in a world of opportunity, because any time I saw a business miss the point, I'd imagine that I could do it better. Walking down the street, I was surrounded by possibilities to rearrange the world in a more sensible and lucrative fashion. Perhaps I'd see a wine store with the wrong selection for a particular neighborhood; with a keener appreciation for the tastes of their customers, I was convinced I could sharply increase sales. Was a nice family jewelry business hamstrung because it didn't have sufficient capital? Hmm—a nonrecourse asset-based financing structure would free things up for growth. Seeing any business anomaly, I'd always wonder: *Is there a business in this? For me?*

By the time purposeful entrepreneurs start their first business, they've gone through a hundred dress rehearsals in their mind. In my case, there were opportunities everywhere, but none had seemed quite right. Or the timing had been wrong. Or they needed particular skills or resources that I couldn't bring to the table.

I thought of ideas as seeds blowing in the wind: a hundred drift by, landing on rock or pavement—hitting in the wrong place or at the wrong time—for every one that's got a chance to sprout. But for the entrepreneur, it takes only one.

## DOWN A ROAD LESS TRAVELED

When there are a thousand different individual roads to becoming an entrepreneur, none of them can be called typical. But perhaps every example, mine included, is illuminating in its own way.

As a child, I didn't think of owning a business, but I was surely influenced by my father. He was a physicist who did underwater research and then became the general manager of a defense laboratory in California. Although part of General Motors, the lab seemed completely separate. It had nothing to do with the automotive business and was geographically remote from Detroit, so it was as if my dad was running his own company. And it was a romantic one, too, with its own research ship and contracts with NASA. For 10 years I saw my dad as a business combination of Jacques Cousteau and Buck Rogers.

Later my dad was promoted into the heart of GM. He moved us to the Midwest, and he was on his way to eventually becoming a genuine big shot, a group vice president of what was then the largest corporation in the world. Tens of thousands of people worked for him. But it actually seemed a comedown to me. He was a big wheel, but also just a cog in a huge machine. The corporate life, even for a successful executive, didn't seem fun. He never seemed as happy as when he had been running the show in California. It made an impression on me.

In school I loved reading the C.S. Forrester books about the fictional Admiral Horatio Hornblower, which were loosely based on the heroic exploits of Lord Nelson. *A courageous captain of a ship,* I thought, *maybe that was me!* Somewhere along the line I took a left turn and decided I'd like to be a writer, perhaps a poet. That was a notion that carried me through college as an English major at Yale. I had teachers who were encouraging and I wrote poems, short stories, and even a novella. But after college I never really imagined I could earn a living that way. It was something I wanted to do, but not necessarily a career.

Before and after college I tried my hand at a lot of jobs. I learned something from every one of them. Before college they were the usual run of local chores and summer work: mowing lawns, babysitting, lifeguarding, summer counselor. I taught folk guitar for a while in high school to a clientele of three attractive girls. I was only barely better than they were, which turned out to be just good enough. While in college I sold hot dogs at the Yale Bowl, taught tennis at the Madeira School summer camp, cooked hamburgers at Jack in the Box, and worked for the Boy Scouts in New Haven. I took a year off from college and wandered through Europe, living on a little less than $5 a day.

After college I worked on an assembly line in Detroit. When I'd saved up enough to buy a Chevy Chevette—with my employee discount—I quit. Then I drove to Santa Fe, where I arrived with $50, a half a tank of gas, and most of my worldly possessions in the backseat. I camped up in the Sangre de Cristo national forest above the city at night, and during the day I came down to circle help-wanted ads in the paper.

I got my first job in Santa Fe pumping gas at the Capital Chevron. I added a part-time night job as security guard in a nearby Grand Central department store. After a couple of months running around catching shoplifters (a depressing job, especially around the holidays), I was invited to apply for a full-time job as an assistant manager. They saw they had a live one. I took to it like a fish to water, moving up from assistant manager to department manager in about three months, then to assistant store manager running the soft goods half of the store after another three months. At that point I was 23 years old and had 20 people working for me. I liked it, but wasn't ready to settle down.

### An On-the-Job Education

My next job was completely different, and one of the best educations I ever enjoyed. A close friend, Jim Patrick, told me about an old man named John Harkrider, who had a unique background. John had moved to Hollywood in its early days. He'd shared a packing crate on Mount Hollywood with Rudolph Valentino, won an Academy Award for set design for his work with Flo Ziegfeld, ran a successful modeling agency for over a decade, then finally settled in running a location scouting company. My friend said Harkrider could use an office manager. I was ready to go.

John was 80 years old, cantankerous, and as vital as hell. A large portion of my job consisted of answering the telephone and fending off creditors. He was constantly late with his tax payments, but he never skimped on gourmet bread and coffee. He had strong opinions about everything, but especially about the IRS and food.

We wanted to be at the shoot when the crew arrived so we could guard our location. Crews were notoriously sloppy—tracking mud in the house, putting gaffer's tape on the walls, and throwing cigarette butts on expensive carpets. Since John would need to use these locations again, he protected them fiercely. Shoots were often at sunrise, and we'd be there a half hour early. Here was an 80-year-old man, seemingly never at rest, still sweet-talking clients, battling the IRS, and jumping up at five in the morning to brew his special coffee. He cared so much about everything in his life—he was so passionate—that it fundamentally changed the way I saw small business. I admired him immensely.

After working with Harkrider and before joining the bank, I had a few additional jobs. I was a copy editor, and an unarmed guard, and a shoe salesman at a Florsheim store. I couldn't put my finger on what exactly I was getting out of any of these jobs, but in retrospect I have the sense that all of them were important. Without realizing it, I was learning about workplaces, learning about different bosses, learning about people.

## IS THIS THE IDEA? IS THIS THE TIME?

As a would-be entrepreneur, I went through various stages of self-awareness. I think they're pretty typical. At first, I had no specific plan for any business. All I had were observations, life experiences, opportunities to manage people in different circumstances, and a confident impatience. Confidence that I could manage things better than whoever was currently running the show. Any show. And impatience, or a certain restlessness, to get things done. To achieve for its own sake. A specific business, much less a business plan, didn't yet enter into it.

The next stage kicked in during my 20s, when I began considering actual business opportunities, however remote. It might have been a retail shop with a for-sale sign; or one of my business clients at the bank, a family operation with no son or daughter active; or any local business that seemed not to understand its customers and was begging for competition. At this stage, an idea became more than just a fleeting fancy. It would beckon and seem to demand closer scrutiny. I'd feel a tentative excitement that maybe this was the one, this was the idea that would really work. My wife and friends might weigh in. I'd pursue a little casual research. I'd wonder: *Is this more than just another idea? Is it the idea to commit to?* The answer had always previously been no.

But the idea of the Brooklyn Brewery wouldn't go away. It wouldn't take no for an answer. For every initial objection, either Steve or I could think of a plausible response. The second stage of closer examination kept extending itself and expanding. It morphed into a much more serious third stage: drafting a business plan.

This is when it hit me. Maybe this idea was *the one.* Compared to previous ideas, this one seemed doable. Friends were enthusiastic and offered more reasons why it would work. My wife carefully acknowledged that this was not a half-bad idea. A year-end bonus from the bank might provide a few months of time to try it out . . .

For any entrepreneur, this is the poignant moment. Terror, agony, and unbearable excitement all build. Doubts about leaving a current job creep in. Gee, in just 15 years I'll qualify for a pension. The project I'm working on now is really important, and no one at the company could handle it quite as well. I'm due for a promotion, and probably a raise . . . Then there are the family issues: What happens to the vacation we were planning for July? Is it really responsible to quit my job just when I'm finally paying down my credit card debt? Wouldn't it be better to wait until my son, Billy, was a little older? Aren't I being a little selfish in pursuing this?

The right time to jump is when the agony of jumping is less than the agony of not jumping. You'll know it when you get there. At one point, I asked my wife what she thought I should do.

"If you don't do this, you'll regret it the rest of your life," Gail said. "You've got to give it a try."

She was right. And I knew it.

### Dreams versus Reality

Purposeful entrepreneurs, those who, like me, had dreamed for years of starting their own business, may bring a lifetime of anticipation into the initial business planning process. Their first thoughts may be colored by issues that have more to do with themselves, as potential founders, than with the potential business.

For years I imagined that if I ever started a business, it would really be set up right. In my imagination it would be not only immensely profitable but community-minded. It would attract the best and the brightest employees, who would work feverishly long hours with an exuberant and comradely sense of shared purpose. No one would ever have to be fired because the internal training would be so amazingly effective that everyone would be a high performer. It would be superbly organized—as nimble as a sports car but as sturdy as a truck—and there would never be any bureaucratic crap. Employees could go home to make lunch for their kids.

On a personal level, my dream continued, the business would answer most of my big issues. It would be enough of a financial success to guarantee lifetime security. The hours might be long in the short run, but eventually excellent managers would allow me to take long and interesting vacations—or perhaps even a withdrawal from daily management into longer-term strategic thinking. While there might be profiles in *Fortune* and *Forbes,* and an *Inc.* ranking that was the envy of the industry, a certain amount of discreet personal privacy would be maintained.

Do these sound like your dreams, too? The reality might be a little different. The business wants what the business wants, not what you want.

A little while ago I was asked for advice about a business plan. I thought it was a good idea, an exciting proposition. But when I talked with the potential founder, I realized there was a huge disconnect between the business plan and his personal goals. He was looking for a business that would enhance his quality of life immediately. What he'd described was instead a business that would devour his life for the next few years. It was a big idea, one that would require huge commitments of time and money; success or failure would necessarily come on a dramatic scale.

The potential founder described how he could minimize his commitment and still give it a try. In my opinion, that was impossible. A good idea is never lonely. Even if he was the first to recognize this opportunity (which he didn't know for sure), he would surely not be the last. And his competitors would certainly not minimize their own commitment. Then what?

When Steve and I started the Brooklyn Brewery, there were only a few dozen other microbreweries and brewpubs in the United States. Over the next 10 years, 2,000 were started. Some of them were very good companies, with smart people who worked hard and with a lot of imagination.

You can count on competition. Your new business, in order to succeed, will need resources and strategy and execution to answer the competitive market. It will want what it wants, need what it needs, whether it fits your personal agenda or not. To some extent, it's useless to try to make a business fit your dreams. Instead, you need to decide, honestly, whether it can fulfill them (some of them, anyway) naturally.

### Don't Let (Lack of) Money Stop You

I've participated in many entrepreneurial forums. The number one concern that most people express is finding the capital to finance their business. It certainly is a legitimate issue, but most people have it backward. Their pessimism about raising money keeps them from even trying to write a business plan. Without a persuasive plan, how do they know they can't raise the money? How do they know they have an idea that's even worthy of funding?

Your last name doesn't have to be Rockefeller to start a business. We are fortunate to live in a wealthy country. There is potential investment capital everywhere. Individuals, families, businesses, local development authorities, and venture funds all have far more money to invest now than a decade ago. The number one complaint of venture funds is that there is too much money chasing too few good ideas. Granted, a venture fund may have a rarefied view of what constitutes a good idea, but I don't think they are off the mark.

If your idea needs money that you don't have, it doesn't mean you can't follow through. It just means you'd better get comfortable with sharing your idea. You'll have to convince other people—partners, investors, banks—to share your dream, both the risks and the rewards.

**LESSON ELEVEN**
### THERE ARE NO ENTRANCE EXAMS FOR ENTREPRENEURS

No one but you can tell you not to start a business. There are no gatekeepers, no personnel directors, and no entrance exams that will keep you out of the entrepreneur's circle. You don't need an MBA; you don't need to have been class president; you don't have to have money. But you do have to decide if you're up to the challenge. You have to honestly judge your achievements and experience. You have to add up all of your skills, your personal resources, and your motivations. Do you really have the right idea? Right now? For you, are the potential rewards worth the very substantial risks?

Of course, you're reading this book. That's a clue, isn't it? ★

## STEVE WEIGHS IN

 November 22, 1995, was the day before Thanksgiving. It was a chilly morning. In our crowded warehouse office, there was a sense of excitement about the impending holiday weekend vacation. We had ignited the industrial gas heater at the end of the room to fight the chill. I was sitting at my desk, working behind a hutch at the rear of the office when I heard screams from the three women working inside. I stood and looked around the hutch. Two men in hooded sweatshirts were waving handguns and shouting, "Get on the floor!" to the seven or eight people in the office. One held Rich Nowak, one of our salespeople, by the scruff of the neck, pointing his gun at Rich's head. He pushed Rich to the floor.

I walked into the room with my hands in the air, saying, "I'm your guy. Don't hurt anyone. What do you want?" The lead gunman grabbed me by the shoulder and spun me around, ripping my sweater.

"We want the money. Get me the money," he shouted. I said the money was out in the warehouse in a safe. "Come with me," I added.

"Don't try anything funny," he said, pushing me out the door. I walked a few steps to the small iron safe that was bolted to the concrete floor. I leaned down and started spinning the combination lock. Then it struck me. I couldn't remember the combination. I had not unlocked the safe in more than a year. Our office manager had long since taken over that responsibility.

"I can't remember the combination," I said.

"Don't bullshit me, man," shouted the gunman. He cocked his 9mm pistol menacingly. "I'll blow your brains out, man. Open that goddamn safe!"

I racked my brain for the numbers, but they would not come. "I can't remember. I haven't opened the safe in more than a year," I said weakly. He pushed the cold barrel of the gun into the side of my head.

"Open the goddamn safe," he shouted.

"I think the controller knows the combination," I said.

"Get the goddamn controller, then," he said.

He pushed me back into the office. I asked Leland Gelman, our controller, if he could open the safe.

"No," protested Leland. "Karen handles the safe."

Everyone was hugging the floor. I did not see Karen. Someone said, "She's under her desk."

The lead gunman dragged Karen out from under her desk.

"We need you to open the safe," I said. "I can't remember the combination."

He took Karen and me out to the safe. Karen squatted down and started rolling the tumblers. The gunman held his pistol at her head.

"If you take that pistol away, maybe I could think," she shouted at him. He complied. She opened the safe. The two men got away with $30,000 dollars in cash.

We soon discovered we did not have reliable theft insurance. I subsequently spent about $25,000 more on security fences, cameras, and alarms. At significant expense, we hired an armored car service to pick up our cash every day. I was determined that we would not be robbed again. Tom winced at the added expense. It was clear that there was a difference between me—who had had the gun to my head—and Tom, who had not. On Christmas Eve, the gunmen returned.

This time, they grabbed our warehouse manager, Gerald Cogdell, and demanded he take them to our office. Jim Munson saw the gunmen enter the warehouse and ran out a side door. One gunman chased him, shouting, "Stop!" But he did not fire, and Jim got away. Cogdell stopped at one of the security fences and pressed the doorbell. Seeing the cameras, the robbers relented and ran away.

The added security, and Jim Munson's brave dash, saved the day. The added security also assured our employees that we were serious about protecting them. Incidents like these really test your commitment to your business. They were terrifying. Lydia Ward, one of the employees who had endured both ordeals, said to me, "You are used to this sort of thing because of your experience in the Middle East. I can't live with this sort of danger."

I assured her that I was not accustomed to having a gun at my head. I explained the steps we had taken to deter robbers. I told her that I had been every bit as scared as she and the rest of the employees. But in fact, I was almost euphoric after the second incident. I remember that Winston

Churchill once said, "There is nothing quite so exhilarating as being shot at without effect."

And also, I felt I had been living with a deeper terror for years: the fear and loathing of failure. Wilson Harrell, of *Inc.* magazine, called it "entrepreneurial terror." It is a more profound terror than the physical terror we felt facing the robbers. It is a terror you feel every day and every night. Since we started the business, I have had few solid nights of sleep. In the beginning, it is the excitement of the business that keeps you awake at night. Later, it is the fear of not being able to make payroll, of juggling 10 different creditors. It is the fear of failure, of having to tell all those people who invested in your company that your idea didn't work, that you have lost your money and their money.

In 1990, Tom and I went for two months without a paycheck. Both of us piled up credit card debt during that period. That debt stayed with us for a long time. There were many sleepless nights. Rather than tossing and turning, I would get out of bed and read a book, usually fiction, to escape my worries. During that period, I started hiking with my family, eventually climbing mountains in the Adirondacks of New York, the White Mountains of New Hampshire, and the Tetons in Wyoming. I got interested in rock climbing and read the books of Rheinhold Messner, the world's greatest solo mountain climber.

I tried not to share my fears with my wife, Ellen. But she could tell when I was under extreme pressure.

"You'll figure it out," she said to me during one of my funks. "You always get yourself into these impossible situations where it seems there is no way out. You'll find a way."

Once I called my dad, then retired in Winter Park, Florida, to share my woes. He listened patiently, and then said, "Did you ever get yourself into a situation where everything is going wrong, where you have taken on more than you can possibly handle, where you are just going to crack?"

"Yes," I replied, holding my breath for his wisdom.

"Yes," he said. "Me, too."

That was all he had to say. But there was wisdom in those words. He was telling me to get back to my job and make it work, which I did.

Having a courageous and intrepid partner like Tom certainly helped. We shared those moments of terror, though there was scant consolation in the sharing. It was just comforting to know that Tom and I were in the same boat. In his bedroom on the floor below mine, Tom always said that he heard my footsteps when I got out of my bed to read on those sleepless nights. He was wide awake, too.

In the winter of 2005, I climbed Mt. Washington in New Hampshire with my brother-in-law, Ed Claflin; Matthew Reich; and a very strong climber from Virginia, Jay Butler. Jay has successfully climbed Denali in Alaska and Aconcagua in Argentina. We were sitting in our lean-to swapping stories, our breath crystallizing in the −10-degree cold.

In a thick southern drawl, Jay said, "Every time I climb one of these peaks, I get myself into a dangerous situation, and I say to myself, "If I get down off this damn mountain, I am never going to climb another damn mountain as long as I live." And then six months or a year later, I find myself climbing another one. Most people would not appreciate why I do this. Just like most people would not appreciate how much fun it is sitting in a lean-to talking to friends when it is −10 degrees."

The fact is that you live a little more intensely when you stick your neck out, when you take a chance. The petty worries, cares, and neuroses of everyday life fade away, and you just concentrate on putting one foot in front of the other and moving on. Whether or not you succeed, at least you have tried. Somehow, that has a cleansing effect on the soul.

It seems that memory transforms the fear and pain of those moments of stress and anxiety into something pleasurable. I fondly remember sitting in a tent on the saddle of Grand Teton with Ellen, Sam, and Lily, as the wind howled and the snow piled up outside. The dehydrated soup we ate that night was one of the best meals I have ever had. And the view from Mt. Washington, with fog and snow blowing down the mountain into Tuckerman's Ravine like it was the gate of hell, was all the more beautiful for us having trudged to the summit in spite of leg cramps and freezing fingers and toes. Climbing that mountain in February is the only way to get that view.

If you are going to start a business, you must be prepared for lonely moments of entrepreneurial terror, for stress and anxiety. There is little consolation in those moments. I haven't slept soundly since I became an entrepreneur. But Tom and I have shared some experiences that only an entrepreneur can appreciate, and I know we both treasure the experience.

**Our Grade:** I doubt that either of us will ever be happy working for someone else. I think we deserve an A− for our efforts as entrepreneurs.

# Timeline

1983    Tom graduates from Columbia Business School to work at Chemical Bank.

1984    Steve returns from Middle East with his wife, Ellen, and their two children. They move to Park Slope. He becomes assistant foreign editor at *Newsday* and home-brews as a hobby.

1985    Tom and his wife, Gail, move into the apartment below Steve and Ellen.

1986    Tom and Steve watch their children in Tom's backyard while drinking Steve's homebrew. In the fall, Tom goes to the 2nd Annual Microbrewers Conference in Portland, Oregon. On his return, Tom and Steve seriously plan the business. Tom begins the business plan.

1987    By March, the business plan is done. Tom quits his job at the bank. Steve and Tom begin to raise money. Steve quits his job at *Newsday* in September. They break escrow, raising $300,000, in October.

1988    They begin selling Brooklyn Lager on March 30 while working out of a Hittleman Brewery warehouse on Meserole Street and an office on Fourth Avenue.

1989    They lease a small warehouse on 2nd Street, leaving Meserole Street. The brewery invades Manhattan. Brooklyn Brown Ale is introduced.

1990    They raise more money in a second partnership offering. Also, they tentatively start distributing other beers. Growth slows.

1991    They give up the office on Fourth Avenue and move into the 2nd Street warehouse. Steve goes back to work at *Newsday* to save money. Distribution operations expand. Tom gives his first-ever speech on distribution at the Annual Microbrewers Conference.

1992    Steve returns to work full time at the Brooklyn Brewery. In December, the company moves to a large warehouse at 118 North 11th Street in Williamsburg. Brooklyn Lager wins the Gold Medal and Brooklyn Brown Ale wins the bronze at the Great American Beer Festival.

1993    Distribution rights for top specialty brands are consolidated. Growth accelerates. The first Beer Fest is held under the Brooklyn Bridge.

1994    They raise more money in a third partnership offering, all from Jay Hall. The growth rate reaches 97 percent. About 70 percent of revenue is now derived from the distribution operations. Brewmaster Garrett Oliver joins the company and introduces Broadway Black Chocolate Stout.

1995    The space at 79 North 11th Street is leased for a future brewery. Steve organizes construction plans.

1996    The brewery opens in May. The company considers going public. Instead, they take on the Ottaway family as primary financiers and their two sons, Robin and Eric, as new managers. They open the Long Island warehouse for distribution. They lose distribution rights to two key suppliers. New York passes a distributor franchise law.

1997   They buy International Beverage, a Massachusetts distributor, which Eric and Robin Ottaway manage. The company considers buying additional small distributors in upstate New York.

1998   Sales reach $15 million. Both brewery and distribution sales grow.

2000   Tom and Steve write a plan for TotalBeer.com. Eric Ottaway moves to New York to help manage it.

2001   The Ottaways make an additional investment. TotalBeer.com is launched. Sales are modest and dry up completely after September 11. Other dot-coms fail. TotalBeer folds. New York State franchise laws change. Brewery growth outpaces distributor growth.

2002   They explore selling the distributorships. They sell the Massachusetts arm in December and some brands in New York.

2003   They sell all New York distribution rights. The total realized for all distribution sales approaches $10 million. The Brooklyn brand moves to Phoenix/Beehive distributors. The Ottaways offer to buy out Tom.

2004   The Ottaways extend an offer to buy out all small investors. Tom sells his voting shares to the Ottaways and resigns.

2005   Steve and Tom write *Beer School* and live happily ever after.

# Index